$7.95

In the fifth part of Bréhier's monumental *History of Philosophy* to appear in English translation the author traces eighteenth-century philosophical speculation in France, England, and Germany.

An introductory chapter on Newton's physics and Locke's metaphysics is followed by chapters on the English deists and on Berkeley, Christian Wolff, Giambattista Vico, and Montesquieu.

The second section covers early thinkers of the "Enlightenment"— Condillac, David Hume and Adam Smith, Vauvenargues, Voltaire, and Rousseau.

In the final section, Bréhier surveys the leading proponents of the return to sentiment and immediate intuition that characterized the last quarter of the century—Lessing, Herder, and others, and concludes with an illuminating analysis of Kantian criticism.

at Southeastern State College, has also edited and translated the philosophical works of Bergson, Voltaire, and Sartre.

# THE HISTORY OF PHILOSOPHY

# THE EIGHTEENTH CENTURY

THE HISTORY OF PHILOSOPHY
VOLUME V

# THE EIGHTEENTH CENTURY

BY ÉMILE BRÉHIER

TRANSLATED BY WADE BASKIN

THE UNIVERSITY OF CHICAGO PRESS
CHICAGO AND LONDON

*Originally published in 1930 as* Histoire de la philosophie:
La Philosophie moderne. II: Le Dix-huitième siècle.
© *1930, Presses Universitaires de France*

*The present bibliography has been revised and enlarged to
include recent publications. These have been supplied by
Wesley Piersol Murphy.*

*Library of Congress Catalog Card Number: 63-20912
The University of Chicago Press, Chicago & London
The University of Toronto Press, Toronto 5, Canada
© 1967 by The University of Chicago
All rights reserved. Published 1967
Printed in the United States of America*

# CONTENTS

# NEWTON AND LOCKE

BETWEEN THE great theological systems of Malebranche, Leibniz, or Spinoza and the massive philosophical structures of Schelling, Hegel, or Comte, the eighteenth century appears to be a moment of relaxation for the synthetic and constructive mind.

Appraisals have differed: the eighteenth century has been scorned by historians of philosophy who—apart from the doctrines of Berkeley, Hume, and Kant—have found its thinking to be sketchy, disconnected, not very original, pamphletary, and biased; from another point of view, the violent reaction which marked the beginning of the nineteenth century tended to make it seem like a negative, destructive, critical century. In short, as many different judgments have been passed on it as on the French Revolution, which is considered to be its direct outgrowth.

The beginning of the eighteenth century was characterized by the rapid decadence and collapse of the great systems in which the intellectual heirs of Descartes had sought to unite the philosophy of nature and the philosophy of mind. The luminaries of the eighteenth century were Newton and Locke: Newton, whose basic teachings, expressed in his *natural philosophy* or physics, are only loosely connected with his doctrines of spiritual realities—doctrines which he was inclined to accept through personal mysticism rather than to subject to methodical meditations as if they were part and parcel of his physics; and Locke, the author of a philosophy

I

of mind not directly related to the contemporaneous development of mathematical and physical sciences in the hands of Boyle or Newton. Locke and, more particularly, some of his successors tried to establish between mind and the material world an affinity like that reflected in the theory of attraction; but such an affinity is distinct from the methodical unity which Descartes had tried to establish between the different parts of philosophy. It is a simple metaphor in which the image of mind corresponds to the model of nature as revealed by Newton, for the illusion persisted that it was possible to achieve in sciences of the human mind success as remarkable as that achieved in natural sciences.

No matter how paradoxical it may seem, this radical separation of nature and mind dominated eighteenth-century thought. The dualistic direction of Locke and Newton governed men's thinking throughout the century, except for the protestations which we shall later examine.

## I   *Newton's Thought and Its Diffusion*

The essential traits of the change of mind produced by the prodigious success and diffusion of Newton's celestial mechanics are worth noting. At the beginning of the eighteenth century a kind of Cartesian orthodoxy virtually dominated instruction in every country, and Rohault's physics was widely diffused. Within thirty years it had completely disappeared; abandoned first in England, it survived in Scotland until 1715. "I believe," wrote Reid (August 24, 1787) of James Gregory, professor at the University of St. Andrews, "that he was the first professor of philosophy who taught Newton's doctrine in a Scottish university; for the Cartesian system was the orthodox system at that time and continued to be so till 1715." Voltaire, who with Maupertuis did much to propagate the Newtonian spirit in France, considered the year 1730 as the date of its definitive success. "It was only after the year 1730," he wrote concerning the philosophy of Descartes, "that there was a withdrawal in France from this chimerical philosophy, when experimental geometry and physics began to receive more attention." It was then that the Newtonians, notwithstanding Fontenelle's faithfulness to Cartesianism, gained admission to the Academy of Sciences. Later, in 1773, Holland wrote that the philosophy of Descartes had few adherents.

Newton's celestial mechanics is characterized by two traits diametrically opposed to those found in Cartesian physics: utmost precision in the application of mathematics to natural phenomena, which allows rigorous calculation of the great cosmic phenomena (motion of the planets, gravity, tides) when their initial conditions are given; and ample allowance for inexplicable phenomena, since their initial conditions cannot be deduced mathematically but are provided only by experience. In Descartes, on the contrary, there were certain instances when qualitative descriptions of mechanisms which did not result in any prediction appeared alongside a mechanical explanation which was intended to be integral. The two traits that characterize Newton's celestial mechanics are interdependent. The first depended on the discovery of differential calculus, the only language adequate to the new mechanics; like analytical geometry, it expresses the state of a magnitude at a given instant; in addition, it shows how the magnitude varies in intensity and direction at that instant. But—and this is the second trait—differential calculus does not contain the conditions that make possible its application to physical reality. It is easy for us to imagine conditions which, if they had been realized, would have ruled out the use of differential calculus and the discovery of the law of attraction: under actual conditions, in fact, the position of a planet in relation to the sun is such that the attraction of the other bodies in the universe to it is negligible in relation to the attraction of the sun, with the result that we need calculate only the reciprocal attraction of two masses; but if the other disturbing forces had been comparable to solar attraction in the chaos of reciprocal actions (typified by the world of Leibniz, in which everything depends on everything) differential calculus would have been inapplicable.

Some initial conditions could have been different, however, without affecting the solubility of the mechanical problem; for example, it makes no difference whether the tangential force of the motion of planets acts in a particular direction or in the opposite direction. The two traits are inseparable: the solution of problems of celestial mechanics requires data which cannot be explained mechanically. In other words, Newton provided no cosmogony—no scientific explanation of the origin of the existing arrangement and velocity of celestial bodies. As the astronomer Faye noted, "Newton stopped short when he came to the constitution, gyratory in origin, of the solar system." [1] But how is this lacuna in his explanation to be interpreted? We cannot fall back on chance, for if planets were flung haphazardly into the field of gravitation of the sun, the probability that they would assume their actual positions and motions is infinitely small. We must have recourse to the power of an intelligent being who set the planets in motion and who, to create isolated solar systems, "placed the fixed stars at immense distances from each other for fear that these globes would fall on each other by virtue of the force of their gravity." [2]

Newton's mechanics is linked to his own theology. His God is a geometer and an architect who knew how to combine the materials of his system in such a way that the result was a stable state of equilibrium and a continuous and periodic motion. The precariousness and instability of this link is obvious. While Voltaire accepted it and made it the foundation of his natural religion, many Newtonians tried to narrow the allowance made for mechanically inexplicable phenomena and to construct cosmogonies—solutions of problems declared insoluble by Newton. How is it that particles actuated by a random motion and subject solely to the Newtonian law of attraction are of necessity shaped into a system like the solar system? That was the question studied by Kant and by Laplace, who showed clearly how the motion inaugurated by Newton could not stop where he had intended to stop it. "On this point

[1] As quoted by Busco, Les Cosmogonies modernes (Paris, 1924), p. 52.
[2] Léon Bloch, La Philosophie de Newton (Paris, 1908), p. 502 f.

[the arrangement of the planets] I cannot help observing how far Newton deviated from the method which he applied so successfully elsewhere . . . ," wrote Laplace. "When we trace the history of the progress of the human mind and its errors, we see that the final causes are continuously pushed beyond the limits of its knowledge."[3]

Thus many who accepted Newton's physics rejected his metaphysics. Furthermore, even in his physics we find a type of intelligibility quite different from the Cartesian type. To explain a phenomenon was, for Descartes, to imagine the mechanical structure from which it issued, but such an explanation is likely to introduce several possible solutions inasmuch as the same result can be obtained through quite different mechanisms. Newton repeatedly stated that all the "hypotheses" of the Cartesians—that is, the mechanical structures imagined to account for phenomena—ought to be avoided in experimental philosophy. *Non fingo hypotheses* means that I do not invent any of the causes which may well explain phenomena but which are only probable. Newton admits no cause except the one that can be "deduced from phenomena themselves." When he enunciated the law of universal gravitation, Newton was under no illusion that he had arrived at the final cause of the phenomena explained by his law. He was only showing that it is in accordance with the same law that heavy bodies are drawn toward the center of the earth, that the liquid masses of the seas are drawn toward the moon in tides, that the moon is drawn toward the earth and the planets toward the sun. Proof of the law of universal gravitation rests solely on experimental measures. For example, we can demonstrate Newton's thesis by calculating according to the laws of Galileo the motion which actuates a heavy body placed at the distance of the moon and by determining that this motion is precisely that of the moon (the length of the degree of the terrestrial meridian is one of the elements that enter into our calculation, and it was because Newton accepted a false estimation of its length that he almost abandoned his theory, which

[3] As quoted by Busco, *op. cit.*, p. 52.

nevertheless was confirmed by a more exact measurement accomplished at a later date). It was by analogy with terrestrial gravity that he gave the name of gravitation or attraction to the unknown cause of all these phenomena. But he was by no means certain that gravitation was the cause of these phenomena, and he went so far as to posit as unassailable the principle that any action from a distance is impossible. Since the principle applies to God himself, Newton was led to declare that God is present at every point in space and that inasmuch as this is the presence of an active, intelligent being, space is the *sensorium* of God. Consequently gravitation could be explained only by collision and contact; but knowledge of phenomena was insufficient to permit deduction of the effects of collision and contact; therefore he posited, at the periphery of his experimental philosophy and by way of example, an ether in which matter was suffused and whose properties would explain gravitational phenomena by impulsion.

But the master's suggestion was not followed. "His desires have not been fulfilled," wrote D'Alembert in 1751 in his *Discourse on the Encyclopedia,* "and probably will not be fulfilled for a long time." On the contrary, there was a tendency to regard Newton's crowning achievement as the discovery of attraction and to make attraction an irreducible property of matter, like extension or impenetrability. This is clearly the interpretation favored by D'Alembert, who answered those who accused Newton of having introduced occult qualities: "What harm would he have done to philosophy by giving us grounds for believing that matter can have unsuspected properties and by disabusing us of the ridiculous confidence which allows us to think that we know them all?" This is the exact opposite of Cartesianism. Descartes began with a clear and distinct idea which gave him intuitive knowledge of the essence of matter and to which nothing could be added; it was by "consulting" this idea that one could determine the properties of matter. The Newtonians found in their master a completely different rule for determining the universal properties of matter: "The qualities of bodies which can neither increase nor decrease and which belong to all bodies that can be investigated," says the fourth rule in the *Regulae philosophandi,* "ought to be treated as qualities of all bodies." Thus experience and induction alone are decisive. Newton's rule is confirmed by the reflections on substance in Locke's *Essay.* Locke, too, assumes that substance is known to us only through an accumulation of properties which experience alone reveals to us as being rigidly interlinked. It is then permissible and even necessary to attribute attraction—which, as Newton proved, has the same coefficients regardless of the bodies under consideration—to matter. Thus measurement alone assures us of the identity of a quality. "The first means employed by nature," said Voltaire, "are not within our reach when they are not amenable to computation."

Thus attraction, though it defied explanation, was to Newtonians an incontestable property of matter. Voltaire was expressing a widely held opinion when he said that physics consists in starting from a very small number of properties of matter revealed through the senses and discovering through reason new attributes such as attraction. "The more I reflect on it," he said, "the more I am surprised that men are afraid to recognize a new principle or property in matter. It must have an infinite number of them, for in nature everything is distinct" (*Philosophie de Newton,* Part II).

Through this approach also, the philosophy of nature was separated from the philosophy of mind. The primitive data by means of which nature was interpreted were the data of experience, but the mind could not penetrate them or identify their cause. In the course of the century a long series of difficulties arose from this empiricism.

From the philosophical standpoint, Newton's science leaves us in a quandary: his mechanics can direct us toward theology or materialism, and we are not told explicitly where explanation stops or whether the mind can go beyond the opaque qualities ascribed to experience. There is a striking contrast between the precision of his results and the imprecision of his principles—a contrast which was the underlying theme of a major part of eighteenth-century philosophy.

## II Diffusion of Locke's Ideas

"Locke can be said to have created metaphysics in much the same way that Newton had created physics," wrote D'Alembert in his *Discourse on the Encyclopedia*. The word "metaphysics" is used here, as it was often used in the eighteenth century, to designate the subject of Locke's *Essay*—the study of human understanding, its powers, and its limits. In discussing the understanding in his *Essay,* Locke spoke of subjects peculiar to metaphysics—the idea of infinity, the question of liberty, the spirituality of the soul, the existence of God and the external world—but he dealt with these subjects not so much because of his interest in them as because of his desire to determine how far the human mind can go in such questions. "The aim of metaphysics," said Father Buffier (1661–1737), "is to make such an exact analysis of the objects of the mind that all things can be conceived with the greatest possible exactness and precision." [4]

By the beginning of the eighteenth century Locke's ideas were widely diffused on the continent. The *Essay* was known in its French abridgment published by Leclerc (1688), in numerous editions of Coste's translation (1700), and in the French translation of Wynne's English abridgment. It was discussed in learned journals: *Nouvelles de la République des lettres* (August, 1700 and February, 1705), *Mémoires de Trévoux* (June, 1701), *Histoire des ouvrages des savants* (July, 1701), and *Bibliothèque choisie* (Vol. VI, 1705). Long before Voltaire, in 1717, Claude Buffier wrote in his *Treatise on First Truths:* "Locke's metaphysics has led a part of Europe away from certain illusions disguised as systems." He was of course referring to the systems of Descartes and Malebranche, which are to Locke's system as fiction is to history. The *Philosophical Letters* (1734) which Voltaire brought back after his stay in England (1726–29) crowned what was already an established success.

---

[4] *Éléments de métaphysique* (ed. Bouillier), p. 260.

# Bibliography

Becker, C. L. *The Heavenly City of the Eighteenth-Century Philosophers.* New Haven, 1932.

Bloch, L. *La philosophie de Newton.* Paris, 1908.

Carré, M. H. *Phases of Thought in England,* pp. 225 ff. Oxford, 1949.

Cassirer, E. *The Philosophy of the Enlightenment,* trans. F. Koelin and J. Pettegrove. Princeton and London, 1951.

Copleston, F. *A History of Philosophy.* Vol. 5, *Hobbes to Hume.* Westminster, Maryland, 1964.

Faguet, E. *Le XVIIIe siècle.* 1890.

Flamenc, L. le. *Les Utopies prérévolutionaires et la philosophie du XVIIIe siècle.* Paris, 1934.

Gillispie, C. *The Edge of Objectivity: An Essay in the History of Scientific Ideas.* Princeton, 1960.

Hazard, P. *La crise de la conscience européenne (1680–1715).* 3 vols. Paris, 1935.

———. *The European Mind, 1680–1715,* trans. J. L. May. London, 1953.

———. *European Thought in the Eighteenth Century, from Montesquieu to Lessing,* trans. J. L. May. London, 1954.

Koyré, A. *From the Closed World to the Infinite Universe,* pp. 155 ff. Baltimore, 1957.

Lalande, A. *Les théories de l'induction et de l'expérimentation,* pp. 110–45. Paris, 1929.

McLachlan, H. *The Religious Opinions of Milton, Locke and Newton.* Manchester, 1941.

Mauzi, R. *L'idée du bonheur au XVIIIe siècle.* Paris, 1960.

Mornet, L. *Les sciences de la nature au XVIIIe siècle.* 1911.

Rosenberger. *Isaac Newton und seine physikalischen Principien.* Leipzig, 1895.

Vernière, P. *Spinoza et la pensée française avant la Révolution.* Vol. 2, *Le XVIIIe siècle.* Paris, 1954.

Whittaker, E. T. *Aristotle, Newton, Einstein.* London, 1942.

9

# FIRST PERIOD
## 1700–1740

# DEISM AND ETHICS BASED ON
# INNER FEELINGS

IT WAS in the absolute that seventeenth–century rationalists sought to establish the rules of thought and action: Cartesian reason sought "true natures" whose immutability was guaranteed by God himself; Malebranche saw ideas in God; and in Leibniz principles of knowledge are also principles of divine action. Seventeenth-century rationalism preserved the idea that the rule of thought, like the rule of action, transcends the individual. Acceptance of apriorism or innatism resulted from the desire to avoid having these rules depend on chance and accidental discoveries through individual experience.

The rationalism of the eighteenth century is quite different. Many literary critics attribute it to Descartes on the ground that he was the first to assert the rights of reason against authority, but they are mistaken. The rules of thought and action were sought in individual experience and reason, the supreme tribunal, and they required no other guarantee: through his own efforts man must find order in chaos and organize his knowledge and action. It is true that many of the thinkers of the period were inclined to find in this experience a principle of order, a benevolent reality which would support their efforts or make them possible—reality in the form of nature or God, manifested in the regularity of external things or in man's innermost tendencies. There is a striking contrast between the excessive finalism of the century of nonbelievers and the reserve with which the century of believers treated the designs of God. This finalism was not in any sense a rational principle but was rather a kind of divine complicity, with the result that the God who was its support remained in the background and became, in materialistic systems, simple nature—our own nature. There was a strong tendency to view transcendental authority, whether imposed from without by the church or monarch or from within by innate ideas, as something wholly arbitrary—a human invention justified only by reasons all too human, a stratagem of priests and politicians, a set of philosophical prejudices. It was thought that true generality—a standard—could be found by proceeding in just the opposite direction: toward nature as it is revealed to the unprejudiced observer. God himself, according to Lord Bolingbroke, resembled an English monarch whose acts were always in keeping with the conditions that result from the nature of things: he was limited by the rules which his infinite wisdom imposed on his infinite power.[1] Remarkable examples of this state of mind are provided by deism and ethics based on inner feelings.

## 1 Deism

Fénelon described with precision the scope and nature of the deist movement which was so important in England and even more so in France during the first part of the eighteenth century: "The great vogue of the freethinkers of our time is not to follow the system of Spinoza. They credit themselves with acknowledging God as the creator whose wisdom is evident in his works; but, according to them, God would be neither good nor wise if he had given man a free will—that is, the power to sin, to turn away from his final goal, to reverse the order and be forever lost. . . . By adhering to a system that eliminates any real freedom, they divest themselves of any merit, blame, or Hell; they admire God without fearing him, and they live without remorse, swayed first one way and then another by passions."[2] If, as we read these words,

---

[1] *Letters on the Spirit of Patriotism* (London, 1752).
[2] *Lettres sur divers sujets de métaphysique et de religion.* Letter 5.

we disregard the bishop's hostility toward the new spirit, we see clearly that a new conception of man, wholly incompatible with the Christian faith, had been introduced: God the architect who produced and maintained a marvelous order in the universe had been discovered in nature, and there was no longer a place for the God of the Christian drama, the God who bestowed upon Adam the "power to sin and to *reverse the order*." God was in nature and no longer in history; he was in the wonders analyzed by naturalists and biologists and no longer in the human conscience, with the feelings of sin, disgrace, or grace that accompanied his presence; he had left man in charge of his own destiny.

Thus, in his definition of a deist, the Anglican bishop Gastrell stressed the new morality that had replaced the dictates of the human conscience: "The deist is one who, while he accepts a God, denies Providence or at least restricts it to such a degree that he excludes any revelation and believes that his obligations are determined solely by public or private interest, without consideration of another life" (*Certainty and Necessity of a Revelation*).

The situation could have appeared all the more serious to the defenders of the faith because there was no one among them to counter the pretensions of reason with pure and simple fideism. All were advocates of a *natural religion* based on dogmas demonstrated by reason; they clashed with their adversaries over the issue of determining whether, as they believed, natural religion by itself leads to revealed religion. Gastrell, for example, posited the thesis that, if a deist is not at bottom an enemy of natural religion, it is impossible in a Christian land for him not to accept revealed religion. Samuel Clarke, who typified this spirit, was not content like the rationalists of the seventeenth century to expound for their own sake rational truths concerning God and the soul or even to go one step further and determine whether they would agree with revelation; he was always wavering between reason and faith, and in spite of the apparent rigor of his demonstrations, he took pains to erase the lines of demarcation between them.

The result was a singular situation: in England especially, deists and orthodox Christians used the same weapons, or rather deists had only to borrow from their adversaries. It was an orthodox theologian, Sherlock, who said in a sermon in 1705 that the religion of the Gospel is the true primordial religion of reason and nature, and that its precepts introduce us to the primordial religion which is "as old as the Creation." These words, which are in such perfect agreement with Locke's *rational Christianity*, enunciate one of the ideas which became a favorite theme of all eighteenth-century deists. They took delight in contrasting the simplicity and naturalness of the ethics of Jesus with the theological superstructures which brought on mankind so many conflicts, often bloody but in any case insoluble. An earlier example was Toland,[3] with his primitive Christianity, based solely on reason, with neither tradition nor priest. The same theme appears in *The True Gospel of Jesus Christ Vindicated* (1739) by Thomas Chubb, who made the teaching of Jesus an exposition of fundamental truths such as that of Socrates, and in *The Moral Philosopher* (1737–41) by Thomas Morgan, who sought the true religion in primitive Christianity.

In spite of their rationalism we generally find an extraordinary affinity between English deists and Scripture. Although they insisted that their doctrines were completely rational, these men, many of whom were scholars or clergymen, seemed unable to dispense with the revelation provided by Scripture. This accounts for the ambiguous character of the men and their thinking. Matthew Tindal (1656–1733), for example, the most celebrated of the deists, had a high position in the national clergy. At the end of a long life devoted to the defense of the rights of the church in its relations with the state, he published a work which borrowed its title from Sherlock's statement, quoted above—*Christianity as Old as the Creation, or the Gospel a Republication of the Religion of Nature* (1730). He called upon all the arguments of Clarke and Wollaston, and drew this conclusion concerning the comparison of natural religion and the Gospel: The religion of nature and external revelation correspond exactly to each other, with no difference between them except the manner in which they are communicated. Was it

---

[3] See Émile Bréhier, *The Seventeenth Century* (Chicago, 1966), p. 285.

not obvious that this sole difference should rule out completely any revelation, together with the historical tradition which was its consequence? If Tindal did not draw this conclusion, implicit throughout the book, it was through an obvious inconsistency. On the other hand, one of the great enemies of the Anglican clergy, Thomas Woolston (1669–1731), chose to interpret allegorically the miraculous accounts of the Gospel and to see in them pure truths of reason rather than to abandon Scripture altogether.

Thus confusion of philosophical knowledge and revelation had reached the point where the only means of freeing religion was to demonstrate that revealed religion could produce all its benefits without the motives for acting proposed by reason. Such was the goal of William Warburton (1698–1779), who became Bishop of Gloucester in 1759. In *The Divine Legation of Moses, Demonstrated on the Principles of a Religious Deist* (1737–41), he showed that one of the rational truths thought by deists to be essential to the Mosaic religion and Christianity—a truth on which ethics is grounded, namely the immortality of the soul—was not taught by Moses to his people. What conclusion could be drawn except that God gave him supernatural power and made him capable of dispensing with means indispensable to law-makers who employ only reason?

In his *Analogy of Religion, Natural and Revealed, to the Constitution and Course of Nature* (1736) Joseph Butler, Bishop of Durham in 1750, chose a different course in an attempt to mitigate the conflict. He addressed himself to adversaries—the deists—who supposedly assumed that God was the author of the system of nature, and he then undertook to demonstrate that the difficulties raised by this hypothesis were the same in nature and just as refractory as those raised against the religion, natural or revealed, which affirmed that the providence of God was reflected in the lives of men. If there were identical difficulties, it followed that there were identical presumptions on both sides, if the special proofs of religion were disregarded. His method is illustrated by his treatment of determinism or fatalism: if true, it can be used as a valid argument against both deism and religion, and the argument can be refuted in the same way in both instances. This is true because one cannot deny the existence of a finality and consequently of a will in nature but can only say to the deist that this will acts through necessity; yet the institution by the author of nature of a system of rewards and punishments, such as that taught by religion, is not made less probable by the supposition of fatalism, since our moral judgment which causes us to expect either rewards or punishments, according to the circumstances, is a fact of experience no less obvious than finality. On the whole, then, Butler's work was designed to show the equivalence between the probability of religion and the probability ordinarily associated with other things: "The natural course of things always makes it necessary for us to act in our temporal affairs in accordance with proofs similar to those which establish the truth of religion." [4] Butler's doctrine transposed a conflict that was insoluble in the terms in which it had been stated. His aim was not, like Clarke, to establish an absolute, rational, universally equivalent certainty, but to define motives for believing by comparing them with motives ordinarily accepted by men.

Shortly after Butler's work appeared, Marie Huber published a book designed to provide religion with a principle of certainty which sound judgment would adopt at sight and which would therefore eliminate all traditional opinions contrary to the nature of God or man. To accomplish her aim the Genevan writer—in *Letters concerning the Religion Essential to Man; as it is distinct from what is merely an accession to it* (the French version, also published in 1738, was printed in Amsterdam)—imagined an untutored man who discovered the First Being through self-examination, and who was then introduced into society and persuaded to accept the Christian religion. In her supposition we recognize the same spirit that led Condillac to his hypothesis of the statue. The object was to remove man from his historical and traditional milieu, from the influences that might interfere with the natural course of his thought. She had to imagine a man with respect to whom, as she put it, "no authority can be used other than the intrinsic char-

[4] *Works*, ed. W. E. Gladstone (1896), Vol. I.

acteristics of truth which an unbiased observer finds in revelation."
As for revelation itself, a distinction must be made between historical data amenable to the ordinary rules of evidence—clear and
indubitable truths of common sense—and accessory elements tinged
with obscurity, such as the harsh evangelical advice which was
sometimes given by Jesus and which goes against man's natural
inclinations; finally, revelation contains impenetrable mysteries,
many of which contradict our elementary sense of justice—for example, the notion of imputative righteousness, ransom, or substi-
tution, which attributes the merit or demerit of an act to someone
other than the performer. Marie Huber's unhistorical man obviously
accepted only the unhistorical part of Christianity, for he did not
intend to be overburdened by the weight of tradition. Deism is but
one aspect of a general tendency—the tendency of the individual
to find all the elements of his moral and intellectual life in his own
experience and reason.

The conflict continued for many years. Orthodox Christians accused deists of being atheists in disguise, since, according to them,
through a series of logical consequences the affirmation of the
existence of God leads to faith; and the deists accused the orthodox
Christians of adding arbitrarily to the data of reason. The conflict
was speculative only in appearance. Deism may have seemed to its
adversaries to be the same thing as atheism, but only because it
could not replace the religion which François de la Chambre, a
French disciple of Clarke and a noted enemy of the deists, describes
thus in his *Treatise on the True Religion* (1737): "Nothing is more
desirable for princes, for societies, or for the individuals of which
societies are composed." For princes, it "encourages people to do
their duty"; for societies, the notion of a God of retribution pro-
motes virtue; for individuals, God is a comforter. Although he first
says that atheism denies the distinction between good and evil, and
then admits that there is an atheism which recognizes the distinction and confidently follows whatever reason prescribes, De la
Chambre quickly adds that religion provides much stronger support for this distinction. Thus when deists spoke of reason and

freedom of thought, their adversaries countered by emphasizing social policy and the instruments of government. In consequence, deism and atheism were linked to every demand for tolerance, to every tendency toward reform. Deism was linked both to empiricism and to individualism; the "inner feeling" was the archenemy of orthodox Christians, and De la Chambre distrusted it, even when he saw La Bruyère put it to the service of religion. Criticizing the proof of God's existence which La Bruyère based on an inner feeling, he wrote that religion "is of no use in proving the divine existence to those who deny it, since one person cannot manifest his inner feelings to another and since the inner feelings of one person are no model for the inner feelings of another." Here he anticipated the Savoyard Vicar's criticism of religion. But his remark also may refer to a movement which paralleled deism and which, like deism, was linked to empiricism and individualism. We shall now follow the development of this movement during the first forty years of the century.

## II  *Ethics Based on Inner Feelings*

To Hobbes man was naturally an egotist and could be induced only by external coercion to accomplish virtuous acts, that is, acts useful to society. Significantly, both affirmations were contested and criticized in England at the beginning of the eighteenth century, the first by Shaftesbury and the second by Mandeville.

The views of Shaftesbury (1671–1713) contrast sharply with those of his contemporaries. He believed that natural social inclinations in each animal species were directed toward the good of the species, that these inclinations were the work of a providence which, through them, maintained the perfect harmony of the universal order, and that man possessed a "moral sense" which made him aware of good and evil.

Francis Hutcheson, professor at the University of Glasgow in 1729, gave a more systematic turn to Shaftesbury's ideas in several of his works, particularly in *An Inquiry into the Original of Our*

*Ideas of Beauty and Virtue* (1725). He, too, came under the influence of Malebranche. His proofs of the existence of the "moral
sense" are worth noting: it issues from the disinterested judgment
which we bring to bear on acts, or rather on the person who has
accomplished them; otherwise we would have the same feelings for
a fertile field as for a generous friend; we would no more admire
a person who lived in a distant land or century than we love the
mountains of Peru; we would have the same inclination toward
inanimate beings and rational beings. This moral sense has no religious foundation; we have lofty ideas of honor without knowing
the Divinity and without expecting any reward from him; furthermore, without our moral sense divine sanctions could make us
reach decisions only by coercion and not by obligation. Nor is it
related to the social good, for we despise a man who betrays his
country in the interest of our own, and we esteem a generous
enemy. Finally, it is grounded on a quality truly inherent in the
person whom we are judging, for it is foolish for us to assume that
the virtue of another person depends on our approbation of him.
We should add that the word "sense" is appropriate, and that it
does not presuppose any innate idea.

This faith in man's natural benevolence toward man was widely
accepted in the eighteenth century. In 1745 Diderot translated (not
without some modification) *The Essay on Merit and Virtue,* in
which Shaftesbury's stated aim was to show that virtue is almost
indivisibly linked to knowledge of God and that man's temporal
happiness is inseparable from virtue. The second clause in his
sentence makes the first one almost redundant.

The second of Hobbes' theses is implicitly criticized in a work
which was immensely popular throughout the eighteenth century:
*The Fable of the Bees, or Private Vices, Public Benefits* (published
in 1705 and reprinted, with additions, in 1714 and 1723), by Bernard
de Mandeville, a Dutch physician residing in London. He argues
that "Envy itself," pride, and human passions in general are "Ministers of Industry," and that the suppression of vice, which ethics
seeks to destroy, would put an end to industry and commerce

(p. 11). As Adam Smith indicated in his critical exposition of Mandeville's ideas,[6] the heart of his thesis is an extreme moral rigorism which, like Cynicism, views as sensuality everything that deviates from ascetic severity and as luxury everything that is not a prime necessity; thus in the burgeoning industrial civilization around him he sees evidence of vicious passions, and he thinks that seemingly disinterested acts, such as the devotion of a Decius to his country, can be obtained only through the legislator's skill in exciting vanity; vanity, the strongest of the personal passions, surpasses the egotistical pleasures which we must sacrifice when we act for others. What the eighteenth century retained was not Mandeville's rigorism, however, but the perfect harmony between natural egotism and social utility.

III  *The Philosophy of Common Sense: Claude Buffier*

Clear evidence of the same state of mind is provided by the work of the Jesuit Claude Buffier, of whom Voltaire wrote: "In his treatises on metaphysics there are sections which Locke would not have disowned." The work attracted little attention until the end of the century, when Reid and the Scottish philosophers showed that Buffier had anticipated their own philosophy of common sense. The English translation of the *Treatise on First Truths* (1717), published in 1780, even accused them explicitly of plagiarizing Buffier.

We shall see later that the Scottish school was hostile to Locke as well as to Descartes, and it is certain that in spite of Buffier's sincere esteem for Locke, the central idea of his system is totally alien to Locke. This idea is that first truths are not linked to the inner sense, as Descartes supposed, and that the affirmation of such a union leads to an extravagant skepticism which can be overcome only at the price of inconsistency. For to say that, primitively, we are aware of the actual modification of the soul only as this modification is revealed to us by the inner sense, is to say that we can legitimately doubt external things, the events of our past, and the

[6] *Theory of Moral Sentiments,* VIII, ii.

existence of other men, since none of these things could be the object of the inner sense; and it is illusory to think that we could begin with the modifications and demonstrate rationally the existence of the things. The Cartesian proof of the existence of God through the idea of God is a typical example of illusory thinking, for if we "begin with what we experience within ourselves—our thoughts, ideas, or feelings," we cannot, as this proof would have us do, go beyond "the perception of our own thoughts."

All the insoluble problems that issued from the initial fallacy of methodical doubt are, therefore, fallacious problems. There are truths relating to existences outside us (called "external truths") which are "first" just as surely as the inner sense—the reality of the external world or of other men, for example. For Buffier's first truths are in no sense the common notions which Descartes (cf. *Principles,* I, 49) utilized in his reasonings, such as "the whole is greater than the part," which is a simple logical or "internal" truth, a mere linkage of ideas from which existences could never be deduced. First truths posit existences outside us.

The faculty which perceives these truths is "common sense." Here what is meant is not innate ideas but "a simple disposition to think in a particular way at a particular juncture"—for instance, to affirm, when we are in the act of perceiving, that external objects exist. Common sense is the same thing as nature, since "it is nature and our awareness of nature that we must recognize as the source and origin of all truths of principle." That nature should mislead us is unthinkable, and the sole function of the philosopher is to rid common sense of the obscurity diffused by "those who are not familiar with objects beyond the senses and popular ideas" or by "scholars who misconstrue the most important truths." How could it be otherwise, when "excessive curiosity, vanity, bias, the brilliant succession of a great number of consequences . . . conceal the falsity of their principle?"

Buffier had no difficulty in refuting the reiterated objections of the skeptics concerning the reality of the external world. He pointed out that sense data are "adequate guides in daily life" even if they are not certain enough "to procure for us a science of pure curiosity," that whatever seems probable to us generally conforms to truth if the ordinary needs of life are at issue, and that in the opposite case reflection readily corrects the situation.

Buffier was a theologian, and we should not fail to note the close union which he established between the philosophy of common sense and religious truths. "Out of consideration for certain turns of mind," he wrote at the end of the foreword, "I have restricted myself exclusively to the purely philosophical sphere; but it will lead to the most solid principles of religion." We should note especially the end of the first part of his treatise on the certainty of the testimony of the senses (Chapters XIV–XVIII) and of human authority (XIX–XXIV), particularly his discussion of Locke's opinion on the second point. Here he reprimands Locke for saying that the argument of authority reached only probable conclusions whereas, in certain questions of fact, it is equivalent to certainty; he also censures him for saying that the probability of testimony is lessened in proportion to the number of intermediaries through which it is transmitted—obviously false when all witnesses are equally credible. It is clear that his aim was to ground the authority of the Catholic tradition—that is, of testimony traceable ultimately to direct perception of the acts and words of Jesus—on the first truths of common sense, and that in his view apologetics had everything to gain by relinquishing Cartesian philosophy and returning to common sense.

It is in the second book of his *Treatise* that Buffier relies mainly on Locke, in his analysis of the ideas of essence, infinity, identity, duration, substance, and liberty. He joins Locke in condemning the Cartesians' attempts to resolve the problem of the origin of ideas and of the relation of mind and body, and he declares in particular his hostility to any physiological explanation of human faculties. "The most substantial fruit of metaphysics," he concludes, "is the clear recognition of the limits of our mind and the vanity of so many philosophers, ancient and modern."

# BIBLIOGRAPHY

Bartholmès, C. *Histoire critique des doctrines religieuses de la philosophie moderne.* Strasbourg, 1855.

Brett, R. L. *The Third Earl of Shaftesbury.* London, 1951.

Broad, C. D. *Five Types of Ethical Theory.* London, 1930.

Carrau, L. *La philosophie religieuse en Angleterre depuis Locke jusqu'à nos jours.* 1888.

Espinas, A. "La philosophie en Écosse au XVIIIe siècle: Hutcheson, Adam Smith, Hume," *Revue philosophique*, XI, 1881.

Flew, A. *Hume's Philosophy of Belief.* New York, 1961.

Hutcheson, F. *Works.* 5 vols. Glasgow, 1772.

Lanson, G. "La transformation des idées morales et la naissance des morales rationnelles de 1689 à 1715," *Revue du mois,* January, 1910.

———. "Questions diverses sur l'histoire de l'esprit philosophique avant 1750," *Revue d'histoire littéraire de la France,* 1912.

Lefèvre, A. "Butler's View of Conscience and Obligation," *The Philosophical Review,* 1900.

Leroux, E. and Leroy, A.-L. *La philosophie anglaise classique.* Paris, 1951.

Leroy, A. *La critique et la religion chez David Hume,* pp. 1-3. Paris, 1929.

Lyon, G. *L'idéalisme en Angleterre au XVIIIe siècle.* Paris, 1888.

Mackintosh, J. *On the Progress of Ethical Philosophy, Chiefly during the XVII and the XVIII Centuries.* Edinburgh, 1872.

Martineau, J. *Types of Ethical Theory.* 2 vols. 3d ed., rev. Oxford, 1901.

Montgomery, F. K. *La vie et l'œuvre du P. Buffier.* 1930.

Raphael, D. D. *The Moral Sense.* Oxford, 1947.

Schlegel, D. B. *Shaftesbury and the French Deists.* Chapel Hill, N. C., 1956.

Scott, W. R. F. *Hutcheson, His Life, Teaching, and Position in the History of Philosophy.* London, 1900.

Seth, J. *English Philosophers and Schools of Philosophy.* London, 1912.

Sidgwick, H. *Outlines of the History of Ethics for English Readers.* London, 1931.

Sorley, W. R. *A History of English Philosophy.* Cambridge, 1920. Reprinted 1937.

# BERKELEY

GEORGE BERKELEY (1685–1753), born of English stock at Dysert, in Ireland, entered Trinity College, Dublin, in 1700. He took his degree of Master of Arts, became a fellow in 1707, was ordained, and lectured on Greek, Hebrew, and theology. Few philosophers have been more precocious or formulated a doctrine at an earlier age. His *Treatise concerning the Principles of Human Knowledge,* published in 1710, contains all the features of his doctrine, of which a part had been expounded a year earlier in *An Essay Towards a New Theory of Vision.* His notebook, the *Commonplace Book,* written between 1702 and 1710, shows his doctrine in its formative stages, and his *Three Dialogues between Hylas and Philonous,* published in 1713, presents it in a new form, intended for a very wide public. Berkeley attempted, through rectification of the philosophical errors which he was combating, to revive moral and religious feelings and to refute freethinkers. During his sojourn in London he made a direct attack on Arthur Collins, one of the most eminent of the freethinkers, in his articles in *The Guardian* (1713). The following years were given over to travels in France, possibly in Spain, and especially in Italy and Sicily, where he evidenced an interest in geology and geography as well as in archeology. It was in France (in Lyons, as he was returning to England) that he wrote *De motu* (1720), in which he attacked Newton's physics. In 1726, after he had served for two years as Dean of Derry, he inherited a part of the fortune of Esther

Vanhomrigh. His first thought was to use his inheritance to propagate Christian civilization and thought in the American possessions of England, and he made public his intention to found a college in Bermuda. On the strength of a promise of an important subsidy from the government of Robert Walpole, he set out in 1728 and took up residence in Rhode Island, where he waited in vain; the money was not sent to him and he became less enthusiastic about the project. During his sojourn in Rhode Island, which lasted until 1731, he first became intimately acquainted with the Neo-Platonic philosophers Plotinus and Proclus, who had a profound influence on his last works; he wrote *Alciphron, or The Minute Philosopher* (1732), which continued the polemic against freethinking initiated in *The Guardian*; and he met Jonathan Edwards, who propagated his ideas in America. After his return to England in 1732, *Alciphron* and the third edition of *An Essay Towards a New Theory of Vision* caused him to become involved in a polemic with the mathematicians, which inspired his defense and explanation of the theory (*The Theory of Vision . . . Vindicated and Explained,* 1733) and *The Analyst* (1734). During the same year he published a new edition of his *Dialogues and Principles,* which contained important doctrinal additions. He was named Bishop of Cloyne, an Irish diocese populated mainly by Catholics. The plight of Ireland caused him to take up economic questions (*The Querist,* 1735–37; *Letter on the Project of a National Bank,* 1737) and moral questions (*A Discourse . . . Occasioned by the Enormous License and Irreligion of the Times,* 1738). On several occasions (notably in 1745, during the Scottish revolt in favor of the Stuarts), he affirmed his desire to reach an understanding with Catholics: (*The Bishop of Cloyne's Letter to the Roman Catholics of the Diocese of Cloyne,* 1745; *A Word to the Wise,* 1749; *Maxims concerning Patriotism,* 1750). The outbreak of an epidemic in Ireland, in 1740, provided him with an occasion to experiment with tar water, a remedy which he had discovered in Rhode Island and in which he thought he saw the universal panacea. This was the point of departure of his last philosophical work, *Siris: A Chain of Philosophical Reflections and In-*

*quiries concerning the Virtues of Tar-Water and Divers Other Subjects Connected Together and Arising One from Another* (1744), in which his guest for the reasons for the efficacy of the marvelous remedy brought him to Platonic metaphysics.

## I  *Philosophical Ideas in The Commonplace Book*

*The Commonplace Book* contains a number of short notes intended mainly for the preparation of the work which Berkeley was contemplating—his *Principles*. These notes refer not only to the projected Introduction and to the first book—the only parts of the work to appear—but also to a second book, which was to deal with the applications of the doctrine in geometry and physics ("My end is not to deliver metaphysics altogether in a general scholastic way," he wrote, "but in some measure to accommodate them to the sciences and show how they may be useful in optics, geometry, etc."), and to a third, which was to deal with ethics. Thus in the *Principles* (as in the *Dialogues*) we find only the elementary part of the doctrine; *De motu* substitutes in certain respects for the second book, and *Alciphron* for the third. Berkeley never actually carried out the project of his youth, however, and *The Commonplace Book,* in which he set down his fleeting reflections, many of them never used, is all the more interesting because it reveals the breadth and scope of his project. The last note sums up his aim in these words: "The whole directed to practice and morality—as appears first, from making manifest the nearness and omnipresence of God; secondly, from cutting off the useless labor of sciences, and so forth."

Still, we find nothing here that resembles the heavy war machine used by Clarke and his like to advance the good cause. Berkeley lived in a happy, buoyant atmosphere, and his manner, though less tense and harsh, recalls that of Malebranche. Nor do we find anything that resembles the Cartesian attitude, wholly antinatural, of peaceful meditation beyond the level of the senses. It is "ridiculous in the mathematicians to despise sense," for without it "the mind can have no knowledge, no ideas. All meditations or contemplations . . . which might be prior to the ideas received from without by the senses are patent absurdities (328)." The famous Cartesian *Cogito* is tautological (731) or, if it means that knowledge of our own existence is prior to that of things, contrary to truth (537). To Berkeley the pretended spirituality of mathematics is merely an illusion: "The folly of mathematicians [is] in judging of sensations by their senses. Reason was given us for nobler uses" (370).

The stable realities which geometers pretend to identify are shown by Berekley to be changeable, undergoing countless modifications and blending together in the flow of consciousness. If it has the fixed measurement ascribed to it by physicists, why is "time in pain longer than time in pleasure" (7)? If a succession of ideas is attributed to the Eternal Being, one may wonder whether, to God, "a day does not seem to God a thousand years, rather than a thousand years a day." Time is a sensation, and it is solely in the mind. But the same is true of space: a line, to the eye, is a thing that changes with our position, and this, according to Berkeley, ought to prove highly embarrassing to mathematicians in defining such simple notions as the equality of two triangles, for if sight is to be the judge, "then all lines seen under the same angle are equal, which they will not acknowledge." Touch cannot be the judge, however, for we cannot touch or feel these lines without length and these surfaces without depth imagined by the mathematicians. To the objection that "pure intellect must be judge," he replies that "lines and triangles are not operations of the mind" (521).

Berkeley's spirituality then is not that of a Plato or a Descartes for whom mathematics is a step toward the intelligible. How could it be otherwise in a man who wrote: "Vain is the distinction [which Locke had postulated] between intellectual and material world" (528)? There is no necessity to pass from one to the other, no dialectic since no opposition exists. This is why Berkeley criticizes Locke for making a distinction between ideas of sensation and ideas of reflection. Is there "any real difference between certain ideas of reflection and others of sensation"—for example, between "perception and white, black, sweet"? Just how "does the perception of white differ from white" (575)? The distinction between "an idea and perception of the idea has been one great cause of imagining material substances" distinct from spiritual things (599). Unless we suppose that perception is "somewhat different from the idea perceived"—that is, that it is "an idea of reflection," whereas the thing perceived is "an idea of sensation"—why posit the distinction between the two worlds?

The mind then does not have to win its victory by detaching itself or isolating itself, for nothing exists other than mind, considered in its concrete reality—as a person who wills and acts. "Nothing properly but persons, that is, conscious things, do exist. All other things are not so much existences as manners of the existence of persons" (24).

Berkeley's main task then was to show that the obstacles—opaque, impenetrable realities—seen by philosophers were specious. Locke's *Essay* began with prudent reservations concerning the limits of our faculties and our definitive ignorance of the intimate essence of things. Berkeley's *Principles* begin with the assurance that these limits and this ignorance relate only to the misuse of our faculties: "We have first raised a dust, and then complain we cannot see" (*Principles,* Section 3).

## II *The New Theory of Vision*

Is it not possible for us simply by opening our eyes to apprehend, through sight, external objects and material things which have certain dimensions, which are separated by determinate distances, and which constitute a world totally alien to the mind? Berkeley answers our preliminary objection in his *New Theory of Vision*. Our mistake is in thinking that we *see* distances, dimensions, and displacements or positional relations; we do not *see* distances, since a point, regardless of its distance, can always be projected on the same point of the retina; we do not see dimensions, since the relative dimensions of objects can be estimated only through knowledge of their remoteness—knowledge which we lack; finally, we do not see displacements, since they depend soley on changes in relations involving distance.

His theory then eradicates the distinction, traditional since Aristotle, between particular sensibles—colors, sounds, and so on—and common sensibles such as magnitude and extension. There are only particular sensibles, according to Berkeley; the old common sensibles—those studied by the geometer—are really peculiar to touch; the object of geometry is tangible extension (Section 139 ff.).

Why, then, do we think we see external objects when color is just as internal as pleasure or grief? The reason is that we learn from experience that infinitely small changes in the gradation of light and colors correspond to changes in distance; if we try to imagine ourselves without this experience or prior to it, we are like "a man born blind, being made to see. . . . The objects intromitted by sight would seem to him (as in truth they are) no other than a new set of thoughts or sensations, each whereof is as near to him as the perceptions of pain or pleasure" (Section 41). We have learned from repeated experiences that a particular adaptive sensation of the eye corresponds to a particular distance, that an object is distinct in proportion as it is near to us; these differences in the visual scheme are like signs in which we read the properties which touch will cause us to perceive directly.

Thus we can dismiss sight, for it does not enable us to become acquainted with a reality inaccessible to the mind. But Berkeley is led to a much more important conclusion: between these signs or visual aspects and the things signified there is obviously no more resemblance or necessary connection than between a word in our language and its meaning; we must learn to spell this language just as we spell words: "I see, therefore, in strict philosophical truth, that rock only in the same sense that I may be said to hear it, when the word *rock* is pronounced" (*Alciphron,* Fourth Dialogue, Section 11). Nothing would cause us to foresee a priori the link between a change of clarity and a change of distance. All languages are instituted by minds, and a universal language such as the one under discussion here could have been instituted only by a universal mind, by an arbitrary decree of Providence which rules over us. Consequently the study of vision, far from turning us toward material things, leads us first to our own mind, then to the supreme mind which governs all things. It is still possible, however, that touch might provide us with direct knowledge of material objects. Does it?

## III  *Immaterialism in "The Principles" and "The Dialogues"*

The visual language instituted by God can help us or harm us. It helps us if we simply consider it as a sign of tangible qualities; it harms us if we mistake signs for realities and forget the mind that animates them. That is true of any language. *A New Theory of Vision,* the source of important psychological works, is important to Berkeley only because it calls attention to one of the illusions of language, even in knowledge which seems most immediate. In the *Principles* he shows at the outset that language is the source of the very errors that he has discovered and condemned in visual perception. Coming after Locke and Malebranche, he was preoccupied from the outset by this question of language, which is interposed like a veil between us and our ideas: "Locke's great oversight," he writes, "seems to be that he did not begin with his Third Book [or] at least that he had not some thought of it at first. Certainly the two first books don't agree with what he says in the third" (*Commonplace Book,* 710). Many times in his notebook he engages in speculation (his hypothesis is similar to that of the man blind from birth) concerning the thought of a solitary man who, "put into the world alone with admirable abilities . . . would know without words" (555).

It is in such a state, prelinguistic in a sense, that the Introduction to *Principles*[1] seeks to place us: "Whatever ideas I consider, I shall

---

[1] A first draft of his Introduction, written before the end of 1708, is published in Frazer's edition (I, 407).

endeavor to take them bare and naked into my view; keeping out of my thoughts, so far as I am able, those names which long and constant use has so strictly united with them" (21). Later he writes: "I entreat [the reader] that he would make my words the occasion of his own thinking, and endeavor to attain the same train of thoughts in reading that I had in writing them" (25).

What, then, are the dangers of language? Briefly, language is the source of belief in abstract ideas, and this belief is the source of the fundamental philosophical error or belief in an independent reality of mind—an error which is the source of all scientific and moral aberrations. The *Principles* were intended to show this filiation.

It was in Locke that Berkeley found the doctrine of abstract ideas which he criticized. To Locke an abstract idea was properly a fabrication of the understanding, peculiar to human reason, which he substituted for the real but unknown essence of things in order to be able to give a meaning to the words of language and, consequently, to be able to reason and to communicate his ideas; a substitute for the substantial form, it owes its existence to the fact that we disregard everything peculiar to individual objects which resemble each other in certain qualities and preserve only that which is common to all of them.

The abstract idea, as defined here, is an invention of philosophers and is neither possible nor useful. It is not possible, because it is obviously contradictory for us to have the idea of a motion which belongs neither to one body nor to another, which is neither fast nor slow, neither straight nor curvilinear; at least one of the contraries must belong to the abstract idea, yet it excludes both. It is not useful: much importance is attached to the geometer's demonstrations, which are said to apply to triangles in general and not to a particular triangle, but the question is to determine whether it is not possible for us to speak of triangles in general, without recourse to the abstract idea of the triangle—that is, without imagining a triangle which is neither isosceles, nor scalene, nor equilateral. It is entirely possible for us to draw a particular triangle which will represent all other triangles, if (as Berkeley explains in the second edition) we pay no attention to "the particular qualities of the angles, or relations of the sides" (16). It follows that we do not need an abstract idea for demonstration but only a particular idea which will be the *sign* of other particular ideas—a positive idea of great importance in Berkeley's system. To think is not to apprehend an abstract, real, or nominal essence but to pass from one idea to another, thanks to the function of sign assumed by the idea.

The source of this error, according to Berkeley, is in language or, more exactly, in the manner in which language is interpreted. A man who had been "put into the world alone . . . would know without words. Such a one would never think of genera and species or abstract general ideas" (*Commonplace Book*, 555). It is wrongly assumed that language would be meaningless if each word did not signify an abstract idea. This is untrue for two reasons: first, a word such as "triangle" signifies not an idea but the unlimited multiplicity of all figures which are plane surfaces bounded by three straight lines; next (a profound observation which later proved to be very useful in the psychology of thought), in ordinary conversation most words evoke no idea at all but are employed like letters in algebra, which always stand for particular quantities—quantities that we need not keep in mind in order to reason clearly. Furthermore, language is often intended to suggest, not ideas but, as in discourses, emotions or attitudes. These observations tend to loosen the bond between language and ideas: a sign is not a label attached to a thing but is rather the instigation of a complex train of thought which retains a certain determination and a certain suppleness.

The abstract idea is a monster of logic wrongly linked to the use of language. But Berkeley's prime target—the doctrine of the existence of a thing independent of the mind—had its source in faith in abstract ideas. In his notebook Berkeley observed that inasmuch as modern philosophers had set down exact principles, it was surprising that they had gone so far astray in drawing their consequences. The modern philosophers to whom he refers are Descartes, Malebranche, and Locke; their principles are the theory of knowledge which reduces external things to ideas—that is, to modalities of mind; and the false consequences are their corpuscular physics. Berkeley saw (this stands out in all his critical remarks) a conflict between the theory which reduces all external things that are perceived to modalities of mind, and physics, which affirms the existence of matter as a substance distinct from mind. This conflict was expressed in Locke by the distribution of qualities into primary qualities—such as extension and solidity—which pertain to things, and secondary qualities—odor, heat—which are modalities of mind.

Berkeley does not dwell on principles which, after Locke's analysis, seemed almost obvious to him. All external objects are composed of what Locke called "ideas of sensation"—odor, color, solidity, and so forth—or of what Berkeley (who, as we noted earlier, refused to acknowledge ideas of reflection distinct from ideas of sensation) calls simply "ideas." It is obvious, however, that an idea exists only if perceived by a mind and that it ceases to exist as soon as it is no longer perceived. Being without being perceived (*esse* without *percipi*) is merely one more abstract idea, and it is just as impossible as the abstract idea of a triangle or a man. This truth is as self-evident as an axiom: that only minds which perceive and ideas perceived by them exist (*esse est percipere et percipi*) is not a new doctrine; it is the principle recognized by all modern thinkers (1–7).

Immediately they make distinctions, however, which ruin the doctrine. To Locke (and Descartes) ideas are representative; they are copies or images of an external reality. This thesis is absurd, since it is intuitively evident that only an idea can resemble another idea; moreover, these models that they speak of either have been perceived by us and are then ideas, or they are not ideas and cannot be discussed. Locke agreed to this (*Essay,* II, 8, 15) in his handling of secondary qualities; odor, sound, color certainly do not exist except in their perceived being. But this is not true of the primary qualities—figure, motion, solidity—which constitute the body as it is defined by modern corpuscular physics and which exist in matter. The distinction is inadmissible, for if we try to imagine a figure in motion, by itself (that is, divested of color or any other sensible quality), we immediately see the impossibility of our doing so: extension and motion in themselves are then abstract ideas which the mind imagines it can contrive. Furthermore, reasons valid against the reality of secondary qualities outside mind are equally valid against primary qualities. According to the example of the ancient Skeptics, sweetness cannot be a primary quality of wine since wine seems bitter to us when we are sick; if that is true, neither magnitude nor solidity is a property of a body, since magnitude changes according to the distance and structure of our eyes, and hardness or softness depends on the force we exert on the body. In his *Dialogues* Berkeley nevertheless indicates a psychological basis for the distinction between diverse qualities—something later called their emotive tone. Heat, cold, smells, and tastes affect us with the vivacity of a strong feeling of pleasure or pain, in contrast to the rather insipid ideas of extension and motion. The absurdity of placing pleasure and grief outside mind was responsible for the attribution of a separate existence to primary qualities alone, but such a reason is not sufficient, for a sensation is not more or less a sensation in proportion as it is more or less stamped by affectivity. Finally, since these qualities are not in the perceiving mind, a subject to which they can be assigned must be imagined: matter, which serves as their substratum. After Locke's criticism of the idea of substance, it was not hard for Berkeley to show the emptiness of his "something I know not what" of which nothing can be said.

Berkeley's situation here is singular. Descartes had managed to lay the foundation of modern philosophy only by making ideas the immediate objects of knowledge; but in its Cartesian form as well as in the form it had assumed under Boyle and Newton, one essential aspect of this philosophy—mechanistic physics—was intimately linked to the theory of ideas. Then Berkeley made his appearance and declared that by following the first way—the way of truth—uncompromisingly, he had found mechanistic physics to be inadmissible. In Descartes physics was linked to philosophy only by virtue of the distinction between a confused idea and a clear idea which had as its object a true, immutable nature; in Malebranche there was an even more clear-cut distinction between a sensation, a simple modality of mind, and an idea which has its object in God. From Berkeley's point of view, however, this distinction completely disappears, for according to him it issues from a vicious circle. The clear ideas of extension, motion, and number (clear ideas which are abstract ideas and have no true existence) do not provide the foundation for mathematics and mechanistic physics; instead, the latter seek to justify themselves by arbitrarily conferring a special value on these ideas.

Berkeley's doctrine, with its apparently simple and obvious principle, was bound to upset the equilibrium of the science of his time. It is interesting to follow him in the fiery struggle in which he seems at times to typify the reactionary and condemn the surest acquisitions of modern mathematics, at times to possess a singularly new and original conception of science.

Berkeley has little trouble, of course, in refuting the objections raised in the name of common sense. Told that it is impossible to distinguish between reality and the chimeras of our imagination if being consists only in being perceived, he counters that the distinction is easy: there are in me ideas which are independent of my will; they are particularly strong, vivid, and distinct; finally, they are produced according to fixed rules, in such a way that one anticipates the other. It is this mass of ideas that we call a *nature;* the only bodies dictated by common sense (which knows nothing of the corporeal substance postulated by philosophers) are regular combinations of such ideas, which are what we ordinarily call things. It may be objected that common sense holds that things are permanent whereas ideas are annihilated as soon as they cease to be perceived—that the landscape before me is not annihilated when I close my eyes whereas my vision of the landscape is annihilated. This objection is easily answered, however, for the permanence of these ideas may be allowed if their being is related not only to my mind but also to other minds and to the universal mind (25–28).

There remained mathematical and mechanistic physics, which then reigned supreme. Two basic notions were incompatible with his doctrine: the notion of infinitude in mathematics, and in consequence the whole of infinitesimal calculus; the notion of cause or force in physics, and in consequence the whole of Newtonian dynamics.

Berkeley holds that mathematics has a sensible object. Number and magnitude, apart from sensible things, are only abstract and false ideas. To the senses, however, space is not infinitely divisible, for there is a tangible and visible minimum beneath which nothing is perceived and, consequently, beneath which nothing exists. Boldly, he calls in question even the oldest discoveries of the Greek mathematicians: irrationals are inadmissible, for any magnitude is composed of a finite number of visible minima; we cannot, therefore, speak of a polygon tending toward a circle or of having an idea of a space larger than any given space, for since that of which one has the idea must be something given, the thing cannot be larger than itself. The same argument appears in various forms in *The Analyst,* but it always goes back to the principle: *esse est percipi.*

Berkeley's criticism of Newtonian mechanics, from the *Principles* to *De motu,* is linked up with the same principle. We recall that Malebranche attributed any efficient causality to God, giving as his reason the fact that when he examined the clear idea which he had of matter—the idea of extension—he found in it nothing resembling a force or an efficient causality. Here Berkeley's thinking runs parallel to that of Malebranche: the ideas or perceived beings into which the external world is resolved are passive; the so-called internal, active essences which we attribute to things are pure fictions, since we do not perceive them; we observe that ideas follow and replace each other in accordance with general rules revealed to us by experience; we do not see that one idea is the cause of another. On the other hand, experience shows us that true causality pertains to minds; we know ourselves as free agents. Furthermore, it should be noted that, for Berkeley, to be a cause is by the same token to be the cause of an idea; a moving cause is a cause which makes a certain succession of ideas occur in a mind; to say that we are free to move is to say that our minds are capable of producing in us a succession of ideas corresponding to the motion of our arms. Alternatively, there are ideas and series of ideas which occur in us without our willing their occurrence, and which therefore must be attributed to the influence of other minds; and from this, common sense derives its belief in the existence of other persons. Certain motions which are seen, certain words which are heard, are sure signs of the existence of these other minds. According to Berkeley, only prejudice prevents us from generalizing the procedure and knowing God or the universal active mind as surely as we know other minds, for outside the ideas which we produce and the ideas produced in us by finite minds analogous to ours are all the ideas that constitute what we call *nature*—ideas which form groups and series so regular that through experience, the perception of a particular idea becomes for us the sure sign of another particular idea, and natural science is simply a kind of grammar of nature which teaches us the constant relations of signs to the things they signify.

But then the ideas produced in us in this way must be attributed to an omnipotent mind, nature's creator, which acts in accordance with a constant will and infallible rules, which are nothing but the laws of nature. Nature is not, as pagan philosophers assumed, a distinct cause of God; it is the language through which God speaks to us as distinctly, if we know how to interpret it, as our fellow men.

Consequently physics is a science of laws and not of causes, which are relegated to metaphysics. The division of tasks anticipates, in a sense, the positivist conception of science; but we should note that Berkeley's legalistic conception is intimately linked to finalism, which was probably the only reason for its introduction. What matters most is not language itself but what it communicates to us. Rigorous exactitude in reducing each particular phenomenon to general rules hardly concerns Berkeley, who proposes "nobler views, such as to recreate and exalt the mind with a prospect of the beauty, order, extent, and variety of natural things" which these rules evidence in their creator (109). These uniform rules bear the imprint of wisdom but not of necessity, for their cause is a free, omnipotent, and providential will.

Mechanistic physics—"natural philosophy"—boasted of finding in nature itself the active, moving causes of phenomena. Boyle's mechanistic physics indentified the cause of light and sound with the insensible mechanical structures of matter; the Newtonians saw in attraction an essential property of matter and a source of motion. According to Berkeley, in modern physics positive results must be separated from the prejudices which are added to them. Thus the mechanist apprehends a constant relation between certain mechanical phenomena and sound, and he finds a law linking certain ideas of motion to the idea of sound; but to say that he has found the cause of sound is to say that one idea can be the cause of another idea, which is absurd. Berkeley's admiration for Newton is unstinted so long as he limits himself to the discovery of analogies between apparently isolated phenomena, such as gravity and tides, each of which becomes a particular example of a general law of nature, according to his investigations; but to assert that attraction is universal and possessed by all matter transcends or even contradicts experience, and to make attraction a property of matter and a cause of motion is manifestly absurd. The familiar terms of dynamics—*sollicitatio, nisus, conatus, vis*—designate, by themselves, mental acts which are applied to bodies only metaphorically. What does experience show us about heavy objects? That we become tired when we support them and that, when released, they fall to the earth with an accelerated motion. What does this teach us about a force? Gravity, to the physicist, is not a cause but a motion that occurs in accordance with a determinate law, and the same applies to all of the other so-called forces that must always be reduced to mathematical hypotheses (*De motu*, 1–41).

To Newton, of course, these mathematical beings—number, extension, motion, time—had an absolute reality. According to him, there was an absolute space, an absolute place, which was the position of a body in absolute space, an absolute motion, which was the passage from one absolute place to another absolute place. Berkeley's criticism of these notions must be read with particular attention. He does not oppose absolute motion by relative motion in the Cartesian sense—that is, the continual change of location of one body in relation to another body which is supposedly fixed—for this is a purely cinematic notion which does not involve a moving force. His criticism of Newton, which could also be applied to Descartes, is that Newton thought it possible, thanks to the frame of reference provided by absolute space, to define motion without introducing a moving force. The notion of relative motion which he opposes to Newton does of course include the relation of the moved body to another referential body, but it also requires, for completeness, the thought of the moving force (spiritual in nature) which is applied to it. Motion is relative chiefly in the sense that it stands in some relation to this force and does not exist by itself; consequently the idea of absolute motion must be rejected, for it is an abstract idea, a physical notion, which asserts its completeness (*Principles* 110–17). Taken by themselves, mathematical beings—numbers, quantities, and the like—"in their own nature . . . bear no relation at all" to sensible things. They depend on the notion of the one who is defining, with the result that the same thing can be explained in different ways. Mathematics then is only the abstract language through which we express things.

The independent existence of matter and the mechanistic physics associated with it were the surest means of leading men to atheism. This consideration gave rise to the "minute philosopher" who ignored the magnitude of divine works and whom Berkeley attacked in *Alciphron*. He had the general opinion of the orthodox Christians of his time concerning deism and he accepted the dilemma of choosing between Christianity and atheism. But the reason given is quite personal, and his thinking is singularly profound: "It was always my opinion . . . that nothing could be sillier than to think of destroying Christianity by crying up natural religion. Whoever thinks highly of the one can never, with a consistency, think meanly of the other; it being very evident that natural religion, without revealed, never was and never can be received anywhere but in the brains of a few idle speculative men" (V, 29). Natural religion then cannot serve as an introduction to revealed religion, although this common illusion persists, for by itself it would be understood only rarely. "Precepts and oracles from heaven are incomparably better suited to popular improvement and the good of society then the reasonings of philosophers; and, accordingly, we do not find that natural or rational religion, as such, ever became the popular national religion of any country" (V, 9). This is the very essence of immaterialism: the abstract and the mediate have reality only through the concrete and the immediate, mathematical notions only through sensation, reason only through revelation.

## iv  *The Platonism of Siris*

A universal mind that expresses itself to other minds through a constant and orderly language, a physics that teaches the signs of this language, and a metaphysics that teaches their meaning—such is the image of the universe provided by the *Principles* and *Dialogues*. Nothing in these works prepares us for the speculations of *Siris*. In this work of Berkeley's old age we find a universe which, like that of the Stoics, is an animate being whose motions are all sympathetically interrelated and ruled by a subtle fire, a kind of vital fluid which suffuses every part of it. The fire is an instrumental cause which does not act by itself but is in the power of a Supreme Being, which is at once the force that produces all things, the intelligence that regulates them, and the goodness that makes them perfect.

This image of the Universe was borrowed by Berkeley from the mass of Neo-Platonic and Neo-Pythagorean writings in which it had already appeared during the Renaissance: first Plato and Plotinus (with the commentary by Marsilio Ficino), then Proclus' *Platonic Theology,* Iamblichus' *Mysteries,* the *Hermetic Writings,* and some other works. All these works, which he meditated upon during his sojourn in Rhode Island, seemed to him, according to an opinion prevalent among historians of the period, to reveal a very ancient tradition rooted in the earliest ages of the world

(Sections 298–301). Here we again find the idea that a body of mysterious knowledge was transmitted alongside the official doctrine—an idea which was widespread during the seventeenth century and which played an important role at the end of eighteenth. At that time, however, this body of Platonic doctrines was not very popular: the seventeenth century had not shared the sixteenth century's infatuation with Platonism, which was misunderstood, and Voltaire's jibes simply accentuate this scorn for the extravagant imagination of the Platonists. Cudworth, though completely sympathetic toward the Platonists, distrusted their doctrines, which seemed to him to be pantheistic and atheistic: they seemed to merge nature and God into one whole, or to place at the summit of the universe the One, devoid of intelligence and consciousness. Leibniz was certainly influenced by them, but he objected violently to their thesis of an animate world or a world soul.

What Berkeley attempted was nothing short of a complete renovation. In his thinking Platonism was above all else detachment from sensible things and attachment to the purely intellectual things which should serve to counterbalance the philosophy of his day. For philosophy affects "not only the minds of its professors and students, but also the opinions of all the better sort, and the practice of the whole people, remotely and consequentially indeed, though not inconsiderably . . . and have not fatalism and Sadducism gained ground during the general passion for the corpuscularian and mechanistic philosophy, which has prevailed for almost a century? Certainly had the philosophy of Socrates and Pythagoras prevailed in this age among these people who think themselves too wise to receive the dictates of the Gospel, we should not have seen interest take so general and fast hold on the minds of men." Thus, in opposition to Cudworth, he upholds the Christian character of this divine tradition: the unity of God and nature is not pantheism, for the Hermetic books, which affirm it, acknowledge a directive intelligence; and the Supreme Principle—the One—is devoid of intelligence only in the sense in which, in the Trinity, the Father is prior to the Word he engenders.

Does this Platonism continue the immaterialism of Berkeley or does it not rather contradict it? We should note at the outset that this universal force or soul, this subtle fire, is quite different from forces such as universal gravitation: it is not a property which is distributed equally throughout matter but a life which is diffused; it is not a cause of blind mechanical actions but an instrument of Providence, and Berkeley first discovered it at work in tar water, the universal panacea given by nature to man; by itself, then, it is not truly a cause or a source of activity, and God is the sole universal agent; finally, it does not seem to have any mode of existence except that which Berkeley gave to nature, that of being perceived. The new element in *Siris* is the metaphysical theory of Mind, but it is superimposed, without contradiction, over the theory expounded in the *Principles*. In the first edition of the *Principles,* Berkeley showed that we do not have an idea of Mind and its operations, since the word "idea" designates a passive thing; he remained silent concerning the mode of knowledge that we have of it, though his whole system is designed solely for this knowledge; in the second edition he said that we have a "notion" of it. This thesis is developed in *Siris*. From Plato he learned the distinction between the senses and intellectual knowledge, which properly is not knowledge of sensible things derived through intelligence but rather knowledge of spiritual realities—knowledge of this world which, according to him, would have been inaccessible to human stupidity without a divine revelation.

## v  *The Immateriality of Arthur Collier*

In 1713 Arthur Collier published his *Clavis universalis*. His conclusions, derived mainly from meditation on the works of Malebranche and Norris, are the same as Berkeley's. He is, however, more of a dialectician and theologian than Berkeley. For example, he proves that the very notion of an external world is self-contradictory because both its thesis and its antithesis have been proven: philosophers have demonstrated that the external world is finite and that it is infinite; that matter is infinitely divisible and that there are simple bodies; that motion is both necessary and inconceivable. Furthermore, he uses immaterialism against the Catholic dogma of transubstantiation, which assumes the reality of matter.

To him the negation of the existence of the external world is one of the most fruitful principles ever discovered, even in the domain of knowledge. But in his mind and in Berkeley's two points of view were fused: a criticism of scientific knowledge predicated upon a return to immediate experience, which does not reveal to us anything similar to the pretended powers of "experimental philosophy"; a certain spirituality and a profound sense of the omnipresence of mind. The two aspects are inseparable in a mind such as Berkeley's, for its warmth dissolves and mollifies rigid mechanisms. Furthermore, their union, under various guises, became one of the essential traits of the century: in Rousseau, for example, the return to immediate impressions was linked to the criticism of scientific mechanism and to finalism. Yet the two aspects can be separated, for if mind is eliminated—an idea which Berkeley refused to entertain—there remains a representation of a universe which has neither substance to support phenomena nor a cause to produce them, and in which, as in the universe of the Skeptics of antiquity, regular succession is the sole reality. Later we shall note the results of this separation.

BIBLIOGRAPHY

## Texts

Berkeley, George. *Works: Including many of his writings hitherto unpublished, with prefaces and annotations, life and letters and account of his philosophy,* ed. A. C. Fraser. 4 vols. 2d ed. Oxford, 1901.
———. *The Works of George Berkeley, Bishop of Cloyne,* ed. A. A. Luce and T. E. Jessop. 9 vols. London, 1948–57.
———. *Philosophical Commentaries,* ed. A. A. Luce. Editio Diplomatica. Edinburgh, 1944.
———. *The Principles of Human Knowledge,* ed. T. E. Jessop. 1945.

## Studies

Broad, C. D. *Berkeley's Argument about Material Substance.* London, 1942.
Cassirer, E. *Berkeley's System.* Giessen, 1914.
Fraser, A. C. *Berkeley.* (In the series "Philosophers' Classics.") Edinburgh and London, 1881.
Gueroult, M. *Berkeley, quatre études sur la perception et sur Dieu.* Paris, 1956.
Laky, J. J. *A Study of George Berkeley's Philosophy in the Light of the Philosophy of St. Thomas Aquinas.* Washington, 1950.
Luce, A. A. *Berkeley and Malebranche: A Study in the Origins of Berkeley's Thought.* New York, 1934.
———. *Berkeley's Immaterialism.* London, 1945.
———. *Dialectic of Immaterialism.* Verry, 1964.
Maheu, R. "Le catalogue de la bibliothèque des Berkeley," *Revue d'histoire de la philosophie,* III, 1929.
Ritchie, A. D. "George Berkeley's 'Siris'." British Academy Lecture. London, 1955.
Sillem, E. A. *George Berkeley and the Proofs for the Existence of God.* London, 1957.
Warnock, G. J. *Berkeley.* London, 1953.
Wild, J. *George Berkeley: A Study of his Life and Philosophy.* 2d ed. New York, 1961.
Wisdom, J. O. *The Unconscious Origins of Berkeley's Philosophy.* London, 1953.

## Publications Commemorating the Bicentenary of Berkeley's Death

*British Journal for the Philosophy of Science.* Edinburgh, 1953.
*Hermathena.* Dublin, 1953.
*Revue internationale de philosophie.* Paris, 1953.
*Revue philosophique de la France et de l'étranger.* Paris, 1953.

# CHRISTIAN WOLFF

CHRISTIAN WOLFF (1679–1754) was one of the few renowned philosophers of his time to teach philosophy regularly in the universities. His books are handbooks and collections of his lectures. Named professor at Halle in 1706, he was discharged by Frederick William I, at the request of his Pietist colleagues, Francke and Lange, in 1723. He taught at Marburg, then was recalled to his professorship at Halle in 1740, following the accession of Frederick the Great. On the surface, the doctrine of Leibniz' disciple and popularizer seems to be an exception to the obvious vacillation that we have witnessed in all quarters at the beginning of the eighteenth century: in a series of treatises which he wrote, first in German (*Vernünftige Gedanken von Gott, der Welt, und der Seele, auch allen Dingen überhaupt,* 1719; *V. G. von der Menschen Tun und Lassen,* 1720; *V. G. von dem gesellschaftlichen Leben der Menschen,* 1722), then in Latin (*Philosophia rationalis sive logica,* 1728; *Philosophia prima sive ontologia,* 1729; *Cosmologia generalis,* 1731; *Psychologia empirica,* 1732; *Psychologia rationalis,* 1734; *Theologia naturalis,* 1736–37; *Jus naturae,* 1740–48; *Jus gentium,* 1750; *Philosophia moralis,* 1750–53; *Oeconomica,* 1750), he provided German philosophy with a language, a program, and methods which were to endure for a long time.

But this contribution is infused with the spirit of his era. The cause of his dismissal in 1723 was the uneasiness provoked by his intemperate determinism and his oration "On the Practical Phi-

47

losophy of the Chinese," in which he placed Confucius, along with Christ, in the ranks of the prophets. Chinese thought had been in the ascendant since its introduction by the Jesuit missionaries—in their *Confucius, Sinarum philosophus,* for instance. Here, they said, they had found a moral philosophy "infinitely sublime, simple, sensible, and drawn from the pure fountains of natural reason." [1] Their statement was promptly appropriated for their own purposes by the philosophers who affirmed the existence of a morality independent of any belief in God. Wolff (who, on this point, took a position quite different from that of Leibniz) was concerned with finding rules of action which would retain their value even if God did not exist. His basic rule, "Do whatever makes you and your neighbor more perfect, and abstain from the opposite," is the epitome of an individualistic and naturalistic ethic, devoid of any authority except the rational knowledge of what we are.

Wolff's intransigence on this question is rooted in his over-all philosophy. According to him, the aim of philosophy is happiness, which man attains through clear knowledge. Everything then is subordinate to the widest possible diffusion of philosophy and to the maximum of clarity, by which he means not so much the intellectual and inward clarity of a Descartes as orderliness and consistency. Wolff, whom Kant called an "excellent analyst," was before all else a teacher, and a teacher has a tendency to attach more value to the formal precision with which a conclusion is deduced from its premises than to the premises themselves; but in this way one risks abusing an excellent precept and confusing the principle of logical precision with the very principle of being. That is what happened to Wolff when he defined philosophy as "the science of all possible things, showing why and how they are possible." For to him the possible is the noncontradictory, and the sole principle of philosophical knowledge is the principle of contradiction—that is, the principle of precision in reasoning. Significantly, he discards (or he reduces to the principle of contradiction) the Leibnizian

---

[1] Cf. P. Martino, *L'Orient dans la littérature française au XVII<sup>e</sup> siècle* (Paris, 1906), p. 311.

principle of sufficient reason which, in the mind of the master, was the principle of truths of fact or existences.

The result was a whole series of analyses, ranging from ontology to law and economics. Ontology is the study of propositions valid for any possible subject: it is a useless science, according to Descartes, who managed on the basis of a certain intellectual intuition to apply a predicate to a being—for example, extension to matter; it is an indispensable science, according to Wolff, who thinks he can affirm that "discoveries in mathematics and physics—even experimental physics—can be deduced through certain artifices from ontological presuppositions."

Ontology, in fact, does not simply deduce the predicates of being; it demonstrates them. According to Wolff, we know demonstratively that only wholly determined things exist, that matter is extended, that it is an aggregate composed of simple substances which contain their own principle of change. Cosmology, which follows ontology, begins with the definition of the world as the totality of finite beings and their relations to each other, and demonstrates that the world is composed of extended, mobile bodies. These bodies are composed of simple elements which have neither magnitude nor mobility, and which are distinct although they differ only through their powers or qualities; the active powers with which they are endowed provoke external changes in them; they are truly the atoms of nature, occupy a distinct place, and are capable of acting on each other through physical influx. Rational psychology assumes that the soul is a force capable of representing the world to itself and deduces that it possesses knowledge—that is, confused or distinct representations—and the desire or penchant for a new representation; this penchant is governed by pleasure, which is knowledge of a perfection, true or imagined, and by grief, which is knowledge of an imperfection, true or imagined; these ideas of perfection or imperfection, when clearly identified, become ideas of good and evil, of beautiful and ugly. Natural theology completes theoretical philosophy: the existence of God is necessary as a basis for the possibility of other beings which do not contain their own justification;

this is the proof *a contingentia mundi,* generally accepted during the period; finally, from the nature of God whose sole aim in creating is to be known and honored by rational creatures—that is, by men—Wolff believes that he has the right to conclude that everything in the universe is made for man, and he typifies the intemperate finalism then prevalent.

More than anything else Wolff seeks "to demonstrate the reality (that is, the noncontradictory nature) of the concepts" he uses, and in a long critique which has become a classic (*Theologia naturalis,* Sections 617–716), he accuses Spinoza of having failed to do this. One feature in particular is worth noting: to Spinoza, a finite being is one that has its limits in other finite beings and is in essence the same; but according to Wolff, if we assume that an existing being is a completely determinate being, then we must say that a finite being is one that cannot increase beyond certain limits which are determined by its own nature and result from inner determinations.

Here we see the antithesis between Spinoza's geometric approach and Wolff's, and the distinctive character of the latter. Wolff's system causes him to set beings apart from one another and to refuse to recognize any whole except one formed by individual beings. He accepts neither Leibniz' pre-established harmony nor the notion that the powers in these atoms of nature are representations; thus the unity of the universe can no longer be anything but the external unity of God who rules over it. An analogous motive governs the whole of Wolff's practical philosophy. We have already seen that his sole ethical maxim is the perfecting of ourselves as individuals. This also accounts for a significant contrast in his political views: on the one hand a liberal individualism which sees the sovereignty of the people as the unique basis of government; and on the other a state which, to maintain unity, rigidly controls even the most minute details of life, an enlightened and providential sovereign who compels his subjects to work and save, and who also takes measures against deism and atheism. Wolff's state is an enlightened despotism modeled on the Chinese system, which was also favored by Voltaire—and which was not too remote from the ideal of the new Prussian state.

Wolff's philosophy was immensely successful. It not only invaded the universities but spread through mundane circles. Diderot praised Wolff's philosophy in the *Encyclopedia*. Books such as those of his disciple Bilfinger, a professor at Tübingen (*Dilucidationes philosophicae de Deo, anima humana, mundo et generalibus rerum affectionibus*, 1725), were widely read and often cited, even in France. At the same time, the idealism of Berkeley and Arthur Collier was beginning to attract attention; consequently Bilfinger was disturbed over the resemblance that might be detected between his philosophy and the philosophy of Leibniz, who also seemed to reduce everything to minds (monads) and their representations; but he noted that the simple entities to which Leibniz reduced all things were quite different from minds, that they did not possess representations but only moving powers, and that Leibniz' *corpus phoenomenon* (Sections 115-18) is really an aggregate of monads and not a perception. Thus his refutation of idealism, which was to be the rule among German philosophers until the *Critique of Pure Reason*, eliminated the element which accounted for the profound continuity and unity of the Leibnizian universe.

There was still too much Leibnizianism among the Wolffians, however. They were admired for the order, the analysis, the precise delineation of concepts, which were the passion of the era; but their admirers wished to have the elements of this analysis drawn from experience and not decreed a priori. That is why their apriorism was subject to criticism, even in Germany. Andreas Rüdiger, professor at Leipzig and at Halle, indicates in his *De sensu veri et falsi* (1709, second edition, 1722) that he does not believe that possibility can be shown other than through the testimony of the senses, that we do not at first possess the essence of things, and that truth is but the agreement of our concepts with sensible perceptions; mathematics borrows its own notions from sensible intuition, for any proof (here Rüdiger's words indicate the method used by Condillac in *The Language of Calculi*) is reduced to computation. The mathematical method, therefore, contributes no support to philosophy apart from the external arrangement of materials. These criticisms show clearly the points on which Wolff's analysis differed from the analysis exemplified by Newton: whereas Wolff still subscribes, somewhat reluctantly, to the belief that essences can be identified through analysis, in Newton's analysis, which consists in reducing seemingly different facts to one basic fact discovered through experience, the mind intervenes only between two experiential terms —the facts to be reduced and the irreducible fact.

# BIBLIOGRAPHY

## Texts

Wolff, Christian. *Philosophia rationalis, sive logica methodo scientifica pertractata et ad usum scientiarum atque vitae aptata.* Frankfurt and Leipzig, 1728.

————. *Philosophia prima sive Ontologia.* Frankfurt, 1729.

————. *Cosmologia generalis.* Frankfurt, 1731.

————. *Psychologia empirica.* Frankfurt, 1732.

————. *Psychologia rationalis.* Frankfurt, 1734.

————. *Theologia naturalis.* 2 vols. Frankfurt, 1736–37.

————. *Philosophia practica universalis.* 2 vols. Frankfurt, 1738–39.

————. *Gesammelte kleinere Schriften.* 6 vols. Halle, 1736–40.

————. *Ius naturae methodo scientifica pertractata.* 8 vols. Frankfurt and Leipzig, 1740–48.

————. *Ius gentium.* Halle, 1750.

————. *Oeconomica.* Halle, 1750.

————. *Philosophia moralis sive Ethica.* 5 vols. Halle, 1750–53.

## Studies

Arnsberger, W. *Wolffs Verhältniss zu Leibniz.* Heidelberg, 1897.

Bergmann, J. "Wolffs Lehren vom Complementum possibilitatis," *Archiv für systematische Philosophie,* II, 1896.

Campo, M. *Cristiano Wolff e il razionalismo precritico.* 2 vols. Milan, 1939.

Ludovici, K. G. *Kurzer Entwurf einer vollständigen Historie der wolffschen Philosophie.* Leipzig, 1736.

————. *Ausführlicher Entwurf einer vollständigen Historie der wolffschen Philosophie.* Leipzig, 1737–38.

————. *Sammlung und Auszüge der sämmtlichen Streitschriften wegen der wolffschen Philosophie.* Leipzig, 1783.

Pichler, H. *Über Wolffs Ontologie.* Leipzig, 1910.

Utitz, E. *Ch. Wolff.* Halle, 1929.

Wundt, M. "Christian Wolff und die deutsche Aüfklarung," *Das Deutsche in der deutschen Philosophie,* ed. T. Haering, pp. 227–46. Stuttgart, 1941.

Zeller, E. "Ueber Wolffs Vertreibung aus Halle," *Preussische Jahrbucher,* X, 1862.

# GIAMBATTISTA VICO

"PHILOSOPHERS HAVE numbed minds with Descartes' method by claiming, with their clear and distinct perception, to rediscover without expense or fatigue everything found in libraries. . . . Descartes has acquired a great following, thanks to this weakness of our human nature, which seeks to know everything in the shortest possible time and with the least possible effort." [1] This was the criticism which Giambattista Vico (1668-1744) directed in 1726 against the Cartesianism of his young Neapolitan compatriots, who had made it a short cut to philosophizing. In Vico's view, clear ideas undoubtedly have a sphere of application, but a very limited one; they are appropriate to mathematics and to the most abstract notions of physics—those fabricated by the minds; he began with them and held fast to them. Elsewhere, however, clarity and distinctness are universally "the vice of human reason rather than its virtue." A clear idea is a finite idea, but not all ideas are finite: "For example, I cannot apprehend, the form and limit of my suffering; my perception of it is infinite, and this infinitude gives testimony of the grandeur of human nature."

All this obscure, profound, infinite side of nature, which is penetrated by the intuition of historians and poets and which explains the religious, moral, and political life of man, is examined in Vico's *Principi di una scienza nuova d'intorno alla commune natura delle razioni* (1725). In his book, itself obscure, disorderly, and long mis-

---

[1] As quoted by Maugain, *Étude de l'évolution intellectuelle de l'italie*, p. 196, note.

understood, Vico tried to determine the general traits common to the development of all nations. Praise showered upon him by the philosophers of progress (Herder, Michelet, and even Comte) is likely to create a false impression of the doctrine of a man who was before all else an idealist.

Vico was first of all a Christian. There is a Christian conception of history: that of St. Augustine and that of Bossuet. Vico accepted it but, for this very reason, deliberately excluded it from his investigations, for he wished to determine the natural laws of history, independently of any miraculous intervention (thus depriving himself, moreover, of all the documentation that might have been provided by the Bible).

Secondly Vico was a Platonist. He sought the eternal order of the universe, "the ideal History of eternal Laws on which depend the Destinies of all nations, their birth, their progress, their decay, and their end." What he had in mind was not a law which formulates the infinite progress of mankind as a whole, as in Condorcet or Comte, but an ideal law in which each nation participates separately and for the duration of its own life. For example, Roman history from the fabulous time of the kings until the destruction of the Empire by the Barbarians, constitutes one complete cycle of which the successive phases can and must be rediscovered in the history of every other nation. Time then moves in cycles, winding and rewinding itself (*corsi e ricorsi*), and history begins anew with each nation: this is the familiar vision of time common to Plato, Aristotle, and the Stoics.

This fundamental idea shaped Vico's method of investigation—a method which, in spite of his many mistakes, is the true predecessor of the most modern investigations. For, as he observed, philology must be reconciled with philosophy. It must be demonstrated by comparison of documents from different nations—from Egypt, Greece, or Rome, for example—that the law of development is identical for each of them. The significance of this comparative method must be emphasized. Rationalists acknowledged no unity among men except the unity of reason common to all; everything but reason, everything relating to imagination or passions, could only separate men from each other; furthermore, in their thinking they transported reason to the dawn of mankind—because, "incapable of formulating an idea of things that are remote and unknown, they picture them according to the things they know," and also because of "the pride of scholars who would like everything that makes up their science to be as ancient as they are." From the dawn of antiquity, the Greeks attributed their laws to the reason of wise legislators. According to Vico the whole theory of the social contract, then prevalent, testifies to the same mistake.

The primary aim of *Scienza nuova* is to refute just such views. Drawing support from philosophy, Vico tries to demonstrate (Montaigne had made a similar observation) that there is an identity among men which is not based on reason, "a *common sense,* that is, an *unreflective judgment* which is generally borne and felt by a whole class, a whole tribe, a whole nation, or by all mankind." The result is that *"uniform ideas* spring up simultaneously among *whole tribes unacquainted* with each other." Consequently there can be uniform laws in the formation of nations, without reason as their origin. A certain intuition (Platonic) even assures us of the existence of the ideal law realized by each nation, but only the inductive study of civil and political facts—like Bacon's study of nature—can reveal to us what these laws are.

The materials used by Vico in the inductive study of the distant past were the popular mythological traditions in which are inscribed, though in a distorted form, the most remote history of peoples, the most ancient poems such as those of Homer, the most primitive laws such as those of the Twelve Tables. Whatever illusion Vico may have entertained concerning the original character of his data, we should not fail to note the spirit in which he chose them and the superiority of his thought in contrast to similar speculations of the Renaissance. In fact, he discarded all the documents which, during the sixteenth century, were supposed to reveal a fabulously ancient science—Chaldean oracles, Orphic poems, golden verses by Pythagoras; he recognized these as forgeries from a later era. Armed with the idea that the origins of mankind are "paltry, obscure, and crude," he rejected everything that might lend support to the view that there existed from the beginning a science formulated in enigmas; nor did he have any use for the allegorical method which discovered in myths, by a convenient interpretation, the whole of rational science. In short—and it is on this that his incomparable greatness rests, when one considers that he was marking out a new course—he studied the documents of the past only to determine what they could reveal of the history, religious beliefs, legal practices, customs, and language of those who transmitted them. Of course the basis for his induction was narrow—even narrower than might have been expected under prevailing circumstances—since he disregarded biblical documents and the data that was beginning to flow in on savage tribes and the inhabitants of the Far East, but his method was consistently perfect. It consisted in defining mankind and his progress inductively instead of searching for a static, immediate definition or a hypothetical construction.

The contrast between his results and those achieved by Hobbes or Locke is no less striking than the contrast between their methods. According to Hobbes and Locke, the formation of society was the solution to a rational problem—a solution sought and discovered by rational men; everything was due to human wisdom. To this Vico objects that there would be no wise men or philosophers if a state and a civilization did not already exist, and that a wholly different view of things is provided by the concrete wealth of our documents. These indicate that, after the flood, men began to roam through the vast forest of the world; only religious terror, the fruit of the imagination, could begin to subdue these barbarous, ferocious giants; fear of Jupiter's thunder forced those who experienced it to hide in caves. Such was the genesis of the first permanent dwellings and, with them, the religious practices and rites prescribing the conduct of each individual—the institution of monogamous marriage, for instance, in which Vico sees, from its beginning, a legal institution encumbered by rites, each designed to instill reverence. Also on this order was the genesis of families: each evolved in its own shelter, isolated from the others and bound only by the ties of religion. The result was a theocracy, or rule by gods. To each family was added a variable group of vagabonds who remained in the primitive forest, without law or religion. Then families gathered together in cities; the city was formed by family chieftains, among whom there existed rights and laws, and the plebian group who lived outside the law. Each city was originally aristocratic, composed of patricians and plebians, who were at first treated as beasts and had a right only to the necessities of life; for a long time in Rome, patricians withheld from the plebians even the legal consecration of their marriages.[2] Finally a third age came, the age of reason, in which the rule of law was applied universally to relations among men—a state realized in the Roman Empire, which crumbled with the Barbarian invasions.

The scheme of succession is clear: the age of the gods, the age of heros, the age of men; theocracy, aristocracy, human government (which is sometimes a monarchy in which the monarch—as Voltaire, Mabley, and many other apologists later remarked—guarantees equality of rights). Vico, who was a lawyer by profession and never ceased to concern himself with Roman jurisprudence, characterizes each of the ages according to its law: religious law, which makes everything the property of the gods, heroic law, which uses religion to temper the law of force, and human law, which is based on reason. But it must be added that each of these states of law derives from a perfectly distinct and original state of mind. Without entering into the details of the contrast between poetic wisdom (wisdom which comprises economics, politics, and even science, and which the poems of Homer exemplify) and philosophical wisdom, should note that what sets them apart is chiefly the inverse development of imagination and reason. Vico's essential characteristic is his attempt to define an era in which all social relations were based on beliefs originating almost solely in man's imagination, and

[2] *Histoire de l'ancien gouvernement de la France* (1727), by Henri Boulainvilliers, contains an analogous thesis concerning the French nation, originally composed of the victorious Frankish nobles, governed by their own laws, with native inhabitants reduced to servitude.

to demonstrate that without this providential law humanity would not have been able even to subsist; for only the violence of fear provoked by a strong imagination can curb the violence of appetite. Thus he rehabilitated imagination, which Malebranche had subjected to sarcasm. Of great importance to mankind is the fact that reason appeared belatedly rather than prematurely, for young men who are initiated too quickly to the sciences of pure reason—metaphysics and algebra—become refined and distinguished, but incapable of great works. The same is true, according to Vico, of nations which have passed over a halting-place without stopping—the Greeks, for example, who passed without transition from barbarity to refinement, and the French, in whom the Atticism of the Greeks reappeared.

# Bibliography

## Texts

Vico, Giambattista. *Opere,* ed. G. Ferrari. 6 vols. Milan, 1835–37. 8 vols. Naples, 1858–69.

————. *Opere,* ed. F. Nicolini. 8 vols. Bari, 1914–41.

————. *La Scienza Nuova seconda, giusta la edizione del 1744, con le varianti del 1730 e di due redazioni intermedie inedite,* ed. F. Nicolini. 2 vols. 3d ed. Bari, 1942.

————. *The New Science of Giambattista Vico,* trans. T. G. Bergin and M. H. Fisch from third (1744) edition. London, 1949.

————. *Giambattista Vico: Autobiography,* trans. M. H. Fisch and T. G. Bergin. New York and London, 1944.

## Bibliographies

*Bibliografia vichiana,* ed. E. Nicolini. 2 vols. Naples, 1947.

## Studies

Adams, H. P. *The Life and Writings of Giambattista Vico.* London, 1935.

Berlin, I. *The Philosophical Ideas of Giambattista Vico: Art and Ideas in Eighteenth-Century Italy.* Vol. 4, Instituto italiano di cultura. Rome, 1960.

Berry, T. *The Historical Theory of G. B. Vico.* Washington, 1949.

Caponigri, A. R. *Time and Idea: The Theory of History in Giambattista Vico.* London, 1953.

Chaix-Ruy, J. *Vie de J. B. Vico.* Paris, 1945.

————. *La formation de la pensée philosophique de J. B. Vico.* Paris, 1945.

Cochéry, M. *Les grandes lignes de la philosophie historique et juridique de Vico.* Paris, 1923.

Croce, B. *La filosofia di G. B. Vico.* Bari, 1911. (Compare with Jankélévitch, S. "La philosophie de Vico d'après B. Croce," *Revue de synthèse historique,* XXIII.)

Gentile, G. *Studi Vichiani.* Messine, 1914.

————. *Per il secondo centenaria della Scienza nuova.* Rome, 1925.

————. *Giambattista Vico.* Florence, 1936.

Vaughan, C. E. *Studies in the History of Political Philosophy.* Vol. 1, chap. 5. Manchester, 1925. 2d ed. 1939.

# MONTESQUIEU

## I  The Nature of Laws

Charles de Secondat, Baron de la Brède et de Montesquieu, born near Bordeaux in 1689, became counselor (1714) and deputy president (1716) of the *parlement* of Bordeaux; in 1726 he sold his office, and in 1728 he set out on his travels through Italy, Switzerland, Holland, and England. He published his *Considerations on the Causes of the Grandeur and Decadence of the Romans* in 1734 and *The Spirit of Laws* in 1748. He prepared the article on "Taste" for the *Encyclopedia*. He died in 1755.

Although *The Spirit of Laws* appeared in 1748, Montesquieu's age (he was then fifty-nine) and education place him in the first part of the eighteenth century. He was practically the only thinker of his time to consider political problems by themselves, without relating them to an explicit conception of mind and nature.

From the Greek Sophists to Montaigne and Pascal the diversity of laws had been the pretext for skeptical doubt concerning the stability of human justice. This diversity testified to the conventional character of laws. It was in natural rights, common to all, that unity should be sought: either natural and consequently universal law, or diverse, changeable, and consequently arbitrary laws—such was the dilemma. But Montesquieu's thinking was on a plane where this alternative no longer made any sense: "I first examined men and decided that in this infinite diversity of laws and customs, they

61

were not led solely by their whims. I set down the principles and saw that particular cases readily fell into place, that the history of every nation was but their consequence, and that each particular law was linked to another law or depended upon a more general law" (*Spirit of Laws,* Preface). Montesquieu's whole method consists in examining the mutual relations of positive laws, showing how one law by its nature implies or excludes another law, with the result that there are natural relations of exclusion and inclusion between positive laws, governed not by the arbitrariness of a man or an assembly but by the necessity of things.

This explains the paradox of a book which, though it deals only with positive laws and excludes almost any investigation of natural rights and the origin of society, begins with the celebrated statement: "Laws, in the broadest sense, are the necessary relations which derive from the nature of things. . . . There is a primitive rationality; and laws are the relations that exist between it and different beings, and the relations of these diverse beings among themselves. . . . A basis for legal relations existed before laws were made." These statements remind us of Malebranche or Clarke, but whereas the latter had in mind only universal laws common to all mankind, Montesquieu is referring to the necessary concatenation of positive laws. For example, a particular form of government implies a particular political legislation (Book II), particular laws on education (Book IV), particular civil and criminal laws (Book VI), sumptuary laws (Book VII), particular laws concerning war (Books IX and X). In this series of books the variable, so to speak, is the form of government, and political legislation, civil legislation, and similar matter are its functions. But other variables can be selected: for example, constitutional, civil, and financial laws are functions of political liberty, as we observe them in England (Books XI–XIII). We must also observe how laws are transformed by certain natural forces, such as climate or the nature of the terrain, or by certain acquired factors, such as customs, commerce, monetary practices, population density, and religious beliefs (Books XIV–XXV).

It is important for us to note that Montesquieu establishes a unifying bond between the various aspects of the political life of a country. He is not a fatalist: "Those who have said that a blind fatality produced all the effects that we see in the world have spoken foolishly; for what is more absurd than the notion that a blind fatality might have produced intelligent beings?" (I, i). Man is free, and "as an intelligent being he constantly violates the laws established by God and constantly changes those established by himself." Consequently the necessity of the relations that unite diverse kinds of laws in a society must not be interpreted as being inexorable and independent of any human will; it is wholly rational, for God is the author of these laws; he "made them, because they are related to his wisdom and power." With all the imperfections of human nature, man also uses shrewdness and reflection in discovering the laws which are best in a given historical situation; he is guided by a kind of forced expediency. We should not think, for example, that Montesquieu ever said that a physical factor such as climate determines constitutions: "Bad legislators have favored the vices of climate while the good ones have opposed them. . . . The more physical causes incline men to rest, the more moral causes should repudiate rest" (XIV, iii). Legislative systems are like mechanical contrivances which are governed by the eternal laws of motion but require an inventor for their realization. If Montesquieu frequently compares the constitution of a society to a mechanism, he does so in order to call attention to the intervention of human art, which uses natural laws to provide a rather adroit solution to the problem of maximum effect. He points out (III, v) that "in monarchies, politics accomplish great things with the least possible effort, just as art uses as few motions, forces, and wheels as possible in the finest machines." Speaking of the English constitution, he adds: "To form a moderate government, powers must be combined, regulated, made to act; one power must be given ballast, so to speak, to enable it to resist another; this is a masterpiece of legislation rarely achieved by chance (V, xiv)." The machinery often grates: "Of course there is friction in mechanics, and this often changes or stops the effects prescribed by theory; politics also have their friction" (XVII, viii). Montesquieu's plan might be said to be to discover mechanical models that would inspire legislators. His aim is clearly practical: "If I could help those who govern to augment their knowledge of what they ought to prescribe, and those who obey to find a new pleasure in obeying, I would think myself the most fortunate of mortals." To discover these models, he used historical induction. Classical antiquity, the histories of nations, the Oriental countries, even China and Japan revealed to him, in a more or less perfect state of realization, the connections or relations which he sought to prove necessary; at the same time, however, he utilized a sort of deduction that brought to light the natural character and appropriateness of these connections. "What I say is confirmed by the entire course of history, and is in strict conformity to the nature of things" (III, iii). These words, written by Montesquieu of one of his theses on democracy, show the importance he attached to the ideal of a complete proof.

## II  *The Liberalism of Montesquieu*

Montesquieu was not a mere speculator who viewed indifferently the machinery of constitutions but a man who had a definite, practical ideal: to determine the system of laws which, under given historical and physical circumstances, produces the maximum of liberty which he defines as "the right to do whatever the laws allow" (XI, iii). The problem is different for each nation, for laws "must be peculiar to the people for whom they are made, with the result that it is highly improbable that the laws of one nation will suit another" (I, iii). Analysis of the English constitution provides a near perfect example of the ideal constitutional mechanism for deriving the maximum of liberty. The principle of this analysis is the following: there is a minimum of liberty when public powers act arbitrarily and follow no established rules; it is therefore necessary for each of these powers to be limited and controlled by a force that will bring it into equilibrium. Montesquieu does not believe that such control can be exercised by the governed: "The people are in no way equipped to discuss public affairs" (XI, vi). The force used to limit the arbitrariness of a public power itself must be homogeneous and must be another public power; political liberty exists when completely independent powers reciprocally limit each other. This happens in the English constitution. The three constitutive powers of a state are the legislative power, the executive power in matters concerning the law of nations or government, and the executive power in matters concerning civil law or judicial power. If these powers depend upon the same will—whether it be that of an individual, a body of nobles, or the people—all liberty disappears. In most of the states of Europe liberty exists because the monarch, if he combines the first two powers, leaves the third to his subjects; in a monarchy such as France, according to Montesquieu, the independence of courts of justice (*parlements*) is an essential condition of political liberty. In England, however, the three powers are separate; in particular, the legislative power, which belongs to the representatives of the people and to the lords, is independent of the executive power, which is entrusted to a hereditary monarch who has the right to assemble and prorogue the legislative body, whereas the latter can control the execution of the laws established by him (XI, vi).

Montesquieu was particularly concerned with the maximum of liberty compatible with the historical situation in France. His work dates from an era when there were numerous studies of the origins and nature of the French monarchy. He was one of a number of men who, upon appraising the preceding century, the minstry of Richelieu, and the century of Louis XIV, saw a great danger in the absolutist tendencies which threatened to change the French monarchy into an Oriental-style despotism, and a goodly part of his book is explained by his desire to check these tendencies. It was this concern that gave rise to his novel distinction between the three forms of government—democracy, monarchy, and despotism. Democracy—an obsolete system of government of which almost the only example is afforded by antiquity—receives scant attention, but he stresses the distinction between monarchy and despotism. Democracy is a government in which the people, knowing no will except their own, are supported solely by their own virtue (here the word means political virtue, that is, spontaneous attachment to their native country). Monarchy is characterized by rank, precedence, orders, and a hereditary nobility, but the whole system is governed by law: consequently the monarchy draws its main support, not from virtue or the love of the state per se, but from honor, that is, the zeal with which each individual—the noble, the member of parliament, the ordinary citizen—clings to his rank and his privileges. Monarchy then is the antithesis of despotism, which can be maintained only through fear, since it requires passive obedience. "The force of laws in one," he said, "and the arm of the prince, always upraised, in the other, rule and contain everything" (III, iii). But monarchy always runs the risk of degenerating into despotism, and it is obvious that many of Montesquieu's maxims, such as the following, are warnings to the rulers of France: "Monarchies degenerate when the prerogatives of the bodies [read 'nobility' and 'parliament'] and the privileges of towns are eliminated. . . . A monarchy collapses when a prince thinks that he is showing his might by changing the order of things rather than by following it; when he takes away the natural functions of some and bestows them arbitrarily on others" (VIII, vi). His pessimism extends to the whole of Europe: "Most of the people of Europe are still governed by customs. But if, through long abuse of power . . . , despotism should be established at a certain point, no customs or climates could prevail against it; and in this beautiful part of the world, human nature would suffer, at least for a time, the insults inflicted on it in the three others. . . . Rivers are lost in the sea, monarchies in despotism" (VIII, xvii). One circumstance favoring this corruption is territorial extension through conquest: "A monarchical state ought to be of average size."

In addition, Montesquieu devoted his two last books to the defense of his position on the controversial question of the origin of the French royalty. He was convinced that it was the Barbarians who brought liberty to Europe: "Jordanes, the Gothic historian, called northern Europe the crucible of the human race; I shall call it rather the crucible of the instruments which broke the irons forged in the South. There were formed the valiant nations who left their land to destroy tyrants and slaves" (XVII, v). This contrast between the Nordic Barbarian, free and independent, and the civilized Meridional, enslaved by Roman despotism, is the basis for his philosophy of the history of France. Abbé Dubos had just published his *Establishment of the French Monarchy among the Gauls,* in which he maintained that in France the first kings, elected by the Frankish tribes, were merely substitutes for the Roman emperors whose rights they had assumed; consequently royal power was grounded on a kind of contract between them and all the people; the privileges of the nobility were instituted afterwards. To Montesquieu the king of France is primarily the German chief surrounded by his faithful supporters, who assure his supremacy through conquest; fiefs, first amovable and then hereditary, are the king's gift to the nobility; thus the power of the king is in no way arbitrary but is regulated by decisions made in the convocations of his lieges. To Montesquieu a moderate monarchy, such as he envisions, is possible only if its origin is independent of popular consent (we recall that to Hobbes the logical consequence of the contract was the despotism of rulers). Montesquieu's sense of historical complexity serves his liberalism; in politics, the concurrence of independent causes is the condition of liberty.

Locke believed that laws and constitutions were created through a free, arbitrary agreement of wills. Montesquieu introduced into the study of legislation the natural method which links facts together in a series so that, starting from an initial fact—a given historical situation or certain physical conditions—one readily recalls the others. Here he was faithful, to the degree that his subject permitted, to the spirit of his century. That is why, to use the language of a later era, he created a social statics dealing with the simultaneous grouping of facts and the equilibrium of forces in a stable society at each given moment; in the same way Condillac created a psychological statics, and the authors of natural series, a biological statics. But Montesquieu had no notion of social dynamics or of the genetic succession of social forms that we find in Vico. This accounts for the distinctive character of his liberalism; to him the exigency of liberty was not a universal exigency of human nature but rather an equilibrium of all social forces, none of which should be sacrificed. Whenever one of these forces diminished, compensatory and substitutional phenomena appeared. Thus a religious law (XXIV, xvi) like the Truce of God in the Middle Ages could suspend civil wars; or, as in Greece (XXIV, xviii), the imputation of religious defilement to a criminal could inspire horror over his crime, apart from any legal repression.

# BIBLIOGRAPHY

## Texts

Montesquieu, Charles Louis de Secondat, *Œuvres complètes,* ed. E. Laboulaye.
    7 vols. Paris, 1875–79.
———. *Œuvres inédites,* ed. E. Laboulaye. Paris, 1892–1900.
———. *Œuvres complètes,* ed. A. Masson. 3 vols. Paris, 1950–55.
———. *Cahiers* (1716–55), ed. B. Grasset and A. Masson. Paris, 1942.
———. *De l'esprit des lois,* ed. G. Truc. 2 vols. Paris, 1945.

## Bibliographies

Cabdeen, D. C. *Montesquieu: A Bibliography.* New York, 1947.

## Studies

Althusser, I. *Montesquieu: La politique et l'histoire.* Paris, 1959.
Carcassonne, E. *Montesquieu et le problème de la constitution française au XVIIIe siècle.* Paris, 1927.
Dedieu, J. *Montesquieu, l'homme et l'œuvre.* Paris, 1943.
Leroy, M. *Histoire des idées sociales en France.* Vol. 1, *De Montesquieu à Robespierre.* Paris, 1946.
Mirkine-Guetzevitch, ed. *La pensée politique et constitutionnelle de Montesquieu.* Paris, 1952.
*Revue internationale de philosophie.* Nos. 3–4, 1955.
See, H. *L'évolution de la pensée politique en France au XVIIIe siècle.* Paris, 1925.
Sorel, A. *Montesquieu.* Paris, 1887.
Vaughan, C. E. *Studies in the History of Political Philosophy,* vol. 1, chap. 5. Manchester, 1925. 2d ed. 1939.

# SECOND PERIOD

## 1740–1775

# CONDILLAC

## 1 General Considerations

The dominant ideas of the eighteenth century emerged and took shape between 1740 and 1745—a period marked by polemics and violent campaigns which not only roused the learned minority but also interested and impassioned society as a whole, and which often entailed the intervention of the public powers, both civil and ecclesiastical, against philosophers. It was during this interval that Hume, Montesquieu, Condillac, Diderot, D'Alembert, Voltaire, Rousseau, Adam Smith, and Buffon published their principal works.

At that point in time the philosopher was not a seeker of knowledge for its own sake but was before all else the enemy of "prejudices" inimical to the happiness of men, the propagandist of "enlightenment" which would renovate opinion and morals, public and private. This was, as the Germans say, the *Aufklärung*. It was hard to attack prejudices, especially social and economic prejudices, without attacking people in high positions or at least the established powers; consequently pamphlets and campaigns accounted for a goodly part of the philosophical literature of the time. Such a philosophy could not dispense with success, and there was a sustained attempt to influence and even to create public opinion. Philosophers had to discard the scholastic or scholarly technique, which many writers of the Renaissance had abandoned, but which the great

73

thinkers of the seventeenth century had taken up again. Still more clarity, still more limpidity—this was the goal sought by optimists convinced that any ordinary mind, when properly guided, could penetrate every subject affecting the happiness of man and that obscure, inaccessible subjects could and should be abandoned in the best interests of man.

There was nothing artificial about this transformation. Philosophy was both the agent and the result of the great social movement to which it gave expression.

It is interesting to follow the gradual displacement, after the Middle Ages, of the social conditions under which philosophers were molded: the close ties which circumstances had established between philosophy and the clergy were gradually broken. Beginning with the sixteenth century, philosophers generally were no longer professors but free writers, men of the lesser nobility or third estate. In the seventeenth century new ties with theology were established, of course, but these were more apparent than real if Spinoza, Leibniz, and even Malebranche sought to incorporate theology into their philosophy rather than philosophy into theology; in the eighteenth century, however, these systems collapsed and were viewed as "visions."

Then a whole breed of philosophers came into prominence. Their classical and scientific training set them apart from the university tradition, and they gradually disseminated a new conception of man and the universe. Most of these philosophers belonged to the third estate, to the middle class which had begun its ascendancy long before and had now reached its apogee; it dominated business, controlled the most important ministries, imposed its ideas and outlook. Its positive mind—reluctant to engage in pure speculation, desirous of achieving practical results, unwilling to separate the sciences from the arts which applied them, trusting in them and their method, upright and honest in problems in which honesty was the condition of success—is reflected in the philosophers of the eighteenth century. Their fervent desire to be useful to men and their concern for their own reputation, the constant and methodical labor which men like Voltaire and Diderot undertook in order to spread their ideas, their persistent fear of any system or any excessively technical language, their wish to transport the spirit of sciences and crafts into philosophy—these are the traits with which countless readers identified themselves and which truly were responsible for their success.

## II *The Analytical Method*

Étienne Bonnot de Condillac (1750–80), born in Grenoble, was from a family of magistrates. Destined for the church, he entered the seminary of St. Sulpice only to leave it in 1740, renounce the priesthood, and move to Paris, where he was associated with Rousseau, Fontenelle, and Diderot. He published his *Essay on the Origin of Human Knowledge* in 1746, *Treatise on Systems* in 1749 (new edition in 1771), *Treatise on Sensations* in 1754 (new edition in 1778), and *Treatise on Animals*—which contained a *Dissertation on the Existence of God,* written before 1746 for the Berlin Academy —in 1755. He became preceptor to the son of the Duke of Parma in 1758 and remained in Parma until 1767, when he returned to Paris. In 1772 he retired to the Château de Flux, where he published a thirteen-volume *Course of Studies* (1775) containing a grammar, an art of thinking, an art of writing, an ancient history and a modern history, and *Commerce and Government Considered in Relation to Each Other* (1776). *Logic* (1780) and *The Language of Calculi* (1798) appeared posthumously.

Condillac strikes at the very roots of the rationalist doctrines of the past century. The general tendency is for us to rely on "reason," treating it as a set of indisputable maxims, a datum beyond which it is impossible for us to go, but this is because our reason was shaped before we engaged in any reflection. "When we begin to reflect, we do not see how the ideas and maxims which we find within us could have been introduced there," and without doubting them we give them the name of reason, natural light, innate principles. This is a great mistake on the part of philosophers, for they do not suspect that some ideas are the work of the mind, or if they do suspect it, they are incapable of discovering how such ideas were engendered.

This discovery is not a matter of mere speculative philosophy (as Platonic theories of the origin of intelligence may be), for "our mistakes are due to the fact that our ideas were badly formed . . . ; the only means of correcting them is to remake them." Intelligence or reason is not a natural bloc which can be explained and justified on the basis of its origin; it is a structure or fabric which philosophical reflection allows us to remake more perfectly than it was made spontaneously. Thus the task involves the whole future of the mind.

These preliminary observations are directed toward Descartes as well as Locke, for if Condillac agrees with Locke on one basic point—the existence of ideas—he criticizes him for supposing "that as soon as the mind receives ideas through the senses, it is able *arbitrarily* to repeat them, combine them, unite them, fashion them into all sorts of complex notions. But it is an established fact that in childhood we experienced sensations long before we drew ideas from them." Condillac still has to show, then, how and why these complex ideas are formed and when they are legitimate. His analysis consists in describing the acts or operations through which we fashion ideas. In mathematics, for example, he makes a rule (in *The Language of Calculi*) of introducing no definition or maxim, deriving all truths from the operation of the calculus.

In some ways he is probably closer than he suspects to Descartes, who also tried, in the *Regulae,* to explain combinations of complex natures through the properties of "simple natures." But his interpretation of the term is different. He means "the simplest ideas transmitted by the senses," or a kind of inert matter to be combined by the mind, and their intrinsic properties are unimportant, for one person can see as blue what another sees as green, without there being any confusion, if only they both agree to apply the word "green" to the color of grass.

A simple idea, with the fixed sign to which it is linked, is an element which, by its nature and independent of experience and custom, does not evoke or require any connection with this or that idea: the development of the mind will occur, thanks to the diversity of the connections established on the basis of utility. "There is nothing," wrote Condillac in his *Essay*, "that will not help us to reflect," and the important thing is to be able "to form these connections in accordance with the aims which we have adopted and the circumstances in which we find ourselves." For this we need to multiply our contacts with the outer world; inner meditation is a bad method of philosophizing. It is not necessary "to take the precaution, as some philosophers do, of withdrawing into solitude or seeking refuge in a closed cellar. . . . If someone seeks seclusion in darkness, the slightest noise or the least flicker will be enough to distract him. . . . But if I reflect on a subject in broad daylight and in noisy surroundings, the sudden elimination of the light or noise will suffice to distract me.[1] Far from their being a hindrance, "We need only familiarize ourselves with them in order to turn them to great advantage." A more perfect antithesis to the intimate dialogue of mystical contemplation and the solitude of Cartesian meditation could not be imagined. Inward invention is less ample and more limited than reality. "As soon as we cease to search for nature in our imagination," wrote Condillac concerning Galileo's reform, "the study that we propose ceases to have bounds; it embraces the universe. Philosophy ceases to be the science of a man who meditates with his eyes closed and embraces all the arts."[2]

The problem of the origin of ideas, identical to the problem of method, consists in discovering a first, indubitable experience in which the materials, employment, and instruments of our knowledge are accessible to the senses. This concrete, complete experience, of which all other knowldege is but the indefinite repetition, is the linking of ideas to the signs of language and the interlinking of ideas. According to Condillac the only flaw in knowledge is that, between signs and ideas, we do not find the perfect correspondence that exists in geometry, in which the meaning of each word is determined in a precise, invariable way. To rectify this, we would

[1] *Essai*, Part II, sec. ii, chap. iii, par. 37.
[2] *Histoire moderne*, II, xii.

have to put ourselves in the situation of a man created by God with such well-developed organs that he had perfect use of his reason from the very first; he would invent signs only as he experienced new sensations and made new reflections; he would combine his first ideas according to his circumstances; he would use a particular name to identify each combination; and when he wanted to compare two complex notions (this is the essence of knowledge), he could easily analyze them.

The hypothetical man in the *Essay* singularly resembles Adam in his terrestrial paradise, and the goal of philosophy is to place us in a state of spiritual innocence, safe from prejudices and traditions.

Condillac's language changes somewhat in his *Logic*. Here the object is to rediscover the method which our minds unknowingly followed when necessity forced us to develop our knowledge, and after meditating upon this method—that is, after returning through reflection toward natural spontaneity—to become so familiar with it that we use it without thinking about it, just as spontaneously as in the beginning. There is a sort of optimism in this view, which shows us methodical order, not as a conquest of the will but as a slackening of pace which brings back to the natural, primitive operation of the mind. In fact, it is not necessary for me artificially to construct a model of a well-organized whole, for I find it already realized; in ordinary situations characterized by definite needs, every man possesses well-organized knowledge for the simple reason that his judgments follow the order of his needs and extend only to the relations of things to himself, not to essences. The intellectual order is providentially subtended by an affective order; the order in which we ought to study things depends on the order in which things satisfy our needs.

The synthetic method, which proceeds through definitions and deductions, and which philosophers (wrongly) supposed that they borrowed from geometers, according to Condillac, has nothing to which it can cling; it can only be arbitrary, for otherwise it is confused with analysis; any idea (here Condillac follows Locke) is either simple, and therefore undefinable, or compound, with the result that only analysis can show the manner and substance of its composition. A definition, unless it indicates the simple meaning of a word, pertains to doctrines which purport to apprehend the essence of things and therefore falls short.

Analysis, on the contrary, never goes beyond what is given. It consists in beginning with a confused whole, perceiving its details successively and separately, first the most important points, which stand out independently, then the intermediate parts, and achieving finally a simultaneous, distinct perception. In short, it consists in passing from a simultaneous and confused perception of a whole to a simultaneous and distinct perception of the same whole through the intermediary of the successive perception of its parts. The process involves both decomposition and recomposition. That is how we ordinarily proceed in the perception of an unknown landscape, which becomes familiar to us little by little; that is how we ought to proceed in all the sciences. Condillac does not believe in intellectual epigenesis: everything has been given to us *in nuce.*

The analytical method, we learn from Condillac's *Treatise on Systems,* points up the faults of the great systems of the previous century. These pretended systems were built synthetically on pretended principles, actually quite arbitrary; they issued from the Cartesian and Malebranchean maxim that one can affirm of a thing whatever is seen to be included in the clear and distinct idea of that thing—an inapplicable maxim since we cannot be certain that our ideas are ideas of complete things. Take the idea of extension. Is it not the idea of a substance in Descartes, of an attribute in Spinoza, of an incomplete thing in Leibniz? Recourse to evidence or to innateness then is unjustified. Cartesian physics is no more successful when it seeks its principles in hypotheses concerning the mechanical structure of things; the mind can only proceed at random to imagine these suppositions unless it is assumed, falsely, that our knowledge of nature is sufficient to enable us to exhaust all of them.

Condillac does not condemn systemization per se. According to him, a system is "the arrangement of the different parts of an art or a science in such an order that they sustain each other, and that

the last parts are explained by the first, which are the principles."
These principles must also be well-known phenomena, as they are
in Newton's physics, which is for Condillac the perfect model of
method. Newton showed how one known phenomenon, gravitation,
engenders other known phenomena—tides, the motions of the planets. What Condillac finds praiseworthy is the definitive and progressive attainments of such a system; gravitation remained certain as
a fact and continued to be the principle of the phenomena which if
first explained, for it was not affected by the discovery of facts which
could not be reduced to it. It is the same kind of system that Condillac undertook to realize in metaphysics.

III *The Treatise on Sensations*

*The Treatise on Sensations* is the application of Condillac's thesis
of the origin of ideas and his method, and it is sure testimony to their
universality. There is, in fact, a whole category of ideas the origin
of which Locke did not attempt to explain and which Condillac
himself, by his very silence, seemed to abandon as unanalyzable in
the *Essay* of 1746. These are ideas which Locke called ideas of reflection, that is, ideas of the faculties of mind—sensation, imagination, memory, judgment, reason. The indications which Condillac
gave in the *Essay* concerning the reduction of imagination and
memory to an association of ideas (traditional descriptions since
Descartes and Malebranche) did not prevent him from considering
abstraction and judgment as irreducible operations. On the contrary, in *The Treatise on Sensations* he follows his method to the
end, showing that there is no mental operation which is not a *transformed sensation*. This procedure was probably suggested by Diderot who, in his *Letter concerning the Blind* (1749), pointed out the
ambiguity of the *Essay,* which provided no escape from Berkeley's
idealism.[3]

Returning later to the meaning of this celebrated thesis (in his
*Logic,* II, viii), Condillac explained that *The Treatise on Sensations*

[3] Cf. Georges Le Roy, *La Psychologie de Condillac,* chap. iii.

was comparable, on the whole, to the solution of an equation which proceeded from one identity to another in order to reveal the unknown. The *transformation* involved here relates, then, not to a verifiable psychological datum, nor to the inner observation of a development, but to a transformation in the algebraic sense of the term. We have known terms in the form of our diverse faculties—attention, comparison, judgment, sensation, and the like—and an unknown term which is the source and generator of these faculties; we prove that sensation is the source of all the other faculties since it is blended with all of them and since the variations through which it passes produces all of them. Thus psychological observation is of use to us in positing the known terms of the problem, but it is of no use to us, at least in the author's view, in solving the problem. The clarity of the comparison is perhaps more apparent than real, for how can sensation be compared to an algebraic variable, and another faculty—attention, for example—to a determinate value of this variable? In reality, sensation bears a closer resemblance, perhaps, to a person known by different names, depending on the traits observed in him.

To demonstrate his thesis rigorously, he had to show that any sensation, of whatever kind, could engender all of the faculties. This brought him to the hypothesis of a statue on which, separately and successively, he conferred each of the senses, beginning with the one thought to be the lowest of all—smell. He claimed to be able to show that if a man had only the sense of smell, his understanding would have just as many faculties as it would have if all five senses were combined. Condillac's main thesis is the mutual equivalence of the five senses with respect to the generation of the faculties. Investigating the contribution peculiar to each of the senses in the functioning of the mind was a common preoccupation of his era. Condillac generalized the problem and provided a radical solution by affirming the equivalence of all the senses.

But if each sensation contains every faculty, then it is not true, as he said in the *Essay* of 1746, that intelligence depends on the linking of ideas and signs. That all mental faculties are prior to the use of signs was one of the most important conclusions of the *Treatise*. Of course they exist at a lower stage; for example, with respect to number we cannot apprehend more than three objects prior to our use of signs, and "it is the art of signs that has taught us to advance our knowledge." In general, the faculties which seem to be superior at this primitive stage "are only these same faculties after they have been applied to a great number of objects and developed further." The role of signs is to make possible the extension of these faculties. Thus in a sense his *Treatise on Sensations* provides the differentials of the faculties whose integration is made possible by signs. The problem of mind is resolved, as economically as possible, through sensations and signs.

Hence the lean, skeletal character of the *Treatise*. Its emphasis is on analysis rather than psychology. Suppose we try to determine which faculties will develop in a man who has only the sense of smell. First we need to understand clearly the significance of this hypothesis: at first only one thing exists in the consciousness of the statue, a smell—the smell of a rose, for example. Nothing exists at this moment except a consciousness of the smell of a rose; the statue is wholly the smell of a rose; it becomes the smell of a rose, just as it will become the smell of jasmin, then the smell of a carnation. Suppose there is in the statue only one sensation, to the exclusion of all others: attention. The smell does not cease to be sensed when the odoriferous body had ceased to act upon the organ. Now suppose a sensation persists as a new smell is introduced: the lingering impression will be memory. If the statue is attentive to both the present impression and the past sensation, this act of giving its attention to two things simultaneously is comparison; if the statue then perceives resemblances and differences, this is judgment; if comparison and judgment are repeated several times, this is reflection; if the statue recalls an agreeable sensation while sensing a disagreeable sensation, the memory will be stronger and will be imagination. The understanding is the whole set of faculties thus engendered.

A sensation cannot be indifferent but is necessarily agreeable or disagreeable. From this characteristic, combined with the faculties of the understanding, spring the faculties of the will: the memory of an agreeable scent, if it occurs at a moment when the statue is disagreeably affected, is a need, and the tendency derived from it is a desire; if the desire is dominant, it is a passion; love and hatred, hope and fear arise in this way. When the statue has attained the object of its desire, and when experiencing the satisfaction of desire engenders the habit of deciding that it will find no obstacle to its desires, desire engenders will, which is merely a desire accompanied by the idea that the object desired is in our power.

Finally, the statue with nothing but the sense of smell has the power to abstract and generalize ideas—for example, by considering the pleasure common to several modifications. It then has the idea of possibility, since it knows that it can cease to be the smell that it actually is and once again become what it has been; the idea of duration, since, knowing that one sensation is replaced by another, it has the idea of succession; and the idea of selfhood, which includes every sensation experienced and remembered. In short, the statue which possesses only the sense of smell, possesses every faculty, and the same obviously is true of any of the other senses.

But this leads us to a singular conclusion: the statue is in possession of all its faculties—it reasons, desires, and wills—yet it does not know that the external world exists or even that its own body exists. Might it have knowledge which cannot be reduced to sensations?

Two problems must be separated. The first one was in vogue (it was Molyneux' famous problem) when Condillac was writing: How do we perceive magnitudes and distances? The second one was peculiar to Condillac: How do we know that a thing is external to us?

Molyneux had proposed this problem to Locke: If an operation enabled a man blind since birth to see, would he then be able to tell the difference by sight, as he formerly had by touch, between a sphere and a cube? Locke had agreed with him in answering that the man would not. This was also of Berkeley's opinion, but Berkeley generalized the question in a singular way, showing that even to the sighted person, magnitudes and distances are never given but only suggested by sight. In 1728, in *The Philological Transactions of the Royal Society,* Cheselden, the surgeon, published the observations of a young boy, aged fourteen, whose cataracts he had removed. These famous remarks confirmed Locke's and Berkeley's opinion on every point. The subject said that objects "touched" his eyes, and he did not understand how his eyes could judge the size of a thing since an object measuring one inch, when placed near his eyes, seemed as large as the whole room. Voltaire presented Berkeley's opinion, which he approved, and Cheselden's experience in his *Philosophy of Newton* (1741). In this way the opinion was spread that the visual perception of magnitudes and distances was an acquired perception, and that touch alone perceived magnitudes directly.

The only part of this vast literature familiar to Condillac, who was not an avid reader (he himself admitted [Section 43] that he had not read Bacon at the time he completed the *Essay* of 1746), were the writings of Locke and Voltaire. He was naturally hostile to the notion of acquired perception because it assumed what he was least disposed to concede—unconscious judgments. It is impossible for us to be made conscious of pretended judgments linking sight to touch; "therefore they do not exist," he concludes triumphantly. "All I need," he says, "is for those who are willing to open their eyes to agree that they perceive light, color, extension, magnitudes, and the like. I need not go back further, for that is where I begin to acquire evident knowledge." Concerning Cheselden's blind subject, he made a critical observation which has been often taken up by his successors: the youth's judgments resulted, not from the absence of acquired perceptions, but from the lack of visual exercise.

Between the *Essay* and the *Treatise,* in 1749, Diderot published his *Letter concerning the Blind for the Use of Those Who Can See.* Taking up Molyneux' problem once again, they cited the conflicting opinions of Locke and Condillac. To him Cheselden's experiment seemed as inconclusive as it had to Condillac because of the confusion produced by an operation on an organ as delicate as the eye;

moreover, it did not seem certain to him that the subject was capable of understanding the questions put to him. In his view there were two distinct parts to the question: Could such a patient distinguish between objects after his operation? If so, could he recognize by sight objects already familiar to him by touch? With respect to the first question, Diderot called attention to the infinite details which a trained eye could see and which escaped the untrained eye; visual perception embraced many confused sensations, and the investigation of the correspondence of touch and sight ought to be of great use in perfecting our knowledge. Still, Diderot did not allow that sight depended essentially on touch, and he thought that sight was capable of apprehending extremely subtle details without the help of touch. With respect to the second question, Diderot believed that a subject's answer would depend on his mental capacity. A comparison of the new visual perceptions and the perceptions of touch, and consequently a certain mental effort, was required; but even if the patient were capable of recognizing two simple figures such as a square and a circle, reflection could provide him only with uncertainties concerning these correspondences; besides, he would be unable to distinguish between objects more complex than these simple geometrical figures.

In his *Treatise* of 1754 Condillac takes up the same problem again. He reverses his opinion and agrees with Locke, but only up to a certain point. Impressed, no doubt, by Diderot's reflections, he distinguishes between primitive, confused, visual perception in which objects are without precise limits and our actual perception of distinct objects situated in a determinate place. The latter results from an indispensable analysis effected by touch, which alone enables us to untangle the confused objects of visual perception. Thus touch first enables us to recognize forms, and it is by virtue of its relations with touch that vision perceives them. But sensation, once it has been perfected in this way, is self-sufficient and does not have to suggest the tactile sensations from which it has drawn support, as in Berkeley; it contains nothing more than was contained in the primitive sensation; "the statue sees the same things that we see," as soon as it opens its eyes, "but it does not have ideas of them"; it sees them but does not take note of them, for it has not analyzed them.

On the problem of knowledge of the external world Condillac also changed his thinking. In the first edition of the *Treatise* (1754) he attributes such knowledge to the coexistence of tactile sensations. When the statue simultaneously senses heat in one arm and cold in the other, a pain in its head, and so forth, it can apprehend these sensations as distinct impressions only if they are external to each other; thus it would seem that knowledge of externality is independent of motion. But in the second edition (1778) he grants that such vague tactile sensations can be simultaneous without spreading and that the notion of exteriority cannot arise without motion; it arises when the motion of our body is arrested by the resistance of solid bodies; in fact, solidity implies two things which are mutually exclusive, and it can be sensed only in these two things. If the solid body in question is a body external to ours, there will be only one contact, but if it is our own body that we touch, there will be a contact in both the part that is touching and the part that is being touched; consequently our body will be known as ours and distinguished from the others. Finally, it is the sensation of touch, united with the other sensations, which begins to make the statue suspect that smells, sounds, and colors are not simple modifications or variations of itself but come from external objects. The experience which makes us attribute these sensations to objects is that of the variation in intensity produced in them, depending on the remoteness or proximity of these objects. Thus judgments of exteriority are reduced to pure sensations.

## iv  *Science, the Well-Made Language*

Every human faculty is contained in sensation and expanded by the use of signs. Between analysis and language there is not only affinity but identity, as soon as analysis begins to assert itself. Even here, Condillac attributes much to nature. Vulgar, spontaneous language is the best analytical method, and philosophers with their technical language have introduced only confusion: "Before them, no one asked whether *substance* signified anything other than *that which is underneath,* whether *think* signified anything other than *weigh, balance, compare.*" [4] The words of the language can legitimately signify nothing except a sensible fact or a concrete operation.

Thus the only means of promoting analysis is "a well-made language." This is what Condillac tried to construct in *The Language of Calculi,* an incomplete work published posthumously. A science, according to his maxim, is simply a well-made language; consequently mathematics is the exemplary language. He begins with the "natural" method of calculation—counting on one's fingers— and undertakes to demonstrate that all other methods are transformations of the first; we progress by substituting other signs for the fingers, choosing the signs in such a manner as to make calculation simpler and simpler and thereby extend it further and further. This gradual extension is characterized as follows: "It is obvious that the means provided us by nature, being the first known, must necessarily take precedence over all those that have been invented, if, in order to find those we still do not know, we reason as we have reasoned to find those we do know. But we can be prevented from this by being ignorant enough or vain enough to flatter ourselves and, especially, to try to create the illusion that we make discoveries by leaping over great distances, when saner judgment would compel us to be humble enough to believe and let others believe that our mind never leaps over anything. . . . It is the method that does the inventing, just as telescopes do the discovering" (I, xvi). Analysis is an avowal of humanity; it teaches that the most refined and elevated methods are forms of the simplest methods, that any mind can be made to pass from one method to another, and finally that the method of exposition is identical to the method of invention.

Until the beginning of the nineteenth century this course was to be pursued, particularly in France and Italy, by those called the ideologists. It appeared to Condillac that it was not more difficult

[4] *Logique,* Part Two, chap. iv.

to apply analysis to metaphysics (in the sense of theory of mind) than to mathematics except that it was the "nature of our languages which, with respect to everything except numbers, give us only ill-defined notions."

## v Charles Bonnet

The Genevan naturalist Charles Bonnet (1720–93) seems, independently of Condillac, to have had the idea of the faculties of the mind and to have imagined the hypothesis of the statue. That is what he affirms in the preface to his *Analytical Essay on the Faculties of the Mind.* "We differ greatly," he says, "in our ideas and in our analysis. In general it seemed to me that the author [Condillac] does not analyze sufficiently; he sometimes goes by leaps . . . bypassing important questions and leaving them untouched."[5] To characterize analysis Bonnet uses an image quite different from that of Condillac, who borrowed the idea of transformation from algebra. Reasoning as a naturalist, Bonnet utilizes the idea of chain and series; analysis consists in "not having his statue take a single unnecessary step, in interconnecting all the links of its existence in such a manner that the chain is exactly continuous everywhere" (Section 71). Continuity does not mean identity, and Bonnet does not grant that activity is completely irreducible to sensation, which is passive. Preference shown for the most pleasing sensation is an action exercised by the statue over sensation; to prefer is not to sense but to define or to act. Pursuit of pleasure and avoidance of pain are quite different from sensation of pleasure and pain, and attention is a faculty distinct from sensation. By these remarks Bonnet seems to introduce, against the abuse of analysis which identifies, the unrecognized rights of direct internal observation. This was precisely the problem which the development of ideology brought to the attention of Destutt de Tracy and Maine de Biran at the end of the century.

[5] *Œuvres complètes* (1782), VIII, 7.

## VI  *David Hartley*

In his *Observations on Man, His Frame, His Duty, and His Expectations* (1749, partially translated into French in 1755), David Hartley also tries to apply to the mind the method of analysis and synthesis followed by Newton. Beginning with Locke's observations concerning the influence exerted by the association of ideas on beliefs, he generalizes the phenomenon and searches for a total explanation of all psychological facts. His work, though written after Hume's, bears no trace of the Scottish philosopher's influence; moreover, it deals exclusively with psychology, not with the critical examination of knowledge. In one sense, however, Hartley is more ambitious than Hume, for he claims that he can explain associational facts, or at least give their physiological counterpart: Sensations, according to a hypothesis advanced in Newton's *Optics,* are in fact produced by vibrations of an ether contained in the sensory organs, nerves, and brain; the joining of ideas has as its substratum and cause the joining, in the brain, of tiny vibrations which preserve a tendency to reproduce themselves in the same order as the vibrations originally produced by the senses. Although his thesis is not supported by any precise physiological research, Hartley's work is noteworthy, for it contains a multiplicity of observations, often ingenious, concerning the senses, automatic and voluntary movements, language, and judgment.

BIBLIOGRAPHY

## Texts

Condillac, Étienne. *Œuvres complètes.* 23 vols. Paris, 1798.
————. *Corpus général des philosophes français,* ed. G. Le Roy. 2 vols. Paris, 1946–51.
————. *Œuvres philosophiques,* ed. G. Le Roy. 3 vols. Paris, 1947–51.
————. *Lettres inédites à Gabriel Cramer,* ed. G. Le Roy. Paris, 1952.
————. *Treatise on the Sensations,* trans. G. Carr. London, 1930.

## Studies

Baguenault de Puchesse, M. G. *Condillac: sa vie, sa philosophie, son influence.* Paris, 1910.
Bizzarri, R. *Condillac.* Brescia, 1945.
Braga, G. C. *La filosofia francese e italiana del settecento,* vol. 1, pp. 100–60. Arezzo, 1920.
Dewaule, L. *Condillac et la psychologie anglaise contemporaine.* Paris, 1892.
Didier, J. *Condillac.* Paris, 1911.
Lenoir, R. *Condillac.* Paris, 1924.
Le Roy, G. *La psychologie de Condillac.* Paris, 1937.
Meyer, P. *Condillac.* Zürich, 1944.

## Works

Bonnet, Charles. *Œuvres.* 8 vols. Neuchâtel, 1779–83.
————. *Mémoires autobiographiques,* ed. R. Savioz. Paris, 1948.

## Studies

Bonnet, G. *Ch. Bonnet.* Paris, 1929.
Claparède, E. *La psychologie animale de Ch. Bonnet.* Geneva, 1909.
Lemoine, A. *Ch. Bonnet de Genève, philosophe et naturaliste.* Paris, 1850.
Savioz, R. *La philosophie de Ch. Bonnet.* Paris, 1948.
Trembley, J. *Mémoire pour servir à l'histoire de la vie et des ouvrages de M. Bonnet.* Berne, 1794.

## Histories and Studies of Eighteenth Century Thought

Belin, J.–V. *Le mouvement philosophique de 1748 à 1789.* Paris, 1913.
Lanfrey, P. *L'Église et les philosophes au XVIIIe siècle.* Paris, 1857.
Roustan, M. *Les philosophes et la société française au XVIIIe siècle.* Paris, 1911.
Sayous, A. *Le XVIIIe siècle à l'étranger: Histoire de la littérature française dans les divers pays de l'Europe depuis la mort de Louis XIV jusqu'à la Révolution française.* 2 vols. Paris, 1861.

# DAVID HUME AND ADAM SMITH

## 1  *Hume's Point of View*

David Hume (1711–76) was born at Edinburgh. After abandoning the study of law and trying his hand in commerce, he took up residence in France, at La Flèche (1734), then returned to England (1737). He failed to attract attention by publication of *A Treatise of Human Nature,* subtitled "An Attempt to Introduce the Experimental Method of Reasoning into Moral Subjects." The first two volumes appeared in 1739, the third in 1740. He published the first two volumes of his *Essays Moral and Political* in 1741 and 1742, and the third in 1748. He had served previously (1746) as secretary to General Sinclair and had gone as an emissary to Vienna and Turin. The success of his *Essays* probably encouraged him to choose this form to expound the abstruse ideas of the *Treatise.* In 1748 he published *Philosophical Essays concerning Human Understanding* (re named in 1758 *An Enquiry concerning Human Understanding*), and in 1751 *An Enquiry concerning the Principles of Morals. Political Discourses* (1752), *History of England* (6 vols., 1754–62), and *Four Dissertations,* which includes "The Natural History of Religion," complete the list of works published during his lifetime. Between 1763 and 1765 he resided in Paris, where he served as secretary to the British embassy and was "covered with flowers," as he phrased it, in the philosophical and literary world. In 1766 he returned to London, accompanied by Rousseau, who sought asylum in England but soon quarreled with his benefactor. Hume was in London as undersecretary of state in 1768, and he retired to Scotland in 1769. *Dialogues concerning Natural Religion,* probably written in 1749, was published after his death, in 1779.

Cartesian rationalism condemned the imagination as one of the greatest sources of error and opposed its fictive beliefs to the evidence of reason. But eighteenth-century critics saw the great systems that had issued from this rationalism as works of pure imagination, and they referred to the "visions" of men like Descartes and Malebranche, who were victims of what was supposedly expelled by Cartesianism. Thus they spoke in the name of a more prudent "rationality," grounded on experience and more faithful to common, vulgar rationality. By showing that this rationality was also the fruit of the imagination, Hume pushed criticism to the limit and thereby deprived it of any point of support. Following the example set by Vico in his study of history, Hume sought to make imagination, rather than reason, the basis for unity among men.

Among so many thinkers eager to make philosophy serve humanity, Hume seems to be a pure speculator, to a degree that the exigencies of philosophical thought are, in his view, diametrically opposed to those of action. For example, in practical matters it would be bad and even impossible not to rely on beliefs as natural and spontaneous as the belief in the external world or causality, and it behooves the philosopher to investigate carefully the nature and validity of criteria used to justify them. It has generally been conceded (since Thomas Reid) that Hume's skepticism is the natural and inevitable development of the philosophies of Locke and Berkeley. After Locke had criticized the notion of substance and Berkely the notion of physical causality, leaving intact only the causality of minds, Hume was ostensibly left with the task of using the same principle to destroy, along with the notion of spiritual substance, that of causality in general. This conception, though not false, fails to stress sufficiently the philosophical attitude of Hume, who is not advocating a cause, tolerance, or religion but who, so to speak, allows himself to be led freely by reflection, with no call to action. One of the least doctrinaire thinkers to appear since the Academics and Skeptics of antiquity, he points out in his discussion of liberty that "there is no method of reasoning more common, and yet none more blameable, than, in philosophical disputes, to endeavor the refutation of any hypothesis, by a pretense of its dangerous consequences to religion and morality. When any opinion leads to absurdities, it is certainly false; but it is not certain that an opinion is false because it is of dangerous consequence." Hume stands apart from all other eighteenth-century thinkers who posited a providential correspondence between truth and human needs. Metaphysical investigations do not have to be justified on the basis of their utility or accomplishments; they are a form of intellectual exercise. These investigations may seem very difficult and tiring, but some minds, like some bodies, are endowed with vigorous, flourishing health; they need violent exercise and find pleasure in labors that seem difficult and burdensome to ordinary men.

His aim was shared by many of his contemporaries and by Condillac in particular: to make metaphysics a science by using, in the study of the human understanding, the procedure used successfully by Newton in celestial mechanics; to pass from our particular judgments of things to their most general principles—principles which should indicate the limits of human curiosity with respect to each science.

This formula, however, clearly reveals Hume's originality. To him philosophy is a critique: a critique of the human understanding, a critique of ethics, a critique of literature and art. Beginning with man's appreciations and beliefs, he seeks through analysis and induction to identify their principle. He is careful, however, not to evaluate the principle of his evaluation, just as Newtonians refrained from explaining gravitation, through which they explained everything else. Consequently Hume's design is quite different from a genealogy or classification of ideas; it concerns the justification of the principles of our judgments.

## 11 *The Critique of Knowledge*

The preceding fact is somewhat obscured in Hume's first work, the *Treatise,* by the clumsy arrangement of his materials, which suggest at first glance a simple reworking of Locke's *Essay:* an opening section on the ideas of relations, modes, and substance, supplemented by a discussion of the association of ideas and a final chapter confirming the Berkeleian criticism of abstract ideas; a second section on the ideas of space, time, and existence; a third section on knowledge and probability. These were the subjects discussed by Locke in his *Essay.* But in the third volume of his *Essays,* published nine years later, Hume discards some of the long discussions (more particularly, the discussions of space and time) and provides a clearer exposition of his own theses.

From the outset, however, the *Treatise* takes us onto new ground. "Idealism," the name given to Locke's doctrine by his adversaries, as a rule reduces all the objects of our understanding to simple or complex ideas. To Descartes, who had introduced the term, the idea was the image or representation of a reality. To the degree that it remained representative in Locke, the idea was only an intermediary between the mind and its object; unable to choose between the idea as an object and the idea as a representation, Locke was obliged to cope with the Berkeleian objection that one idea can only resemble another idea. Hume did not reject idealism, but he solved the problem by making a distinction between impressions and ideas: impressions are originals or models, and ideas are their copies. Impressions are strong and vivid whereas ideas are weak, so that while each idea is representative, it is representative of an impression, which is identical to it in nature and superior only in intensity. In this way Hume steered clear of Berkeley's criticism and retained representative ideas. He even went further and drew a maxim which is indispensable in judging the worth of an idea: no idea is valid, no idea even has an existence unless the thing or the impressions of which it is a copy can be designated, at least with respect to simple ideas, for the grouping of simple ideas into complex ideas does not always have to refer to an identical grouping of impressions. Hume attaches only one reservation to his maxim, but it is most striking: if the eye is presented with a whole series of gradations one of which is assumed to be omitted, it can perceive the missing gradation even though it has never had an impression of it previously; consequently a simple idea can exist without a corresponding impression. This observation seems to indicate that Hume sensed that the mind was not simply a mosaic of impressions and that it was impelled to search for new impressions.

This maxim is at bottom the sole principle of Hume's critique. In the mind itself he found models to validate ideas, and he became an immanentist critic. His object was to study, not impressions, but only ideas or copies of impressions. Their diverse relations with each other and with impressions—one might say, what is given in the problem and not subject to further investigation—constitute the fabric of the mind.

As he read Locke, Hume must have noted a defect mentioned earlier by Condillac: arbitrariness and indecision with respect to the formation of complex ideas. Whereas Condillac had formulated rules to explain what Locke had failed to clarify—how complex ideas are fashioned from simple ideas—Hume seeks to determine through experience the forces which serve naturally and spontaneously to link ideas. Here he rediscovers the universal principles of the order of the imagination which Malebranche and, before him, Plato and Aristotle, had stressed: two ideas become associated because of their resemblance, because the impressions of which they are copies were contiguous, or because one of them represents a cause of something which the other represents the effect. These laws are to our ideas what the Newtonian law of attraction is to bodies; they maintain the order of the mind as the law of attraction maintains the order of the universe, and they account for the formation of all complex ideas. Hume disapproves only of the physiological "explanations" which the Cartesians and especially Malebranche had claimed to find for these laws; to him they are original and primitive.

Yet Hume is not an "associationist" in the sense later attributed to the word. His mental attraction is not universal: first, because attention has the power to stop the series at an idea, next because there is sometimes a veritable irregularity in the imagination and an arbitrary union between two or more ideas not connected in any way. Moreover Hume, like Malebranche, holds that these associative connections are the main causes of our mistakes; resemblance, in particular, often causes us to confuse ideas whenever the actions of the mind through which we consider them differ but slightly.

Thus Hume first tried to fill the gap in Locke's system. The imaginative connection is the intermediary between a simple idea and a complex idea. For example, if we have a complex idea of relation, it is because we are comparing ideas that have been joined through association based on resemblance; the comparison of the portrait and its model—the complex idea of relation—follows the connection which caused the idea of one to suggest the idea of the other; the complex idea of substance—a mass of simple ideas designated by one name—is formed when these simple ideas have been reunited by the imagination through association based on contiguity.

Proceeding further, however, he found a problem which Locke had found as insoluble as the first one—the problem of passage from ideas to knowledge, in the sense attributed to this word by Locke. Knowledge, according to Locke, was either the perception (immediate or mediate) of a relation between two ideas or the intuitive perception of an existence, and it was always certain. Hume's first original contribution was to show the immense portion of knowledge excluded by this enumeration: all inferences in matters of fact, all more or less probable arguments that allow us to affirm the existence of facts outside our actual experience. For whether our aim is to utilize human evidence to rediscover past facts or prior experience to predict future facts, we employ a mode of reasoning which does not fit into Locke's system since it is neither an actual experience nor a relation of ideas. It can be rejected as knowledge under the pretext that it provides a simple probability (this is often true—for instance, when we remain doubtful about the past or the future), but it also includes an element of certainty. We know with certainty that the sun will rise tomorrow, and although this certainty is different from the certainty of mathematics, it is no less perfect in its own class.

This inference, whether certain or probable, rests on the connection between cause and effect. It is by virtue of this connection that we are able to use evidence to infer a past cause from observable effects and to predict an effect that will be produced by a cause of which we have sensory knowledge. Thus we must probe the nature of this connection in order to identify the foundations of our certainty in matters of fact.

There had, indeed, been attempts to trace this connection to one of the relations of ideas which provide the foundation for certitude in mathematics. In such relations—in relations of equality, for example—we need only inspect both ideas in order to discover their relations a priori. Does the same hold true for the relation of cause and effect, that is, do we discover by inspecting a particular cause (such as the lowering of the temperature of water) that it is the cause of a particular effect (freezing)? Obviously not, and, here alone, experience can instruct us. On this point Hume has reference to the doctrine of those whom Locke's adversaries called idealists. Examining from all angles the idea of the thing which is the cause, we find in it no power to produce the effect. But the only question posited was the following: if the power to produce an effect is not in the phenomenon called cause, where is it? We recall how Malebranche attributed it to God, and Berkeley, more generally, to Mind. Hume adopts the same point of departure but posits a wholly new and distinct problem: if we lack sensory knowledge of any force or efficacy in a fact, why and how do we *believe* that this fact will be followed inevitably by another fact which we predict with the greatest confidence? This is a preliminary problem which Malebranche and Berkeley should have posited at the outset, for it is obvious that the question of the source of the power to produce an effect cannot be raised prior to belief in a connection between facts. Hume's main contribution is in having made the investigation of the principles of this belief completely independent of the investigation of their efficacy. It is no longer a question of the dialectic pointing up the inadequacy of sensible things to explain themselves and causing us to leap to the spiritual reality; we are dealing now with an immanentist critique which seeks to identify the motives of our belief in spite of this inadequacy.

What exactly is belief? Hume tells us that the idea of an object is an essential part of the belief accorded to it but not the whole of it, since we conceive of many things in which we do not believe. Only when belief is added to the idea does it become knowledge of something real and no longer a fiction. Prior to this, according to Hume, no philosopher had explained belief.

Here again, Hume has recourse to the properties of imaginative connections: belief, taken by itself, is only the idea with a particularly high degree of vivacity. Believing in an idea adds nothing to the content of the idea; unbeliever and believer have the same ideas in their minds, but in the mind of the believer these ideas have more strength, vivacity, solidity, firmness, and stability—in the mind of a man, for instance, who accepts as true a tale considered fictitious by another. The particular character of the idea which causes us to believe in it derives from its associative links with present impressions; for an impression, which is more vivid than any idea, has the singular property of transmitting something of its vivacity and power to the ideas connected to it, as if thought, animated by it, retained something of its vigor when gliding toward related thoughts; thus, in religions, sensible images and solemn ceremonies strengthen belief.

It follows that whatever strengthens the connection between an impression and an idea at the same time fortifies belief in this idea, to the point of exempting it from doubt.

There we have all the elements which explain our confidence in the appearance of an effect when its cause is present—confidence culminating in the judgment that their connection is necessary. We should note first that we acknowledge a necessary connection only between successive and contiguous facts whose succession we have observed several times. This repetition has no effect on the actual joining of facts, but in our minds it engenders a habit or a *custom*, strengthening the imaginative connection that causes the mind to pass from the idea of one to the idea of the other and, by reinforcing the connection, producing an irresistible belief. The necessary connection, then, is only a progressively more facile transition from an idea—a penchant born of custom for passing from an object to "the idea of that object, which usually attends it." Like any other idea, the idea of a cause is a copy of an impression—not a copy of a power that we apprehend in things but the power of the internal impression or impression of reflection, which is the feeling of custom. But the universal penchant of the mind for spreading itself over external objects makes us suppose that this necessity is in the objects under consideration and not in the mind that considers them.

Is not this "explanation" of causality its destruction instead, since it shows us the illusion of which we are victims? This would be true if human reason were the product of critical reflection and could be established through argumentation; then other arguments could destroy it, and we would finally have to suspend judgment; but man continues to believe and to think and to reason in the ordinary manner even though he can find no mistake in logical arguments. The explanation is that belief in causality depends on feelings rather than on logic, and ideas cannot destroy a sensation or a particular mode of conception. If there is disparity between belief and reflection, this disparity cannot harm belief. There is a great difference between the opinions we form as a result of calm and profound reflection, and the opinions we embrace by a sort of instinct or natural impulse, by virtue of their conformity and harmony with the mind. If these two opinions collide, the outcome is easily foreseen: as long as our attention is focused on the subject, the philosophical, artificial principle may predominate; but whenever our thoughts stray, nature will deploy her forces and bring us back to our first opinion.

Spontaneous belief, stemming from the nature of imagination, is then the judge in the last resort. Reflection can neither confirm nor achieve belief but can go no further than to discover its laws. The search for the principles of imagination and custom must be abandoned.

We must note, however, that custom could not play such a role if external phenomena did not provide it with the opportunity. Belief in causal connections would not exist if we did not find in experience the repetition of an identical or similar phenomenon. A universe is conceivable in which the same conditions would never be reproduced and belief could not take shape. We would be pressing Hume too hard if we said that there is a harmonious relation between our inner nature and the nature of things, for he did not try to justify our confidence in feeling; he simply reported that this confidence exists and thrives, and the unnatural attitude assumed by the philosopher in calling it in question is no argument against the ease and facility of a more natural conception.

Hume makes imagination the basis not only of our belief in causality but also of the skeptical solution of three great problems which had been troubling philosophers throughout the eighteenth century: the existence of the external world, the immateriality of the soul, and personal identity.

Why do we believe in the existence of permanent bodies distinct from us when our senses reveal to us only evanescent objects resolved into pure impressions which, in the form that they are immediately given, are no more external to us than pleasure or pain? Certainly not by reason, for this belief is prior to any reasoning. Imagination alone is involved, and we can be sure that here, too, it can be exercised only on one condition: certain clusters of collections, or series of impressions must be reproduced intermittently. But only the properties of imagination can explain how we can believe each time that these clusters are the same bodies and that they have continued to exist during the intervals of their appearance. A body which is *the same* or *identical* remains invariable from one moment to the next and is perceived in an uninterrupted manner at these different moments; in such a case, passage from one moment to the next is so easy that it is hardly sensed. In the case of a cluster of impressions reproduced intermittently, the transition from one object to another is almost as easy as in the case of identical objects, and the smooth flow of thought causes us to believe in the identity of the two objects; but since their intermittence contradicts this belief, we create the fiction of a continuous existence.

At this point the philosophical reflection of the skeptics comes into play: That the impressions which we would like to think of as independent of ourselves depend strictly on the senses is proved by all our illusions. Now dogmatic philosophy supports spontaneous belief and invents a world of real, permanent objects distinct from our transient perceptions; it concedes to skeptical reason the intermittence of perceptions and attributes to the imagination continuous existence. Hume calls it the monstrous fruit of two contrary principles and shows that belief and philosophical reflection are opposing sentiments. Dogmatic philosophy proves only that nature is obstinate and will not give ground no matter how fierce the attack from reason. The diverse forms given to the theory of the external world by the dogmatists derive from this requisite of the imagination: Aristotle's first matter, identical beneath outward changes, is a fiction intended to re-establish an identity between successive aspects which are said to belong to the same body; its substantial form simply expresses the easy tranition through which we pass from one quality to others when they are habitually reunited. Here the mechanistic theories of Descartes and Boyle—accepted by Locke, who accorded independent existence only to figure, motion, and solidity, and treated such "secondary" qualities as sounds and tastes as mere impressions on the mind—are the same in nature as Aristotle's theory; furthermore, they include an inner contradiction when they seek to determine the mechanical causes of sounds or smells; for in trying to satisfy the penchant of imagination for picturing to itself bodies distinct from us, they deny that there is any trace of validity in a spontaneous imaginative belief which fails to exclude the slightest sensible quality from the external world.

## III *The Critique of Religion*

The foregoing example shows that in Hume's view philosophy is a completely useless superstructure built on the foundation of spontaneous belief. Some of his other dogmas, particularly those relating to the spirituality of mind and personal identity, were viewed in his time as indispensable preludes to the natural religion which, according to men like Clarke, led to revealed religion. In his *Dialogues* Hume gives a substantial account of the nature of this natural religion: it belongs, he says, to ecclesiastical history rather than to philosophy. Many of the Church Fathers adopted a wholly skeptical attitude toward human reason in order to bolster their authority and attributed all forms of heresy to belief in the universal capacity of reason. But in an era when many religions were known, when one authority counterbalanced another, clergymen thought it necessary to have recourse (at least as a preliminary step) to the universality of reason. Consequently this case is wholly analogous to the preceding cases, for it is marked by the pretense of founding spontaneous beliefs on philosophical reflection. To the critique of this pretense Hume devoted two long sections of his *Treatise* (the sections on the immateriality of the mind and personal identity), the tenth section of the *Essay* (on miracles), and his remarkable *Dialogues concerning Natural Religion*.

So-called philosophical demonstrations of the immateriality of mind are worthless. It is said that impressions or ideas, by their nature, can only be inherent in a spiritual substance, but inherence and substance are left undefined. How could we know a substance since we can know only impressions or ideas which are copies of them, and since an impression is a mode and therefore cannot represent a substance? Thought is said to be immaterial because it is indivisible; but if we grant that the materialists are wrong in linking thought to extension, then the "theologians" are equally wrong in stating that an indivisible thought can perceive extension without spreading itself out and dividing. The difference between spiritualism and materialism is really no greater than the difference between spiritualism and Spinozism, for Spinoza's simple substance, of which all existing things are modes, becomes almost indistinguishable from the simple substance of the "theologians" (here we should of course read "Berkeley"), to which is linked the whole system of perceptions, if everything which is not mind is perception. On this question the opposing dogmatisms coincide when pursued to the end, and one of them helps religion no more than the other harms it.

Equally unfounded is belief in the identity of the personal self as a permanent reality, superior to the transient succession of impressions and ideas. In the mind there are only impressions and ideas which are distinct from each other and joined by no perceptible bond. The notion of personal identity arises in the same manner as the notion of the identity of external bodies; because of the associative force of resemblance and, especially, the natural relation between cause and effect, we remember successive states of consciousness, enabling the imagination to create the fiction of our permanence. Still, Hume betrays his dissatisfaction with his explanation in the Appendix of his *Treatise,* in which he admits that he does not know how "our successive perceptions" are united "in our thought or consciousness." In any event, he holds that philosophers were wrong in assuming that we have an intimate awareness of our personal identity.

As for rational proofs of the existence of God, Hume shows that they derive from an incorrect application of modes of reasoning which ordinarily prove successful. In Hume's day the most popular of these proofs was the proof by final causes, which Voltaire repeated again and again. It rests on the analogy between an artificial mechanism and the universe, which resembles a complex mechanism closely enough also to require an intelligent author. One of the most common arguments in experimental science, it differs strikingly from Clarke's a priori proofs since it relies on probability. The exposition of this proof by the rationalist Cleanthes shocks the mystic Demaea as well as the skeptic Philo: Demea on account of its conclusion, since God is likened to a human operator; Philo on account of its principle, since an analogy is established between a mechanism fabricated by man and the universe. To begin with, it can be argued that there can be no analogy between a very limited part due to a limited cause and the immense whole whose nature may or may not be the same throughout. But if this analogy is assumed to be solidly grounded, it can be put to the most fanciful uses, and that is what Philo did with amusing virtuosity. It is therefore necessary to posit a finite God such as the human artist— a God whose cause can be sought, an imperfect God such as an artisan who meets with obstacles, perhaps even a plurality of Gods, since the operation of the world can be a collaborative affair, and in any case a corporeal God who can work with his hands. Cleanthes' method of analogy can be extended further still: a parallel can be drawn between the universe and an organism, and God can be seen as the soul of the world or a vegetative force, like those forces which, without consciousness or design, produce order in plants; and there is no reason to reject Epicurean cosmogony since, in spite of what the theologians say, a motion can begin without a voluntary agent (gravity or electricity, for example).

Clarke's proof is no less open to criticism. In the first place, it is impossible to conceive of a being as existing necessarily. The imagination always remains free to deny the existence of any being whatsoever; furthermore, if a necessary being existed, why could not the universe be explained through matter, whose properties are better known, rather than through God? Finally, why would we try to find the sufficient reason of the universe outside it if we did not suppose arbitrarily that it is a limited whole?

Natural religion claims to demonstrate not only the existence of

God but also his providence, which is contradicted, however, by the existence of evil. We recall the arguments of the theodicy, which attempts to resolve the difficulty. Hume makes two observations regarding this subject, which he repeatedly examined in detail: first, we must accept the paradox of human suffering, which is both a terrible argument against Providence and a means of persuading men in search of consolation to embrace religion; second, notwithstanding the arguments of all the theologians, nothing is easier than for us to imagine a universe in which the sources of evil, as we know them, have disappeared, in which activity is motivated even by the slightest pleasure rather than by pain, in which particular acts of God's will continuously annihilate the bad effects said by the theologians to be linked to his general laws, in which the human faculty of work is further developed, in which finality is more perfect. In a word, no argument proves that the ultimate source of things is not indifferent to man.

We recall that critical reflection on the origin of the principle of causality did not destroy but rather justified the spontaneous attitude of the normal man who believes in a necessary connection between cause and effect: skepticism is for rare moments of reflection, belief for a whole lifetime. Would the same be true of religion? Would skepticism here be the prelude to faith? This conclusion is suggested by the last conversation in the *Dialogues,* in which Philo explains how his critique of natural religion leaves the field free to revelation. These texts, in which he expounds ideas similar to those attributed by him to the Church Fathers, are parallel to those which we have noted concerning natural belief in causality, which subsists in spite of criticism of this notion. Is his declaration a precautionary measure, typical of the eighteenth century? Is it sincere?

Here a distinction is in order. Imagination, according to Hume, is the natural source of our beliefs. It does not follow that every creation of the imagination is justified. We must distinguish in the imagination between principles which are permanent, irresistible, and universal (like causality) and principles which are variable, weak, and irregular; the former are the foundation of all our thoughts and actions; the latter are neither veritable nor necessary nor even useful in the conduct of life. Reasoning which leads to belief in the existence of bodies and the reasoning of one who believes in ghosts are both natural, but the second is natural in the sense that a sickness is said to be natural when it springs from causes which are natural, even though they may be injurious to health. Alternatively, to see that in the positive religions many beliefs depend on this disordered and absurd imagination, we need only read what Hume has to say in the twelfth conversation about the predominant religion: Far from being a social bond, it is a cause of dissension; it leads to frivolous observances, to ecstasy and credulity; and through concern for eternal salvation, it engenders narrow egotism. Also important in his *Essay* is the chapter "On Miracles" in which he seeks to reveal the fallacious reasoning on which our belief in miracles is based: the human testimony which supports our belief, no matter how high a degree of probability it may attain, is still not susceptible of offsetting the certainty that any event must be produced in accordance with natural laws. Moreover, the famous incidents involving the convulsionaries of St. Médard—incidents which occurred during Hume's sojourn in Paris —showed him that perfect agreement among all witnesses to the same fact fails to prove its existence.

Under these conditions, to bring out the full significance of Philo's declarations, Hume would have had to do for religion something similar to what he did for causality: to identify what is essential and natural, in the broadest sense of the word, in religious belief. Hume set down the broad outlines of this task in a remarkable treatise on *The Natural History of Religion,* which is concerned especially with polytheism. Here Hume combats two interpretations then in vogue: the first, very ancient, affirmed that mankind had begun with divinely revealed monotheism and that polytheism was merely a corruption of it; the second, found in Fontenelle, held that polytheism was the first of the sciences and that man had arrived at polytheism through the contemplation of nature and the investigation of its causes. Here, as everywhere else, Hume denies that a simple theoretical speculation can be the root of a profound belief. How could anyone believe that primitive man was interested in the regular order of nature? Sentiment, hope, and especially fear concerning his destiny gave birth to polytheism: to primitive man the gods were benevolent beings or wicked beings—or at least beings whose favor primitive man had to learn to curry before they were causes of the order of the universe.

Here we see the lines along which Hume might have been able to develop a positive theory of religion. In it he would have placed less emphasis on the extension of knowledge than on the satisfaction of the inmost human needs.

## IV  *Ethics and Politics*

Hume's speculations on ethics fit into the same pattern as his doctrines of knowledge and religion, which they probably antedate.[1] They are at once a critique of ethical rationalism and an appeal to belief and sentiment. The rationalism which he criticizes is that of Clarke, then prevalent in England. It assumes the existence of moral relations which are defined as objectively as mathematical relations—for example, the relation of benefactor to debtor, the relation of fraternity, of friendship. Virtue consists in acting in conformity to the relations conceived by reason; the ingrate, or one who prefers his brother to his friend, is mistaken about the nature of these relations. Hume observes that reason can indeed tell us whether an act is appropriate to an end and consistent with a rule, but that there is no attachment to this end in the absence of an approving or censuring heart. For instance, to the understanding, the murder of Laius by Oedipus and of Agrippina by Nero are both parricides; but the feeling of horror provoked by the second makes it a crime, and this feeling depends not on objective relations but on the inner constitution of human nature, just as beauty is not

[1] Cf. the preface of N. Kemp Smith's *Aristotelian Society*. Supplementary volume XVIII (1939).

the symmetry perceived by the mind but the pleasure that accompanies it.

Still, Hume does not belong to the ranks of those who, like Hutcheson, left the decision to a moral sense or feeling. There is in moral judgments (as in the judgment concerning causality) a universality which should be explained. It results, according to him, from the approval or disapproval of our acts by those around us. Virtue is any action or quality of the soul that excites a feeling of pleasure and approbation among those who witness it. Moral sentiment is meaningful only if it has reference to a society which makes judgments according to its own standard. Against this thesis, it may be objected that variations and contradictions in judgment occur when we examine different societies: did not the ancient societies approve of suicide and the exposing of children? Hume maintains that agreement subsists on the main points—sincerity or courage, for example—and that differences in customs result from a deviation due to circumstances. Exposing children is a form of paternal love in a very poor country; patriotism cannot be the same in a free country like England as in France, where it is reduced to love of the "despot"; bravery cannot have the same meaning among warlike and among peaceful nations; and certain sentiments can develop only at the expense of others—for example French sociability, which stifles family sentiments. But the primordial sentiments remain the same, the only exception being, in Hume's view, the "artificial lives" of those who wish to make their own laws on the fringes of society—fanatic individualists like Diogenes, who tried to make philosophy his standard, or Pascal, who was a victim of religious superstitions or philosophical delirium. We see how remote this "sentimentalism" is from nascent romanticism, from heroism seeking to chart its own course, apart from the courses already laid out.

From the beginning to the end of the doctrine, then, imagination and sentiment are essentially factors of generality, union, and truth. They are not the turbid powers feared by rationalism and made triumphant by romanticism.

From the political point of view Hume goes against the Whigs and against Locke's liberalism. He denies that the legitimacy of a government rests on a primitive contract which is revocable and which therefore includes the right to revolt; moreover, unlike the Tories, he denies divine right and absolutism. He reverses the terms of the problem, in the sense that he tries to discover the legitimacy of a government, not in its origin (unknown in most cases but generally marked by violence, to which the contract is alien or contributes only faint support), but in actual social utility. This principle provides a basis for offering resistance, if only to a slight degree (differing in various governments, but greater in England than elsewhere), to a government detrimental to society.

## v  Adam Smith

It was also in sentiment that Adam Smith thought he had found the rules of ethical conduct. Born in 1723, he attended the University of Glasgow, where he was taught by Hutcheson. He became professor of logic (1751), then of ethics at Glasgow. In 1759 he published his *Theory of Moral Sentiments,* and in 1764 he became tutor to the young Duke of Buccleuch, with whom he resided in France, first at Toulouse, then Paris, where he became acquainted with the physiocrats. Upon his return to England he devoted himself wholly to the preparation of *The Wealth of Nations,* which he published in 1776. He died in 1790.

His *Theory of Moral Sentiments* concludes with some curious pages against casuistry, which he treats as the exemplar of intellectualistic ethics: "It may be said, in general, of the works of the casuists that they attempted, to no purpose, to direct, by precise rules, what it belongs to feeling and sentiment only to judge of. How is it possible to ascertain by rules the exact point at which, in every case, a delicate sentiment of justice begins to run into a frivolous and weak scrupulosity of conscience? When is it that secrecy and reserve begin to grow into dissimulation?"[2] Such fine distinc-

[2] *The Theory of Moral Sentiments* (Edinburgh, 1808), II, 373.

tions (and ethics requires them) can be grasped only through the immediate sympathy or repulsion which we feel and which is translated through a judgment of approval or disapproval. This judgment is not dictated by self-interest, since our good opinion of something may lead to actions which are useless or at times even harmful; nor does it spring from reason, as Cudworth and the Cambridge moralists concluded from the generality of moral judgments, which Smith accepts. This generality, like that of an empirical law, is obtained through induction. We do not approve or disapprove any action originally because, upon examination, it seems to accord with or oppose certain general rules; on the contrary, general rules are established because experience shows that actions composed of certain circumstances are generally approved or disapproved. Unlike Hutcheson, Adam Smith does not think that we can have recourse to a moral sense, for while one sense—the sense of sight, for example—must remain the same no matter which color it perceives, our approbation takes different forms, just as the sentiments we approve take different forms. He maintains that the approbation given to a tender sentiment in no way resembles the one given to a lofty sentiment, that one mollifies us while the other elevates us, and that there is no resemblance between the emotions which they excite. Approbation then is at bottom, nothing more than communion of sentiment, or sympathy. This sympathy is ethical only if it is wholly disinterested; thus we first judge others before judging ourselves, and we appraise ourselves correctly only if we know how to adopt the point of view of an impartial spectator.

Adam Smith nevertheless notes something inconsistent in our manner of judging: it seems that if sympathy is tied only to one sentiment, we ought to judge a man's merit or lack of merit only in terms of the intentions that dictate his conduct; but nothing of the sort happens, and fortunate or unfortunate consequences, success or failure, almost entirely determine the judgment that we make concerning the merit or demerit of his intentions. Thus our sympathy corresponds to the sentiment conveyed by a man's actions rather than to the sentiment that he actually experiences within himself. Adam Smith recognizes that this inconsistency and this superficial manner of judging are the conditions of moral life as he understands it. From the example of moralists such as La Rochefoucauld, he knows the extent to which an exhaustive analysis of sentiments casts suspicion on "the most innocent and circumspect conduct."[3] "Sympathy" then is not a kind of intuition which causes us to penetrate deeply into the conscience of another; unlike Rousseau, Smith does not make moral sentiments an ethic of conscience. Here, as in Hume, sentiment has a practical role and is common to all men, but finalism, which remained latent in Hume, manifests itself on every page, and the sympathy that governs moral conduct is one more proof of divine providence. Later, in his work on political economy,[4] Adam Smith showed that if deliberate measures are not imposed by the government, the spontaneous operation of self-interest should be sufficient to increase the wealth of nations.

[3] *Op. cit.,* I, Part Two, sec. 3, chap. iii.
[4] *Inquiry into the Causes of the Wealth of Nations,* 1776.

BIBLIOGRAPHY

## Texts

Hume, David. *The Philosophical Works of David Hume,* ed. T. H. Green and T. H. Grose. 4 vols. London, 1874–75.
———. *A Treatise of Human Nature,* ed. L. A. Selby-Bigge. Oxford, 1888. Reprinted 1951.
———. *A Treatise of Human Nature,* with an introduction by A. D. Lindsay. 2 vols. London, 1928–30.
———. *Enquiries concerning the Human Understanding and concerning the Principles of Morals,* ed. L. A. Selby-Bigge. Oxford, 1902. 2d ed. 1955.
———. *Dialogues concerning Natural Religion,* ed. N. K. Smith. 2d ed. London, 1947.
———. *The Natural History of Religion,* ed. H. Chadwick with an introduction by H. E. Root. London, 1956.
———. *Political Essays,* ed. C. W. Hendel. New York, 1953.
———. *The Letters of David Hume,* ed. J. Y. T. Grieg. 2 vols. Oxford, 1932.
———. *New Letters of David Hume,* ed. R. Klibansky and E. C. Mossner. Oxford, 1954.
———. *Dialogues concerning Natural Religion,* ed. N. K. Smith. Oxford, 1935.

## Bibliographies

Jessop, T. E. *A Bibliography of David Hume and of Scottish Philosophy from Francis Hutcheson to Lord Balfour.* London, 1938.

## Studies

Broad, C. D. *Five Types of Ethical Theory,* chap. 4. London, 1930.
Brunius, T. *David Hume on Criticism.* Stockholm, 1952.
Dal Pra, M. *Hume.* Milan, 1949.
Deleuze, G. *Empirisme et subjectivité.* Paris, 1953.
Elkin, W. B. *Hume: the relation of the Treatise of human nature in Book 1 to the Inquiry concerning human understanding.* New York, 1904.
Glatke, A. B. *Hume's Theory of the Passions and of Morals.* Berkeley, 1950.
Greig, J. Y. T. *David Hume.* London, 1934.

Hendel, C. W. *Studies in the Philosophy of David Hume.* Princeton, 1925.
*Hume and Present Day Problems.* Aristotelian Society, supplementary vol. XVIII, 1939.
Huypers, M. S. *Studies in the Eighteenth Century Background of Hume's Empiricism.* Minneapolis, 1930.
Kydd, R. D. *Reason and Conduct in Hume's Treatise.* Oxford, 1946.
Laing, B. M. *David Hume.* London, 1932.
Laird, J. *Hume's Philosophy of Human Nature.* London, 1932.
Leroy, A. *La critique et la religion chez David Hume.* Paris, 1930
———. *David Hume.* Paris, 1953.
Lévy-Bruhl, L. "L'orientation de la pensée de David Hume," *Revue de Métaphysique et de Morale,* XVII, 1909.
MacNabb, D. G. *David Hume: His Theory of Knowledge and Morality.* London, 1951.
Maund, C. *Hume's Theory of Knowledge: A Critical Examination.* London, 1937.
Meinong, A. *Hume Studien.* 2 vols. Vienna, 1877–79.
Mossner, E. C. *The Forgotten Hume: Le Bon David.* New York, 1943.
———. *The Life of David Hume.* Edinburgh and London, 1954.
Passmore, J. A. *Hume's Intentions.* Cambridge, 1952.
Price, H. H. *Hume's Theory of the External World.* Oxford, 1940.
Sharp, F. C. "Hume's Ethical Theory and its Critics." *Mind,* 1921.
Smith, N. K. *The Philosophy of D. Hume.* London, 1941.
Taylor, A. E. *D. Hume and the Miraculous.* Cambridge, 1927.
Vaughan, C. E. *Studies in the History of Political Philosophy,* vol. I, chap. 6. Manchester, 1925.

## Works

Smith, Adam. *Collected Works.* 5 vols. Edinburgh, 1811–12.
———. *The Theory of Moral Sentiments.* London, 1759.
———. *The Wealth of Nations.* 2 vols. London, 1776.

# VAUVENARGUES

## I Life and Works

Luc de Clapiers, Marquis de Vauvenargues, was born at Aix in Provence in 1715. At an early age he was an avid reader of the ancient moralists, Plutarch and Seneca. He became an officer in the royal army in 1733 and took part in the Italian campaign (1733–36), then in the Bohemian campaign (1741–43). Though he was sick and almost blind when he returned to Aix in 1745, he decided to establish a residence in Paris, where he died in 1747. He was an intimate of the Marquis de Mirabeau, and later of Voltaire and Marmontel. The only work which he published in his lifetime was *Introduction to Knowledge of the Human Mind* (1746), followed by *Critical Reflections on Some Poets*. After his death, in 1747, there was published a second edition of the *Introduction,* followed by *Reflections* and *Maxims*. Each successive edition thereafter (those of 1797, 1806, 1821, and 1874) contained new writings or new versions of writings already known, but these were only sketches, made for the most part during the course of his military career.

## II The Doctrine of Types of Mind

Historians of philosophy often misjudge the importance and depth of Vauvenargues' thought. Vauvenargues was a systematic thinker who was forced by circumstances to leave his exposition in the form of disconnected thoughts. Trying to achieve a coherent notion of the human mind, he found that his century, with its taste for disputation and its passion for "scientific oddities" (he had in mind the collection mania), was completely indifferent to contradictory statements concerning the most important subjects.

Vauvenargues, though he was not initiated to the scientific movement, brought to the study of the mind the Newtonian ideal which we found in Condillac and Hume: "The vast mind considers beings in their mutual relations, apprehending at a glance all of the ramifications of things; it unites them once again at their source and in a common center, and it puts them all under the same vantage point," he wrote. "I like a writer who embraces all times and all countries," he continued, "and who reduces many effects to few causes; who compares the prejudices and morals of different centuries; who, through examples drawn from painting and music, acquaints me with the beauties of eloquence and the close connection between the arts."

But Vauvenargues did not believe in the existence of an infallible and universally accessible method for realizing the universal concatenation envisioned by his century. He found on the contrary (and this must have had its source in his meditation on Pascal) that people normally see only certain types of mind, which are generally mutually exclusive, and that each individual wants his dominant quality to be that of mind in general. Quick mind, penetrating mind, apt mind, profound mind, poetic mind, rational mind —all these minds denote different, incompatible directions and rule out any mutual understanding. The quick mind of the sophisticated man, for example, will scorn the profound mind which it cannot follow along "its dark path." Worse still is the misunderstanding among people with profound minds, "each preferring his own object." This misunderstanding is radical and necessary because it is the condition of creativity—for instance, poetry "hardly allows us to divide our efforts." Thus few minds are capable of embracing simultaneously every facet of every subject, and Vauvenargues cites the example of the politicians of his time who admired the development of the arts and commerce but failed to see the poverty of the greatest part of the nation.

One is forced to choose between the narrow, limited course and a vast but superficial view. Take the gentleman who knows a little about everything: such knowledge is "almost always useless and sometimes pernicious." Those who say (and is he not referring here to Pascal?) that our century has the advantage of having inherited all the knowledge of the past, are disregarding the weakness of the human mind: "Too many objects confound our sight; too much knowledge overwhelms our judgment. . . . Few people know how to use to advantage the minds of others. . . . The effect of opinions, multiplied beyond the powers of the mind, is to produce contradictions and to disturb the certainty of principles."

Thus Vauvenargues speaks out against the ideal common to his age, against progress through the diffusion of enlightenment, which to him is "barbarism" rather than progress. To disprove the equality of intellects—the common theme of his age—he cites the exception of the genius who, alone, knows how to combine types which are usually incompatible: the philosopher endowed with imagination, such as Descartes or Pascal; the poet with sound judgment, such as Racine or Molière. Unity of mind is not a point of departure but is achieved only in the rare case of the genius. But "in the realm of intelligence as in politics, most men have been destined by nature to be members of the lower classes."

This ideal of power, irreducible to any method, applies to ethics as well as to intellectual life. What are we? We are our passions, "which are not distinct from ourselves." Every passion is shaped by our character; ambition is no exception, for it becomes a vice or a virtue, power or servility, depending on the man. Love attaches itself not to an object but "to the idea that we choose to imagine, and it is only this idea that we love." We prefer the beauty which expresses the character "that best suits our own." The reason is that this passion has its source primarily in the "feeling of power" which we wish to increase, in the feeling of "meanness and subjection" which we wish to stifle; the primitive passions are gaiety, whose source is the ordinary feeling of power, and melancholy or uneasiness, due to feelings of powerlessness. It is obvious that the Stoics were mistaken when they posited a free will above our passions. The will is "the hand that points to the hours on a clock," and the motives of our actions sometimes escape us because of the extreme rapidity of thought; but our freedom consists only in the determination of our acts by our thoughts and feelings—that is, by ourselves—for once again "it would be folly to separate one's thoughts or feelings from one's self." The doctrine of those who preach moderation of the passions is also false. They might as well preach sobriety to a man with an upset stomach: "What does a sick man care about the delectability of a feast which disgusts him?" Finally, La Rochefoucauld's egotism is false, for as soon as a passion becomes strong, it makes few allowances for our individualism, our comfort, or our welfare; his "self-love" is counterbalanced by "love of self" which seeks its happiness outside itself and (if Vauvenargues does not use the language of Nietzsche, he approximates it) in the exercise of the will to power. For example, love of glory, one of the strongest stimulants to magnanimity, which gives us natural control over our feelings and quickens our efforts; or avarice, "the greedy instinct which urges us to increase, strengthen, and consolidate our being"; or paternal love, in which the "idea of propriety" predominates; or friendship, which reveals to us "the insufficiency of our being."

But does not virtue appear to be opposed to the cultivation of the passions? In ethics we must not try to define a virtue as being "essentially good," for it is a virtue only in relation to goodness— that is, by definition, in relation to its usefulness to society; goodness, in turn, is not in itself an object of the will but becomes such an object "because religion assures us of indemnities" and because of our "odious fear of torture." Mandeville was wrong in maintaining that vices, as such, are useful to society; vanity and avarice, for instance, serve society only if they are mixed with temperance, probity, and other virtues. If virtue is uniquely defined by social interest, to say that it is a necessary result of our temperament or that it has its source in love for ourselves is not an argument against it, for here only the results matter.

Obviously, then, Vauvenargues considers ethics as having no relation to the intrinsic worth of man. He states this explicitly: "Some great qualities are perversions of virtue." For example magnanimity, the display of power which consists in exercising control over fortune and subjugating other men, made criminals of men like Catalina and Caesar and showed no signs of diminishing after doing so. Heroism, distinct from our ethical values, constitutes the true worth of man and, like genius, ranks above the limited appreciation and apparent contradictions that characterize the vulgar mind.

Thus, like Condillac and Hume, Vauvenargues sought the source and regulator of mind in something more natural, more profound, more intimate than transcendental reason which, according to eighteenth-century thinkers, neglected nature, sentiment, passion, and belief. "My whole philosophy," he wrote to Mirabeau on March 1, 1739, "has its source in my heart. Do you think it is possible for it to withdraw to its source and take up arms against itself? A natural philosophy which owes nothing to reason cannot submit to laws; my philosophy can tolerate only itself; it consists properly of independence, and the yoke of reason would be more unbearable than the yoke of prejudices."

Condillac's statue which is subjected exclusively to sensible impressions, Hume's man who follows the beliefs formed spontaneously within him, and Vauvenargues' hero whose sole rule is fidelity to himself and to his dominant passion are all conceptions of the same kind, no matter how different their inspiration. Vauvenargues, like Hume, was a critic of natural religion, which claimed to show reason traveling independently toward transcendent reality. "Everything that has being has order," he wrote in the fragments published as a sequel to his *Treatise on Free Will,* and this profound statement put an end to any investigation of the author of this order.

Such was the harsh, haughty doctrine of a thinker who is often slighted, to whom the edition of 1806 attributed a "consoling and gentle philosophy," and in whom Voltaire and others found only substance for fastidious discussions of style.

# Bibliography

## Texts

Vauvenargues, Marquis de. *Œuvres,* ed. P. Varillon. 3 vols. Paris, 1929.
———. *Œuvres choisies,* ed. H. Gaillard de Champris. Paris, 1942.
———. *Réflexions et maximes.* London, 1936.
———. *Reflections and Maxims,* trans. F. G. Stevens. Oxford, 1940.

## Studies

Borel, A. *Essai sur Vauvenargues.* Neuchâtel, 1913.
Lenoir, R. *Les historiens de l'esprit humain.* Paris, 1926.
Merlant, J. *De Montaigne à Vauvenargues.* Paris, 1914.
Paléologue, G. M. *Vauvenargues.* Paris, 1890.
Rocheblave, S. *Vauvenargues, ou la symphonie inachevée.* Paris, 1934.
Souchon, P. *Vauvenargues, philosophe de la gloire.* Paris, 1947.
———. *Vauvenargues.* Paris, 1954.
Vial, F. *Une philosophie et une morale du sentiment: Luc de Clapiers, Marquis de Vauvenargues.* Paris, 1938.

# THE THEORY OF NATURE

## 1 Diderot, D'Alembert, and the Encyclopedia

In the group of philosophers known as the Encyclopedists, either because they actually participated in Diderot and D'Alembert's undertaking or because of their affinity with them, we find a spirit quite different from that of the philosophers previously discussed. Generally speaking, they placed little stress on the philosophy of mind, for they were inclined to think that Locke had had the last word on the matter and to look with deep distrust on metaphysical subtleties. They were interested not so much in mental faculties as in nature and society. In Diderot in particular and in his materialist friends, D'Holbach, Helvétius and, previously, La Mettrie, we find an emergent conception of nature.

The history of the foundation of the *Encyclopedia* by Diderot and D'Alembert is well known. Denis Diderot, born at Langres in 1713, studied under the Jesuits at the Collège Louis-le-Grand. Interested in all the sciences and arts, he first translated Stanyan's *Grecian History* (1743), then James's *A Medicinal Dictionary* (1744), and finally Shaftesbury's *Inquiry concerning Virtue or Merit* (1745). In 1746 the publisher Le Breton entrusted him with the translation of Chambers' *Cyclopaedia; or an Universal Dictionary of Arts and Sciences,* published with great success in 1728. The idea of such a work was in the air, and in an oration delivered in 1737 Ramsay, the great exponent of Freemasonry, is reported to have exhorted his colleagues to "unite to shape the materials for a universal dictionary of the liberal arts and all useful sciences." [1] Diderot enlarged the original project and brought in his friend, the mathematician D'Alembert. Jean le Rond d'Alembert, born in 1717, had already written his *Treatise on Dynamics* and was a member of the Academy of Sciences and a friend of Frederick II. Associated with them were various collaborators, men of letters, scholars, and scientists, but Diderot himself wrote a large number of articles. Imprisoned at Vincennes for six months in 1749 for writing *Philosophical Thought* (1746) and *Letter on the Blind* (1749), he published the first volume of the *Encyclopedia* (*Encyclopédie, ou Dictionnaire raisonné des arts et des métiers*) in 1751 (he had also written *The Way of the Skeptic,* published in 1830, and *On the Sufficiency of Natural Religion,* published in 1770). The first volume of the *Encyclopedia,* by a group of men of letters, was preceded by a "Preliminary Discourse," written by D'Alembert. Pious partisans, supported by the *Journal de Trévoux* and Christophe de Beaumont, Archbishop of Paris, took up as a pretext a thesis upheld at the Sorbonne by the Abbé de Prades in which they found condemnable propositions such as the origin of ideas in the senses or the defense of natural morality, and then placed the responsibility for the scandal on the *Encyclopedia* and succeeded in having it interdicted just as the second volume was being published, early in 1752. Nevertheless, with the tacit support of Malesherbes, director of publications, and in spite of the incessant attacks by the enemies of the Philosophes, Palissot and Fréron, five new volumes of the *Encyclopedia* were published between 1753 and 1757. But 1758 was another critical year for the work: as a result of polemics occasioned by his article "Geneva," D'Alembert, with the clandestine approval of Voltaire, abandoned the work, as did Duclos and Marmontel. The *Encyclopedia,* held accountable for the materialism of Helvétius (whose book *Essays on the Mind,* published in 1758, was condemned), was again interdicted by royal decree and condemned by the pope; not until much later, in 1766, did the

---

[1] As quoted by Joseph Le Gras, *Diderot et l'Encyclopédie*, p. 28.

last ten volumes appear. Around the *Encyclopedia* was formed, chiefly from 1753 on, the society which included not only Diderot but also Rousseau, Grimm, D'Holbach, and Helvétius. Several of Diderot's philosophical works—his *Thoughts on the Interpretation of Nature* and *The Dream of D'Alembert,* both written in 1769, and *Supplement to the Voyage to Bougainville,* written in 1772, were not published until after his death. Diderot died in 1784.

"We are witnessing a great revolution in the sciences," wrote Diderot in *The Interpretation of Nature*. "Considering the penchant which intellects seem to me to have for ethics, belles-lettres, natural history, and experimental physics, I would almost dare to assert that within the next hundred years there will not be three great geometers in Europe." What might be called a veritable demathematization of the philosophy of nature occurred as men turned away from the Cartesian ideal according to which every difficulty in physics should be rendered "almost identical to the ideals of mathematics."

The nature and origin of such a new mentality merits investigation. Three reasons for its emergence, all closely interconnected, stand out: (1) the manner in which Newton's mathematical science of nature was interpreted; (2) the transformation of the ideal of the mathematicians; (3) the development, for their own sake, of the life sciences.

The result of Newtonian science was to point up the contrast between the rigor of mathematical reasoning and the merely approximative character of experimental measures. It was wrong for anyone to assume that there was in the law of attraction a principle from which all natural phenomena could be deduced. This law failed to account for the electrical, chemical and biological phenomena which were receiving more and more attention. Moreover, as Diderot, Bradly, and Le Monnier observed, even in the study of the heavens the new mathematical science "did not dispense with observing the sky."

But certainly this new attitude goes beyond the brutal observation which caused Diderot to say that someone should write a

*Treatise on the Aberration of Measures.* It seems, in fact, that through the idea of his science which he fashioned for himself, the geometer took the initiative in dissociating himself from physics, at least in proportion as natural science asserted its originality. D'Alembert, the theoretician of geometry, combines the traits (not incompatible by any stretch of the imagination!) of the empiricist and the logician. On the one hand, mathematics is an experimental science because of its subject matter. It is even the first of the sciences since it deals with figures, the most abstract and general characteristics of bodies: "By successive operations and abstractions, we divest matter of almost all of its properties and somehow consider only its ghost, extension"[2] (we recall that this is the language of Hobbes). Geometry studies matter reduced almost to nothingness, and arithmetic, still more abstract, originates when the object is to find the relation between the parts of that from which we imagine geometrical bodies to be composed. Thus, since it is no longer anything but "a kind of general metaphysics in which bodies are divested of their individual qualities," mathematics relegates to the experience of the physicist almost everything that can be discovered.

On the other hand, as a logician the mathematician seeks to deduce all truths from the smallest possible number of principles. His course, like that of philosophers in general, is the reverse of the course dictated by common sense: "The most abstract notions—those which the common man considers the most inaccessible—are often those through which the greatest light is conveyed. The smaller they are in number, the more fruitful the principles are . . . ; they must be expanded through reduction."[3] The mathematician's virtuosity therefore consists in dispensing with the greatest possible number of concrete notions. This is true, for example, of D'Alembert's work in dynamics, which is the complete opposite of the dynamics attempted by Leibniz, who had reintroduced into Cartesian mechanics the notion of moving cause or force. D'Alembert requires only motion. "Solely from consideration of motion

[2] *Discours sur l'Encyclopédie.*
[3] *Discours sur l'Encyclopédie.*

viewed in the simplest and clearest way," [4] he deduces three principles by means of which reason can obtain results coincident with
those of experience.

Thus the truths of dynamics, contrary to what Leibniz thought,
are necessary and not contingent. Mathematics, understood in this
way, relinquishes the eminent place assigned to it by Descartes and
becomes only one science among others. But if we adopt D'Alembert's interpretation, we see that it has something in common with
the others. Like D'Alembert, almost every other mid-eighteenth
century thinker relied on empiricism and deduction, trying to find
in each science the fundamental fact from which all the rest could
be deduced. For example, nothing bears a closer resemblance to
D'Alembert's ideas on mathematics, than Condillac's theory of
mind. "Anyone who examines a series of geometrical propositions
deduced from each other," writes D'Alembert in his *Discourse on
the Encyclopedia,* "will notice that all of them are merely dis-
figurations of the first proposition; it is distorted, gradually and
successively, as the geometer passes from one consequence to the
next; instead of being multiplied, however, it is simply given different forms." Is this not, *mutatis mutandi,* what Condillac said
of sensation and the mental faculties? This is the same type of
thinking that we find, in another form, in the philosophy of nature
and again in social philosophy.

One of the most characteristic aspects of this type of thinking is
seen in Linnaeus' discussions of the classification of living beings.
Diderot voices the most general criticism of those called "meth-
odists" in these words: "Instead of reforming their notions of beings, it seems that they take it upon themselves to model beings on
their notions." [5] Linnean classes are categories abritrarily fabricated
by the mind and forced to accommodate any living being which
presents the characteristics which define its class; furthermore, any
other characteristics are disregarded, even though they might relate a particular being to other beings placed in a remote class.

[4] *Essai de dynamique.*
[5] *Interprétation de la nature.*

Contrary to the rule established by Locke, Linnaeus thought that he could utilize archetypal ideas of substances.

Diderot is instinctively hostile to any thought that fixes and limits beings. "There is nothing precise in nature. . . . Nothing is of the essence of a particular being. And you speak of essence, you poor philosophers." His work abounds in intuitions concerning nature conceived as a whole in which particular beings are reabsorbed. After being a deist with Shaftesbury, he arrived at a kind of naturalism of which the most vivid expression is given in *The Dream of D'Alembert*.[6] Through Bordeu, the vitalistic doctor of the school of Montpellier, he expounds the thesis that an animal is an aggregate of animalcules which join together and become organs for the whole; the individual has no unity other than the unity of aggregation which is forever varying and being transformed, without any true death occurring and without the whole being affected. He urges us to "steer clear of the sophism of ephemerality," which supports the belief that diurnal forms endure eternally; there is a general flux which must cause the species which constitute the whole to change completely from one planet to the next and from one epoch to the next. Diderot had a presentiment of Lamarck's transformism: "Organs produce needs and needs produce organs." The transient identity of the self exists only through this whole: "Change the whole and you necessarily change me." But there is also in each being (this is the old alchemy of the Renaissance) an image of every other being: "Any animal is to some degree a man; any mineral is to some degree a plant; any plant is to some degree an animal."

To this naturalism is linked an ethic based on the return to nature. Diderot's *Supplement to the Voyage to Bougainville,* in a Tahitian fantasy, describes what human life would be like if entrusted to completely pure, primitive instincts not yet transformed by laws and religion. It contrasts at every point with the naturalism of Rousseau, who stressed the natural, spontaneous character of

---

[6] *Rêve de d'Alembert,* in *Œuvres* (ed. Assezat), II, 139.

conscience and duty. To Diderot the return to nature is the return to instinct.

## II  *La Mettrie, D'Holbach, Helvétius, Maupertuis*

Apart from his scintillating style, there are only slight differences between Diderot's ideas and those of his friends, D'Holbach and Helvétius. Before them came Julien Offray de La Mettrie (1709–51), a doctor who was banished first from France (1746) and then from Holland (1748) because of his publications. He found refuge with Frederick II, who granted him a pension and appointed him court reader. He was always held in bad repute in philosophical circles. Paul Henri Thiry, Baron d'Holbach (1723–89), was born in the Palatinate and spent most of his life at Paris, where he was the friend and host of the Philosophes, whom he assembled in his hotel on the Rue Saint-Roch. He contributed to the *Encyclopedia* articles on chemistry and diverse scientific subjects and, beginning in 1766, published a great number of anti-religious writings. Claude Adrien Helvétius (1715–71) came from a family of physicians of German ancestry. His grandfather, the first of them, settled in France, where Helvétius himself became farmer general. During his lifetime he published only his *Essays on the Mind,* which was condemned; the book *On Man* did not appear until 1772.

The superficial view that La Mettrie's and D'Holbach's materialism is grounded on the sensationalist theory of knowledge was long ago refuted in Lange's *History of Materialism.* Decided sensationalists like Condillac were actually strict spiritualists, and simple chronology rules out the possibility that the first known French materialist, La Mettrie, profited from Condillac's works. Besides, that materialism had existed in England since the emergence of the seventeenth-century "mortalists" is attested by Locke's confession concerning the spirituality of the mind, by Toland's books, and by Collins' polemic.

Materialism asserts the fundamental unity of all phenomena—observable, physical, vital, moral, social, human, or animal—and posits as their common link their relation to the entity which he calls nature. "Everything that is not taken from the very bosom of nature," says La Mettrie, "everything that is not a phenomenon, a cause, or an effect—in short, everything that is not in the realm of natural science—does not concern philosophy and comes from an alien source." [7] Here again the object is not to describe a real genesis of these phenomena but to produce the impression or intuition of their intrinsic relationship.

The thesis of the materialists is simple enough, but the intellectual circumstances under which it is upheld are more complex. Their thesis, though predicated on rigorous determinism, is different from Cartesian mechanics. In *Man a Machine,* for example, La Mettrie refers to the Cartesian thesis of animal-machines, but he thinks that each part of the body has its own structure to allow it to act and to function without the whole; and, as a doctor, he stresses the survival of organs after their separation from an organism (examples then known include the continued beating of the heart of a frog and the reproduction of the whole polyp from one of its parts); it follows, then, that every action of an organism is due to the combined actions of each part, with its own structure and force, as in the automatons then being fabricated by Vaucanson. "If only it is conceded that organized matter is endowed with a moving principle which alone differentiates it from matter which is not so endowed," he says, "and that in animals everything depends on diversity of organization, that is enough to explain the energy of substances and of man."

It is in D'Holbach's *System of Nature* that the thesis stands out most clearly. It is concentrated in an ancient Ionian concept against which Plato and Aristotle had fought persistently and which D'Holbach expresses in this way: "Motion is a mode of being which necessarily flows from the essence of matter." [8] D'Holbach

---

[7] *Discours préliminaire,* in *Œuvres philosophiques* (London, 1752), p. v.

[8] *Système de la nature ou des lois du monde physique et du monde morale* (London, 1770), p. 22.

reprimands the physicists who, like Descartes, thought that bodies were inert and preferred (for instance in the case of heavy bodies) to explain their fall through an imaginary external cause of which they had no idea rather than to attribute an inner force to them, and he undertakes (in a passage that makes little sense) to deduce Newtonian gravitation from the essence of matter. By inherent motion D'Holbach means something that differs qualitatively according to the matter under consideration, for "each being can act and move only in one particular way. . . . Each being has laws of motion which are peculiar to it and acts constantly in accordance with these laws unless a stronger cause interrupts its action" (p. 17). D'Holbach puts primary stress on the Cartesian error of the homogeneity of matter, which he refutes by praising the Leibnizian principle of indiscernibles as stated by Bilfinger. After positing these substances endowed with qualitatively different properties, D'Holbach concludes that each being is a composite of simple beings and that its essence consists wholly in the mingling of these beings.

Like many of his contemporaries, D'Holbach tries to apprehend the series of essences, beginning with matter. But he stresses the philosophy of nature almost solely for the purpose of showing the extent to which his thesis renders natural religion nugatory, and he effectively destroys the argument, then almost unique, used by the Philosophes to demonstrate the existence of God—the argument of final causes. Order in nature is but one rigorously necessary arrangement of its parts, founded on the essence of things; for example, the beautiful regularity of the seasons is not the effect of a divine plan but the result of gravitation.

But D'Holbach was especially concerned with applying his ideas to the moral world and showing how they should be used to construct a new morality not connected with any positive religion. Man, too, is a mixture of matter "whose arrangement is called organization and whose essence is to sense, to think, and to act" (p. 12). The mind of each depends on his physical sensibility, which depends in turn on his temperament. The sole law of his activity is to love pleasure and to fear pain. He is surrounded by sensible beings different from him and unequal among themselves; it is this inequality which supports society inasmuch as it causes men to have need of each other. But of course "men contribute to the well-being of other men only when they are persuaded to do so in order to procure pleasure thereby; they refuse to contribute to it when they are hurt. Those are the principles on which to ground a universal system of ethics, one common to all individuals belonging to the human species." [9] Ethics, then, consists in willing the well-being of others, but the benefits associated with it are in no way natural consequences of the social process; on the contrary, "the powers of the earth must lend to ethics the expedient of rewards and penalties of which they are depositaries" (p. xix). The moral problem is a problem of legislation: the establishment of a system of sanctions in which pleasure is used to incite men to perform virtuous acts, that is, acts useful to others. It therefore implies a political reorganization in which the power of education, until now religious, is replaced by an enlightened, unprejudiced secular power which recognizes, along with the motives of human conduct, social utility.

No morality without social restraint: this notion, notwithstanding appearances, clearly separates the view of D'Holbach and his circle from the teachings of the Epicureans, who were radically isolated from society. D'Holbach, whose books are suffused with the idea of social utility, seeks to achieve the conformity associated with religion, but by surer, more rational measures. Here his views contrast starkly with those of La Mettrie, who states bluntly: "In ethics we have no choice except to resemble others, to live and almost to think as they do. What a comedy!"

Hence the relentless struggle against religion, which philosophy is supposed to replace. In this struggle D'Holbach probably used the arguments common to the philosophers of his time—the absurdity of theological quarrels, intolerance and its dangers, the fragility of traditions—but he relied mainly on the antinaturalistic

---

[9] *La morale universelle ou les devoirs de l'homme fondés sur sa nature* (Amsterdam: Michel Rey), vol. I, p. xviii.

character of Christianity. Religion preaches asceticism and insists that man should not desire what his nature compels him to desire; such principles "produce no effect, or simply reduce man to despair by inciting an unrelenting struggle between the passions of his heart, his vices, his habits, and the fantastic fears through which superstition has sought to crush him"; these principles are wholly arbitrary since they are grounded "on the chimerical will of a supernatural being" (p. 145) and not, like those of the new ethics, "on the eternal, invariable relations subsisting between human beings living in a society." Notions which are inherently as ineffective as these can be fortified only by artificial notions, such as the notion of the soul, of a future life, or of a God who rewards and punishes. Here again, then, man's conduct is motivated by pleasure, yet a purely imaginary pleasure. Who could have contrived and maintained such inventions but those who use them to lead men wherever they will—in other words, priests? That religion is the invention of priests determined to impose all kinds of ceremonies and practices in order to hold men in their power is the thesis transmitted from Toland to D'Holbach.

The doctrines expressed in Helvétius' *Essays on the Mind* (1758) is essentially the same: it is the application, in intellectual matters, of D'Holbach's ethical tenets. He attempts to solve this problem: Everything in the mind originates by means of physical sensitivity, which is identical in all men and even in many animals; but there is a great diversity of minds, which are different both in nature and worth; how can such diversity spring from a single source? This difference derives immediately from the variable capacity of the attention and its orientation or choice of particular objects; furthermore, this capacity and direction exist solely by virtue of passion, and "one becomes stupid as soon as one ceases to be impassioned." Passion itself amounts simply to pursuit of pleasure and flight from pain—that is, to physical sensibility, which therefore proves to be the source of the diversity of minds. As for the worth of a mind, it is based not on something intrinsic but only on the esteem accorded to it by other men, and this esteem is proportionate to the general interest of the members of the society to which the individual belongs; a miser may evidence as much intelligence in his schemes as the leader of a victorious army, but the latter is superior by far to the former. Depending on its nature, each kind of society—commoners, aristocrats, men of letters—confers superiority on a mind which would lose its worth by changing its setting; moreover, since each individual benefits by conforming to the interest of the society in which he lives, this society inspires passions which should produce the minds it esteems. Hence Helvétius deduces the social role of the philosopher, who alone pursues the interests of all—those interests which are truly universal—and not the interests of a particular society: "It was the philosophers who brought societies from the state of savagery to the state of perfection which they have now reached." The "prejudices" of the savage (by this Helvétius means ceremonies such as sacrifices to ancestors or the offering of first-fruits, ceremonies which nineteenth-century sociologists viewed as symbols of the social bond) were imposed for the particular benefit of the priesthood.

No one could outdo Helvétius in deprecating the essential, intrinsic qualities of the mind. A genius is such only by virtue of his worth to society; circumstances are responsible for the reputation of statesmen; as for inventive talents, it must be remembered that no scientist or philosopher is without precursors and that, in consequence, they are merely continuers. Here we have the total reversal of Vauvenargues' theses.

The mind is so dependent on external conditions that education encounters no resistance in shaping it at will. From start to finish the treatise *On Man* (1722), which was written partly to refute Rousseau's *Émile,* purports to show the power of instruction. Helvétius is convinced that man's passions (and consequently his whole mind) are in no way dependent on nature and physiological structure but are due to the circumstances of his education; that is, they are due essentially to the system of sanctions that has been applied to them. Idolatry of education or the artificial fabrication of minds could not be pushed further, and D'Holbach himself criticized Helvétius for not having seen that there are "rebellious, volatile, or dull dispositions" which nothing can improve.[10]

It sometimes happens that materialists try to shirk responsibility for the practical consequences of their doctrine. Helvétius, of course, assures us that ignorance (he means religious prejudice) is no guarantee of the fidelity of those who practice it, that revelation of truth is disastrous only to the speaker, that knowledge of truth is always useful, that its revelation never disturbs states.[11] La Mettrie, on the other hand, presents materialism as a purely speculative doctrine which, though it attains truth, cannot and will not exert any influence on rules of conduct: "It is futile for the materialists to prove that man is only a machine, for the people will never believe anything of the sort. What great harm would result if they did? Laws are so strict that they could be Spinozists, and society would still have no reason to fear the destruction of its altars, which seems to be the goal of this audacious system." [12] And later, speaking of the proof he thinks he has given of the mechanical necessity of all human acts, he says: "All these questions can be put in the same class as mathematical points, which exist only in the geometer's head"; the theory of man as a machine "is so difficult to apply in practice that it proves to be as useless as all the metaphysical truths of the highest geometry," Conduct calls for social restraint, truth for speculation; this is the sense of his reply (at the beginning of *Christianity Unveiled,* 1767) to the objection that "the people must have a religion, good or bad" and that religion "acts as a necessary restraining force on simple, uncouth minds." He says: "The common people read no more than they reason . . . ; if one of them were able to read a philosophical work, he would no longer be a scoundrel to be feared . . . ; fanatics incite revolutions . . . ; enlightened, disinterested, sensible men are friends of peace." It is obvious that indecision reigned in matters that seemed crystal clear. Here we find confusion and indications of an almost irreconcilable

---

[10] *Morale universelle* (1776), II, 70–71.

[11] *De l'Homme,* sec. VI, chap. ii.

[12] *Discours,* p. xvii.

disagreement between speculation and practical necessities; the world, as it was revealed to reason, provided men with nothing to guide their conduct. But this introduces a problem which looms large throughout the remaining part of the history of philosophy.

These books stirred up a violent polemic. The incidents are not important in the history of doctrines; besides, they quickly fell into oblivion, and they seemed for the most part dry and dull. "We did not understand," said Goethe, referring to *The System of Nature,* how such a book could be dangerous. It seemed to us so spiritless, so Cimmerian, so cadaverous that we could hardly bear the sight of it." [13] Critics soon saw that the aim of materialistic naturalism was to replace, by a rational construction, old traditions in the form of government, religion, society, and education. "A hundred times," observed Nicolas Bergier, "philosophers have drawn up plans for politics and for government; every time they have failed because they have always made plans for men as they imagined them, that is, for men who do not exist and who will never exist." [14]

The most profound of these critical examinations is that of Holland in his *Philosophical Reflections (Réflexions philosophiques sur le Système de la Nature,* 1773). Leaving aside facile declamations against atheism, he stresses the radical contrast between materialistic dogmatism and the critical movement that originated with Locke and Hume (one more proof, if such is necessary, of the independence of empiricism with respect to materialism). Whereas D'Holbach represented nature as a necessary concatenation of facts, each deriving from another to infinity, Hume observed that this causality implied only a constant connection, not a necessary one. No one has been able to validate D'Holbach's hypothesis of a geometric deduction of the laws of motion, and the very notion of an infinite series "implies a contradiction since it would have the greatest possible number of terms and no real number can be the greatest possible number" (p. 21). Furthermore, the sufficient reason of a real effect would be relegated to infinity, which means that it

---

[13] *Poetry and Truth,* IX.
[14] *Examen du matérialisme* (1771), I, 386.

would be found nowhere. Here we see the outlines of the finite thesis of the Kantian antimony. Holland found no less intolerable the transformation of attraction into "an undefinable metaphysical being which resides in bodies and acts in places where it is not present" (p. 23), and this despite the anticipated protestation of Newton. Finally and most important, Holland refuses to admit that empiricism leads to egotism in ethics and to negation of the spirituality of the soul and liberty, whereas the opposite theses are linked to innate ideas. As an empiricist Hutcheson posited benevolence as a moral principle, and D'Holbach never proved that a combination of motions can produce thought. As for hostility between philosophy and religion, Holland notes (II, p. 202) that religion is one aspect of the human mind and that it progresses or declines with the mind as a whole; but it neither prevents nor produces progress. "The progress of the sciences was retarded not by religion but by the invasion of the barbarians. . . . It was not religion that caused the fall of Constantinople, a political event to which we are indebted for the renaissance of the sciences and the arts. The state of religion," he adds with profundity, "follows the revolutions of the human mind, which in turn depend on the combination of myriad circumstances totally alien to the mind."

Maupertuis (1698–1759), who was president of the Berlin Academy, remained somewhat aloof from the other materialists, devoting a part of his activity to pure science, mathematics, astronomy, and geography (he directed the expedition charged with determining the shape of the earth). A defender of Newton against Descartes, he believed that it is beyond human intelligence to fashion a system and to "follow the order and dependence of every part of the universe." On the other hand, he imitated Leibniz and used the principle of finality to justify the general laws of nature, least action, and universal attraction. It was in the work first published in Latin under the pseudonym of Dr. Baumann (*Dissertatio inauguralis metaphysica de universali naturae systemate,* 1756) that he upheld a view of materialism complaisantly expounded by Diderot in *The Interpretation of Nature* and castigated by Rousseau in his

*Profession of Faith.* Thought and extension, says Maupertuis, designate not essences but properties which can, without contradiction, belong to a subject whose essence may even be unknown to us; our aversion to attributing thought to matter is traceable to our conceiving thought as a mind similar to our own; in truth (and here Leibniz' influence is again discernible) there are countless gradations of thought, from a clear intellect to the vaguest sensation. The materialism of Maupertuis is a kind of hylozoism which attributes life and sensibility to every material molecule and assumes that any superior life or thought comes from the consensus of elementary molecules. Nevertheless, according to P. Burnet, his most recent interpreter, on some points this doctrine resembles the immaterialism of Berkeley. In particular, Maupertuis does not consider extension as being substantial; like so-called secondary qualities, it is a simple representation. Such indecisiveness is characteristic of Maupertuis' thinking.

## III  *Buffon and the Naturalists*

It is important for us briefly to note the existence of the same spirit in the works of the naturalists, dominated by the personality of Buffon. Georges Louis Leclerc de Buffon (1707–88), superintendent of the Jardin du Roi after 1738, published his *Natural History* between 1749 and 1788. The naturalists looked upon him as a writer and philosopher rather than a scientist: "His work," said one good judge, "is the antithesis of that of Linnaeus." [15] He inspired Diderot's theses against Linnaeus.

In opposition to Linnaeus' hierarchical classification he posits the notion of a *series* or *chain.* Taking species (defined as a group of animals which are physically identical and susceptible of indefinite reproduction through copulation) as the only real units, he proposes to arrange them in a single, continuous file so that each will resemble those close to it more than those remote from it. The

[15] M. Caullery, *Histoire des sciences en France,* in *Histoire de la nation française,* XVI, 117.

Leibnizian axiom of qualitative continuity or the "plenum of forms" is the rule which nature has followed in her production and which the human mind must rediscover. In Buffon's words, "We must assume that whatever can exist does exist." Though he is an exponent of the fixity of living species—which he represents in *Epochs of Nature* (1779) as having been created one by one as the earth cooled and provided the requisite conditions of habitat—he believes in the unity of a living type which exhibits every possible variation and manifests itself through the continuity of species, which is simply the unity of the natural plan. The idea of the series is not linked in any way to the idea of the descent of species, which had almost disappeared in the eighteenth century; it consists rather in asserting that there is an ideal dependence in the moments of the natural or divine plan, and Daudin is justified in saying that the postulate of this theory is that the actual state of the living world has its reason "not in the determinative circumstances of the processes that have brought it to this point, but in certain relations inherent in this state itself." [16]

The same postulate also found support at that time in Daubenton's research in comparative anatomy, which shows, between organs in different groups, relations so essential that they nullify the petty differences on which "methods" are established. It was after citing Daubenton's works, inserted into the fourth volume of Buffon's *Natural History,* that Diderot advanced the idea that there may have been a first being or "prototype of all beings," of which living species are successive metamorphoses.

Another discovery casts a new light on Leibniz' notion of series. Leibniz, according to whom everything is in everything and is organized to infinity, could see in the ascending series of forms only a passage from confusion to distinctiveness. Charles Bonnet's discovery of living beings with a homogeneous structure—the genus *Hydra*—proved that there were living beings without heterogeneous parts; but it also meant that the series of ascending terms

[16] H. Daudin, *Les méthodes de classification et l'idée de série en botanique et en zoologie de Linné à Lamarck* (1926), p. 176.

could no longer be defined by the intrinsic character of a continuous progression toward distinctiveness but only by reference to one term in the series—that term considered, not without an element of arbitrariness, to be the most perfect. According to Bonnet, this being is man, and its degree of resemblance to the human organization gives each animal its place in the series.

This is also the view expressed by J. B. Robinet in his *Philosophical Considerations of the Natural Gradation of the Forms of Being, or Nature's Attempts to Create Man* (1768). He was even more ambitious than Buffon, for he taught that the series in question should embrace every being in nature. Robinet (like Buffon) rediscovers the old antimechanistic ideas of the Renaissance and believes that there is no matter in the universe which is not animated; that is, capable of nutrition, reproduction, and growth. In this sense he resembles Diderot, in whom the idea of the old alchemists reappeared. The problem posed by nature is that of realizing these three functions with the greatest possible perfection, and man is the most elegant and most complicated solution of this problem. According to Robinet, progress toward the realization of man consists in a sort of progressive liberation of activity, which is a substance and which uses matter for the purpose of displaying its effects; in minerals activity is completely enslaved to matter, with the result that all operations are made subservient to the material subject; in that case a spontaneous motion is noted in a living being and "it seems that the active power endeavors to rise above the solid, impenetrable, extended mass to which it is connected and often forced to submit." In man, matter is no longer anything except the organ of this activity, and its progression cannot be said to have reached its limit in him; a phase must be postulated in which this activity, no longer dependent on organs and converted into pure intelligence, "is completely dematerialized." The visible world, therefore, has an invisible world as its counterpart. Thus through the idea of series a type of philosophy of nature known since antiquity is reintroduced—a philosophy of nature which focuses on the living being and extends beyond matter to pure mind.

The thesis of series, however, encountered difficulties of another kind as a result of the extension of experience. The series of beings should be linear and without ramifications if all beings tend toward man, but experience leads Bonnet himself to think that "the scale of nature might not be simple but might shoot out from all sides main branches from which subordinate branches would grow." This was also the opinion of the naturalist Pallas, to whom the linear series became a ramified tree: from the zoophyte spring the two trunks—the animal and the vegetable—and from the animal trunk spring the two branches of insects and birds. Buffon adopts a slightly more complicated image, that of a web, for "nature does not take a single step which is not a step in every direction"; beginning with a given type, nature projects species which are connected to species of all other types; quadrupeds, for example, include species similar to birds, such as bats, and species similar to reptiles, such as the anteater.[17]

Each of these images—the chain, the ramified tree, the web—seems to have a different philosophical signification. The chain is a series of forms obtained through the degradation or attenuation of a supreme type—the old Neo-Platonic image; the tree is a tendency to realize a superior type—a tendency which sometimes misses the mark and results in aberrant, unproductive formations; the web, as Buffon indicated many times, is the realization at each stage of all possible types to the extent that each stage permits their realization. But of prime importance was the common character revealed, at the crux of these divergences, in the statement of the problem. The aim of the naturalists was to establish, among the forms or types of beings under consideration, a smooth, easy connection which would enable the mind to grasp their ideal dependence. They were concerned, not with the real, effective genesis of these forms (which they attributed to nature or to God), but with their emergence from one another and their fusion.

[17] *Ibid.,* pp. 176–87.

## IV  *The Dynamism of Boscovich*

Roger Joseph Boscovich, born at Ragusa in 1711, entered Jesuit novitiate at Rome in 1725. Versed in geometry, optics, and astronomy, he was also an engineer and an archeologist; in addition, he wrote poetry. His *Philosophiae naturalis theoria redacta ad unicam legam virium in natura existentium* is the exposition of a dynamistic theory of nature which closely parallels the theories just discussed. Boscovich, like a true disciple of Locke, thinks that we know neither substances nor the active powers of things; but he makes a distinction between power and force, and, thanks to Newton, he succeeds in defining force solely through determination of motion. In fact, we can speak of forces only when at least two material points are under consideration. These two points are determined by their distance, whether they are moving toward each other or away from each other, and "it is this determination that we call force, by which we mean not a mode of action but the determination itself—regardless of its origin—which changes in magnitude as the distances change." [18]

This force is attractive when the distance between two points surpasses a determinate limit; it becomes repulsive when the distance falls short of the limit. The universe is the whole set of points which mutually attract or repel each other. Each point is a center of force, not by itself but solely in its relations to the other points which it attracts or repels just as it is attracted or repelled by them. This conception bears some resemblance to Kant's *Monadologia physica* (1746) but differs strikingly on one point: Boscovich's center of force has no heart, no spontaneity; apart from the whole to which it belongs, it is nothing. Here as in the conceptions of nature that we have just examined, the nature of each being is determined, but in an entirely different way, by circumstances relating to its place in the whole.

[18] As quoted by Nedelkovitch, *La philosophie de Boscovich* (1922), p. 147.

# Bibliography

## Texts

Diderot, Denis. *Œuvres.* 6 vols. Amsterdam, 1772.
———. *Œuvres complètes,* ed. J. Assezat. 20 vols. Paris, 1875–77.
———. *Œuvres,* ed. A. Billy. Paris, 1952–57.
———. *Correspondance avec Grimm.* 5 vols. Paris, 1829.
———. *Lettres à Sophie Volland.* 2 vols. Paris, 1829.
———. *Diderot: Interpreter of Nature. Selected Writings,* trans. J. Stewart and J. Kemp. New York, 1943.
———. *Selected Philosophical Writings,* ed. J. Lough. Cambridge, 1953.
———. *Early Philosophical Works,* trans. M. Jourdain. London and Chicago, 1916.
———. *Diderot: Selected Writings,* ed. L. G. Crocker. New York, 1964.

## Studies

Barker, J. E. *Diderot's Treatment of the Christian Religion.* New York, 1931.
Billy, A. *Vie de Diderot.* Paris, 1943.
Cresson, A. *Diderot.* Paris, 1949.
Crocker, L. G. *The Embattled Philosopher.* New York, 1964.
Hermand, P. *Les idées morales de Diderot.* Paris, 1923.
Le Gras, J. *Diderot et l'Encyclopédie.* Amiens, 1938.
Luppol, I. K. *Diderot, ses idées philosophiques.* Paris, 1936.
Mauvezux, J. *Diderot, l'encyclopédiste et le penseur.* Montbéliard, 1914.
Mesnard, P. *Le cas Diderot, étude de caractérologie littéraire.* Paris, 1952.
Morley, J. *Diderot and the Encyclopaedists.* 2 vols. London, 1878.
Rosenkranz, K. *Diderots Leben und Werke.* 2 vols. Leipzig, 1866.
Thomas, J. *L'humanisme de Diderot.* 2d ed. Paris, 1932.
Vartanian, A. *Diderot and Descartes.* Princeton, 1953.
Venturi, F. *Jeunesse de Diderot.* Paris, 1939.

## Other Texts and Studies

*Annales de l'Université de Paris,* vol. I, 1952.
Bertrand, J. *D'Alembert.* Paris, 1889.
Boissier, R. *La Mettrie, médecin, pamphlétaire et philosophe.* 1931.
Brunet, R. *Maupertuis.* 2 vols. Paris, 1929.

Buffon, G. L. *Nouveaux extraits,* ed. F. Gohin. Paris, 1905.

———. *Œuvres philosophiques,* ed. J. Piveteau. Paris, 1954.

Cushing, M. P. *Baron d'Holbach.* New York, 1914.

Daudin, H. *Les méthodes de classification et l'idée de série en botanique et en zoologie de Linné à Lamarck (1740–1790).* Paris, 1926.

Du Bois-Reymond, E. *Rede über La Mettrie.* Berlin, 1875.

Evellin, F. *Quid de rebus vel corporeis vel incorporeis senserit Boscovich.* Paris, 1880.

Ganguilhem, G. *La formation du concept de réflexe aux XVIIe et XVIIIe siècles.* Paris, 1955.

Helvétius, C. *Œuvres.* 7 vols. Deux-Ponts, 1784. 5 vols. Paris, 1792.

———. *Choix de textes,* ed. J. B. Severac. Paris, 1911.

———. *De l'esprit,* ed. G. Besse. Paris, 1959.

Hubert, R. *D'Holbach et ses amis.* Paris, 1928.

———. *Les sciences sociales dans l'Encyclopédie.* Paris, 1926.

Keim, A. *Helvétius, sa vie et son œuvre.* Paris, 1907.

Kerkinen, H. *Les origines de la conception moderne de l'homme-machine. Le probleme de l'âme en France à la fin du règne de Louis XIV (1670–1715).* Helsinki, 1960.

Kunz, L. "Die Erkenntnissnteorie d'Alembert" *Archiv für Geschichte der Philosophie,* XX, 1907.

La Mettrie, J. *Œuvres philosophiques.* 2 vols. London, 1751.

———. *La politique du médecin de Machiavel,* ed. R. Boissier. Paris, 1931.

Lange, F. A. *Histoire du matérialismé,* trans. Pommerel, vol. 1, pp. 293–408. Paris, 1910.

Muller, M. *Essai sur la philosophie de Jean d'Alembert.* Paris, 1926.

Nedelkovitch, D. *La philosophie naturelle et relativiste de R.-J. Boscovich.* Paris, 1922.

Plechanow, G. *Beitrage zür Geschichte des Materialismus, Holbach, Helvetius, Marx.* 3d ed. Stuttgart, 1921.

Queprat, N. *La philosophie matérialiste au XVIIIe siècle: essai sur La Mettrie, sa vie et ses œuvres.* Paris, 1873.

Renouvier, Ch. *Le personnalisme,* pp. 440–62. Paris, 1903.

Topazio, V. W. *D'Holbach's Moral Philosophy.* Geneva, 1936.

Vartanian, A. *La Mettrie's "L'homme machine": A study in the origins of an idea.* Princeton, 1960.

Vernière, P. *Spinoza et la pensée française avant la Révolution.* Vol. 2, *Le XVIIIe siècle.* Paris, 1954.

Wickwar, W. H. *Baron de Holbach: A Prelude to the French Revolution.* London, 1935.

# VOLTAIRE

## 1  Life and Works

Voltaire (François Marie Arouet), the son of a notary, was born in Paris in 1694 and educated by the Jesuits. A forced sojourn in England from 1726 to 1729 introduced him to Locke and Newton, who became his masters, and resulted in the publication of *Philosophical Letters* (1734), followed by *Remarks on Pascal*. Condemnation of the *Letters* forced him to leave Paris and take up residence in Circey, in Lorraine, with the Marquise du Châtelet, for whom he wrote *The Philosophy of Newton* (1738). After having honors heaped upon him in Paris, where he was named historiographer-royal and later elected to the Academy, he retired to Berlin in 1750, following the death of Mme du Châtelet. There he was welcomed by Frederick the Great, who gave him a pension and the title of chamberlain. Having fallen out with Frederick as a result of his attacks on Maupertuis, then president of the Berlin Academy, he left Prussia and spent several months at the Benedictine abbey of Senones, where he worked on his *Essay on Morals,* published in 1756. It was in 1759, after he had spent several years at Les Délices, near Geneva, that he took up residence in France, at Ferney, near the Swiss border. There, keeping in contact with the whole of Europe through his correspondence, he carried on his campaigns in favor of Calas, Sirven, and Lally (*Treatise on Tolerance,* 1763) and wrote *Questions on the Encyclopedia* (1764), later known under the title of *Philosophical Dictionary*. He died in Paris in 1778, after the opening performance of his drama *Irène,* on which occasion his bust was crowned on stage.

No philosophical doctrine, in the technical sense of the word, is to be found in Voltaire; he was satisfied with the teachings of Locke and Newton, whom he credits with specifying decisively the powers and limits of the human mind. But does it follow that there is no originality, other than in formal and superficial features, in this vast literary output which has exerted such great influence and which has occasioned so much praise and so much censure? Most of his writings, including the fiction and many of the tragedies, are campaigns against prejudice and propaganda for the new spirit. He sensed a violent contrast between the point to which philosophy has brought the human mind and the pattern of thinking and living of most men who carry their prejudices and beliefs like a dead weight. On one hand is tolerance born of knowledge of the limits of the human mind, a consensus drawn from experience and from the progress of the arts and sciences; on the other hand is intolerance and the coercive means put at its disposition by laws and customs, unending discord and controversy based mainly on private opinions relating to incomprehensible subjects, and finally, stagnation. Voltaire's ambition was to put intellectual, moral, and social life on the level of philosophy and to liberate man from the prejudices that bring him unhappiness. To accomplish his aim, he relied on enlightenment and not on an inner modification of man: man will always be the same, with his egotism and passions; he has his place in the scale of beings and cannot emerge from it; but his egotism and passions are harmful only because of his ignorance and prejudices. Such is the essential thesis of the master of the "philosophy of enlightenment; like Locke, he holds that there is a kind of harmony between the intelligible and the useful. "That which cannot be used universally," he says in *The Ignorant Philosopher,* "that which is beyond the reach of the common man, that which is understood only by those who have exercised their minds the most is not necessary for mankind." It follows that a goodly part of philosophy is useless if "no philosopher has had any influence even on the morals of the street where he lived."

## II  *Theory of Nature*

One central notion underlies the Voltairian spirit, and that is the notion of the fixity of things, of the impossibility of changing things, and of the folly of men who cannot be satisfied with things as they are. It is less a doctrine than a diffuse train of thought, a few examples of which follow.

"I am called nature," he has nature say, "and I am wholly art." [1] The likening of the universe to a clock is a recurrent theme from which he draws his frequently repeated proof by final causes of the existence of God; obvious to all in this work of art are combinations which require an "eternal geometer-God" as its creator. But he discarded the proof of the existence of God by the contingency of the world—the proof put forward by Locke and Clarke—which he had first upheld in his *Treatise on Metaphysics* (written in 1734). That the image of the clock gives to the universe a kind of rigidity in which he delights is incontestable: God, in his view, is the God of nature and not the God of mankind—in other words, his God is asked to guarantee the fixity of the universe but not to save man, who was never imperiled. This is the extreme form of natural religion, which sees God merely as the wise author of a nature useful to man. Voltaire, then, was hostile to Epicurus as well as to Descartes,[2] and in general to all those who, as a result of the concatenation of natural causes, sought a cosmogony, that is, to all those who did not view the actual state of the world as a privileged, unique state. On the other hand, he was fascinated by Newton's physics. This was certain to appeal to him, with its mechanical laws that implied nothing concerning the quantity of matter, the number of stars and planets, the inclination of their axis to the ecliptic, or their circular motion and the speed of this motion, for

---

[1] *Dictionnarie philosophique,* Article "Nature."
[2] *Sur l'Anti-Lucrèce de M. le Cardinal de Polignac,* end.

it was on these circumstances particularly that the distribution of the seasons on the earth and the possibility of animal and human life depended; independent of mechanical causes, they produced effects which showed that they must have been chosen by an omnipotent God.[3] Thus a lacuna in Newton's philosophy, which men like Kant and Laplace sought to fill through new cosmological investigations, was viewed by Voltaire as an asset—as the affirmation of a definitive, permanent state. That is why he was repelled by Leibniz, with his principle of sufficient reason, his relative time and space, his failure to make room for the wholly free decisions of God which are implied, in Newton, by the absolute character of time and space.[4]

In the details of his vision of the world, the same spirit predominates. He was a resolute supporter of the immutability of living species, and also of the immutability of chemical species; to him transmutation was always an illusion.[5] He sometimes doubted, particularly at the beginning of his *Treatise on Metaphysics,* that mankind was a single species, and he thought that the races of man could in fact be different species, but this was mainly on account of the difficulty of assuming that there could have been progressive differentiation of such importance within a single species. He constantly scoffed at those who, like Needham, sought to prove spontaneous generation.

The same skeptical attitude marks his treatment of the theory of the physical revolutions of the globe, which was supported mainly by fossils of marine animals discovered on mountains and by Louville's investigations (1724) of the displacement of the poles. Always suspecting that such theories might be used to prove the Flood, Voltaire resorted to an imperturbable finalism—the beautiful order of the mountains and the indispensable role in the life of animals of the "high aqueducts" from which life-giving water issued.

[3] *Philosophie de Newton,* Part III, chap. x.
[4] *Ibid.,* I, v.
[5] *Ibid.,* I, viii.

This view of things, fundamentally opposed to that of Descartes, led him to believe that the role of physics was to begin with a very small number of properties of matter supplied by our senses and to discover through reason new attributes, such as attraction and gravitation. "The more I reflect upon it," he writes, still refuting those who accused Newton of reintroducing occult qualities, "the more I am struck by the fear that surrounds recognition of a new principle or a new property in matter, which probably contains an infinite number of them. Nothing in nature is like anything else," [6] and rather than yield on this point, he prefers to say that "everything is an occult quality." The tendency is for him always to multiply fixed, inalterable essences.

## III  *Man and History*

The same doctrine of fixity reappears in his conception of man. This perfect writer believed in the almost complete fixity of languages and believed them subject only to superficial changes due to fashions—foreign influences, for example; and he is noted for his precise, rigorous conception of the purity of style. If language itself is fixed, how much more so are the other attributes of the human mind. Here, it would seem, was an important cause of Voltaire's profound hostility toward Christianity. In St. Augustine and Bossuet as well as in Pascal and Malebranche, Christianity constitutes a history of man, for whom sin and redemption are critical events which radically transform him, his faculties, and the conditions of his happiness; the Christian life consists in waiting, wishing, preparing for transmutations of this kind. Indeed, the first adversary pursued by Voltaire in his attack on Christianity is Pascal,[7] the very one who painted such a dark portrait of the wretched condition of man after his sin. In the *Thoughts* of this "sublime misanthrope" are reflected his delicate temperament, his sad imagination, his bad regimen; in reality man is not an enigma; he

---

[6] *Ibid.*, II, xi; cf. chap. vii and III, xii.
[7] *Remarques sur les Pensées de M. Pascal.*

has a place in nature, is superior to the animals and inferior perhaps to other beings, is endowed with passions in order that he may act and with reason in order that he may control himself. The apparent contradictions noted by Pascal are necessary ingredients which can be explained without the Fall; self-love is one condition of societies; preoccupation with the future, the constant desire to act, boredom associated with inaction are all charitable gifts and not, as Pascal said, calamities; the inconstancy of our actions is a trait of human nature, quite often described by Montaigne, but what right have we to interpret it as the sign of a double nature in man?

By his *Remarks* Voltaire extricated himself from the kind of apologetics of Christianity which could have been most embarrassing to him—that which emerged once again in nineteenth-century thinking and which considered belief in Christianity to be an indispensable exigency of human nature. The sense of uneasiness and instability that accompanies it was wholly antipathetical to the Voltairian spirit of an immutable human nature.

Just as Voltaire's *Remarks* contradict Pascal, his *Essay on Morals* is completely antithetical to Bossuet's *Universal History* and St. Augustine's *City of God*. St. Augustine and Bossuet were trying to show the unity of history, the solidarity of the past and the present, the same divine plan spanning events; Voltaire, on the contrary, tends to see in history only the eternal interplay of human emotions. "There are about a dozen battles which I have not mentioned, thank God," he says in a letter to D'Argental regarding his *Essay,* "because I am writing the history of the human mind and not a newspaper." In his vast study of the period between the reign of Charlemagne and the century of Louis XIV, his subject is not historical events but mores, not individuals but the spirit of an epoch with its commerce, its finances, its sciences, its arts. Each of these epochs forms an almost isolated whole which is not closely bound to the past. To him history seems to be bent on keeping the past from encroaching on the present: "Past times are as if they had never been. We must always start from the point where we are and from the point which nations have reached." [8] We must not think that we can proceed from the point reached by the ancients. "The whole of the ancient world," he says, speaking of the Jews, "was so different from ours that no rules of conduct can be drawn from it." [9] That is why he writes in his *Advice to a Journalist:* "Be certain to inspire in the young more interest in the history of recent times, which is a necessity for us, than in ancient history, which is merely a curiosity. . . . I would like especially for you to recommend that they seriously begin the study of history in the century immediately preceding Charles V, Leo X, and Francis I. It was then that there occurred in the human mind, as in our world, a revolution which has changed everything."

Sometimes he advanced the beginning of the new period still further. In 1765, he wrote that the face of Europe had changed in the last fifty years, that governments were fortified by standing armies and good police forces, that there had been a softening of manners, and that philosophy had made headway against fanaticism.

Discontinuity in time, according to Voltaire, is linked to discontinuity in space. Universal history is not limited to Christianity and preparation for Christianity: the independent civilizations of India and America coexist alongside the civilization of the West, and he was the first to treat them at such length in a universal history.

But now a new discontinuity appears. The same period has a double history: the official history which appears in the foreground in documents[10]—civil and ecclesiastical history in which man is seen as a victim of his passions; and, less obvious or rather almost unknown, the history of inventions useful to man—the plow, the shuttle, the saw. The spirit of invention has existed throughout time, for in the face of the officials and the ignorant doctors we find "obscure men, artists inspired by a higher instinct, who invent admirable things which later are discussed by scholars." [11] It was not

[8] *Traité sur la tolérance,* "Comment la tolérance peut être admise."
[9] *Ibid.,* "Si l'intolérance fut de droit divin dans le judaïsme."
[10] *L'A B C, dix-sept dialogues traduits de l'anglais,* "Douzième entretien."
[11] *Lettre sur Roger Bacon.*

philosophy but "a mechanical instinct found in most men"[12] which produced these inventions, and the prodigious use of machinery among the Greeks and Romans contrasts sharply, according to Voltaire, with the absurdity of their beliefs.

Such views simply imply a radical disagreement in principle with Montesquieu, whom Voltaire frequently censured on technical grounds because of his lack of method[13] and the falsity of "almost all of his citations." Voltaire emphatically denies the validity of relations presumed to be necessary, such as the influence of climate on religion, the sciences, and the arts; religions are established "accidentally" rather than by a natural necessity.[14] The historical solidarity of generations on which Montesquieu founded his theory of the liberal monarchy in France does not appeal to Voltaire, who, in one sense, is no liberal; his enemies are the traditional enemies of royalty—an overly powerful clergy and an administration based on the venality of offices—and only the king, with his increased power and the enlightenment provided by philosophy, can spread tolerance and justice; an enlightened despotism such as that of Peter the Great, Frederick II, or Catherine II, or such as that which he attributes to the emperor of China, who makes decisions only on the advice of mandarins chosen for their knowledge and competence, represents the political ideal of Voltaire. The growth of the arts, the sciences, and tolerance is the result not of a continuous, spontaneous development of humanity but of a great ruler and a good government.

Thus Voltaire dissolves and decomposes everything into stable, fixed particles: history has only the meaning and direction imparted to it by human wills and human passions, enlightened in varying degrees by reason; there were no other hidden realities whose designs they might unwittingly execute.

In his conception of the nature of man he displays remarkable consistency and precision. He is said to have had a simplified view

[12] *Lettres philosophiques,* tenth letter, on Chancellor Bacon.
[13] *L'A B C,* "Premier dialogue."
[14] *Pensées sur l'administration publique,* 38 and 42.

of things, but it would seem more appropriate to call it denuded, for his harsh empiricism or realism treats as chimerical everything which is not a definitive reality—a present and actually given reality —and sees in the present, not one moment in a vast history, but the stable, permanent elements of which things are composed. These traits were common to all thinkers of the eighteenth century, which was the century of statics, but here they are manifested with extraordinary precision.

## IV  *Tolerance*

These traits are reflected in the campaigns which filled a major part of Voltaire's life but which we shall not examine here in detail. Intolerance, according to Voltaire, is peculiar to Christianity.[15] Neither the Oriental countries nor the Romans, nor the Greeks, nor even the Jews practiced religious intolerance. Christianity practices it because this religion seeks to dominate both the temporal and the spiritual realm; political primacy of the spiritual authority is the grand pretension of the popes. If we consider only the "physical and moral good of society," it is obvious that this pretension continues to shackle the individual and the citizen. Tolerance is the condition of a strong government, without which, as we noted earlier, Voltaire does not think that progress is possible,[16] furthermore, there can be no strong government with a clergy that pays no taxes and exempts from the royal courts of justice many matters referred to Rome for settlement, and with a religion which through its monasteries deprives the nation of a great number of active citizens and seeks to involve the state in its irritating and incomprehensible disputes over dogma. Nor is an economic life possible.[17] Economic interests were foremost in his thinking when Voltaire requested at least as many rights for Protestants returning to France as were accorded the Catholics in England. Moreover, the struggle

[15] *Traité sur la tolérance,* "Si l'intolérance est de droit naturel et de droit humain."
[16] *La Voix du sage et du peuple.*
[17] *Traité de la tolérance,* "Comment la tolérance peut être admise."

against intolerance is tied to the development of world trade, characteristic of the times: "You condemn," he writes ironically, "the profits made through maritime ventures. . . . You call such commerce usury. The king will have the new obligation of preventing his subjects from trading at Cadiz. This Satanic enterprise must be left to the English and the Dutch, who are already hopelessly damned." [18] Finally, he shows that morality is impossible if religion goes so far as to deny the foundation of all morality by condemning, in the matter or the bull *Unigenitus,* the proposition that the fear of excommunication ought not to prevent us from doing our duty. We see, then, beneath a host of confusing incidentals, the serious and profound idea that dominated Voltaire's attitude: the idea of the independence of the ends proposed to man by his own nature, against which no religion can prevail.

[18] *Remerciement sincère à un homme charitable.*

# BIBLIOGRAPHY

## Texts

Voltaire, *Œuvres complètes,* ed. A. J. Q. Beuchot. 72 vols. Paris, 1829–34.
———. *Œuvres.* ed. L. Moland. 52 vols. Paris, 1878–85.
———. *Traité de métaphysique,* ed. H. T. Patterson. Manchester, 1937.
———. *Dictionnaire philosophique,* ed. J. Benda. Paris, 1954.
———. *Philosophical Dictionary,* trans. H. I. Woolf. London, 1923.
———. *Lettres philosophiques.* ed. F. A. Taylor. Oxford, 1943.

## Bibliographies

Bengesco, G. *Voltaire: Bibliographie de ses œuvres.* 4 vols. Paris, 1882–92.

## Studies

Aldington, R. *Voltaire.* London, 1926.
Alexander, J. W. "Voltaire and Metaphysics," *Philosophy,* 1944.
Bersot, E. *La philosophie de Voltaire.* Paris, 1948.
Brandes, G. *Voltaire.* 2 vols. Berlin, 1923.
Carré, J.-R. *Consistance de Voltaire le philosophe.* Paris, 1938.
———. *Réflexions sur l'Anti-Pascal de Voltaire.* 1935.
Charpentier, J. *Voltaire.* Paris, 1955.
Delbos, V. *La philosophie française,* pp. 153–68. Paris, 1919.
Desnoiresterres, G. *Voltaire et la société au XVIIIe siècle.* 8 vols. Paris, 1867–76.
Fitch, R. E. *Voltaire's Philosophical Procedure.* Forest Grove, Oregon, 1936.
Janet, P. *Histoire de la science politique.* 2 vols. 3d ed. Paris, 1883.
Lanson, G. *Voltaire.* Paris, 1906.
Maurois, A. *Voltaire.* Paris, 1947.
Meyer, A. *Voltaire, Man of Justice.* New York, 1945.
Morley, J. *Voltaire.* London, 1923.
Naves, R. *Voltaire et l'Encyclopédie.* Paris, 1938.
———. *Voltaire, l'homme et l'œuvre.* 2d ed. Paris, 1947.

Noyes, A. *Voltaire*. London, 1938.
O'Flaherty, K. *Voltaire: Myth and Reality*. Cork and Oxford, 1945.
Pellisier, G. *Voltaire philosophe*. Paris, 1908.
Pomeau, R. *La religion de Voltaire*. Paris, 1956.
Rowe, C. *Voltaire and the State*. London, 1956.
Torrey, N. L. *The Spirit of Voltaire*. New York, 1938.
Touchard, J. *Histoire des idées politiques,* vol. 2. Paris, 1959. 2d ed., 1962.
Wade, O. *Studies on Voltaire*. Princeton, 1947.

# JEAN JACQUES ROUSSEAU

## 1 Life and Works

Jean Jacques Rousseau, born at Geneva in 1712, was the son of a watchmaker. His vagabond life began early: in 1728 he resolved to leave Geneva forever to escape the tyranny of the master engraver to whom he had been apprenticed. From 1728 until 1741, the date of his arrival in Paris, after many adventures (he was even a lackey in Turin), he received the support of Mme de Warens, with whose help he was able to educate himself, learn music and Latin, and read the Philosophes; his sojourn with her (1736) at Les Charmettes, near Chambéry, was one of the few happy episodes in his life. In 1741 he settled in Paris, where he tried in vain to promote a system of musical notation which he had invented; he left Paris for Venice, where he was secretary to the French Ambassador. Upon his return to Paris in 1744 he began to become intimate with the Philosophes, particularly Diderot; in 1750 he published his *Discourse on the Sciences and the Arts,* which made him famous; in 1755 he published his *Discourse on the Origin of Inequality*; in 1756 he lived at the Hermitage, in a house that Mme d'Epinay had put at his disposition, near the forest of Montmorency; in 1758 he wrote *The Letter to D'Alembert on Spectacles,* concerning the article "Geneva" in the *Encyclopedia,* in which D'Alembert had censured an article in the Geneva constitution prohibiting theaters. At that time he was in retirement at the home of the Duc de Luxembourg, near Montmorency; it was there that he wrote *The New Heloise* (1761) as well as *The Social Contract* and *Émile* (1762), a work which forced him to flee in order to escape arrest. He took refuge at Motiers-Travers, in Switzerland, then, following his expulsion, with Hume in England. Upon his return to Paris, he began the uneasy, tormented existence described in *Reveries of a Solitary Walker*. Finally he was invited by the Marquis de Girardin to move to Ermenonville, where he died in 1778.

## II *The Doctrine of the Discourses*

In 1762, after *Émile* and *The Social Contract,* Rousseau was condemned by the Archbishop of Paris, placed on the Index in Rome, censured by the Sorbonne, anathematized by the ministers of Berne, Neuchâtel, and Geneva, and drawn into a quarrel with the philosophers of the "Holbachian coterie." A recluse, a thinker who defies classification, he never ceased to exert on other minds a powerful attraction which is manifested in an unmatched array of studies of his thought and life; proof of this is the publication of his *Correspondence* and the recent polemics relating to his religious thought. But leaving aside all systematic attacks and encomiums, we still largely fail to find agreement on the interpretation of his thought. Is there a Roussellian doctrine with a logical sequence and coherence? Or is it not possible that the passionate assurance with which he approaches each new subject hides insoluble contradictions from anyone trying to achieve a comprehensive view? Does he advocate the superiority of the state of nature, as his *Discourse on Inequality* suggests, or does he believe in the supremacy of the social state, as *The Social Contract* leads us to conclude? How is the civil religion of the *Contract,* imposed by the state on its citizens, compatible with the religion of the heart, with *The Savoyard Vicar's Profession of Faith*? Are we to give first place in the *Contract* to the individualism which attributes the birth of the state to unanimity of wills, or to an unbridled communism which dictates the alienation of each individual to the community? In his theory of knowledge, is Rousseau an empiricist or does he believe in innate ideas? Does he base his ethics on reason or on sentiment? These questions are all hard to resolve.

Rousseau's first work, the work that brought him celebrity, is the one that won the prize given by the Academy of Dijon for the best discourse on the subject: Have the arts and sciences contributed to improve morals? Here he rediscovers the ancient theme of the Cynics, which proclaims the misdeeds of civilization. It is the complete antithesis of Voltaire even in its details: the Scythian or German barbarian is superior to the civilized man, Spartan customs contrast with those of the Athenians, and the Roman degenerates as soon as he learns the Greek sciences. In particular, he condemns the universal diffusion of enlightenment: "What are we to think of these compilers of works who have indiscreetly broken down the door of the sciences and introduced into their sanctuary a populace unworthy of approaching them?" In his words we hear biblical overtones; these sciences and arts go against divine order; and the vices that follow them are "punishment for our vain efforts to emerge from the happy state of ignorance in which eternal wisdom placed us. The thick veil it had used to hide all its operations seemed to warn us sufficiently that we were not destined for vain pursuits."

That was a clap of thunder straight from the blue sky of the philosophy of enlightenment. The Academy of Dijon proposed, as the subject for a new contest, the old academic theme: What is the origin of inequality among men? Is it authorized by natural law? Speaking in his *Confessions* of the second discourse which he wrote on the subject, Rousseau says: "I dared, by comparing man's man with natural man, to show them, in his pretended perfection, the true source of his wretchedness." By "man's man" he means man with all the accretions of his social life: a man like Glaucus, the sea divinity whose features are hidden under the shells and seaweed that cover him. It was to Glaucus that Plato and Plotinus compared the soul which had descended from its celestial habitat and been filled with the impurities of the sensible world, and it is a work of purification which Rousseau, like Plotinus, proposes; he aims to separate, in man, "the original from the artificial"; the original is "the state of a being acting always through certain, invariable principles." This is the state of nature, which resembles man's state before his fall as Malebranche might have described it (bear in mind that Rousseau's first philosophical readings were books by Malebranche's disciples)[1]; in this state there is a perfect balance between needs, which are moderate, and their satisfaction; Hobbes was wrong in saying that it was characterized by avidity and pride, passions which are meaningful only in a civil state; living alone in the primitive forest, without any infirmity or sickness, and having no particular instinct but imitating that of beasts, man acquires all the strength, all the agility, all the sensory acuity needed for attack and defense; indifferent to the spectacle of nature because of its uniformity, improvident, having no natural impulse to use fire or invent instruments, he develops neither his understanding nor his industry.

Think of the contrast that Rousseau's first readers must have felt between this description and what the juridical tradition, then quite vigorous, taught concerning natural law: that elementary legal relations are implicit in any human society by the very nature of man, and that society may be treated as a natural fact. Rousseau ignores any such natural law since abstract legal maxims are useless among men who do not need one another. Rejecting the teachings of Socrates and the Stoics, he takes up the ancient theme of the Cynics and finds in man no inclination toward civil life: "Nature's failure to go to great lengths to draw men together through mutual needs and to facilitate their use of speech shows how little she has done to prepare for their sociability and how little she has contributed to all that they have done to establish its bonds." Self-love tempered by pity as natural as egotism—such is the sum and substance of his sentiments.

---

[1] *Confessions,* Book VI. At Les Charmettes he read books "which mixed devotion and science," in particular those of the Oratory and Port Royal. He cites chiefly *Entretiens sur les sciences,* by Father Lamy, "his guide."

The contrast between himself and theoreticians of natural law—
a contrast which he took pains to indicate—implies a profound
divergence of method as well as of doctrine. Jurists see in nature
only the minimal, constant conditions which any positive legislation
should satisfy and which, being simple residuals of analysis, do not
designate a stage traversed by man. But Rousseau, contrary also to
Voltaire, has a historical vision of man: there was in the history of
humanity a presocial stage which man passed beyond as a consequence of circumstances which might not have occurred. Of course
Rousseau carefully removes everything which might lend a mythical
quality to his theory, such as the myth of the golden age or the
earthly paradise, and explains that he is proceeding in the manner
of physicists who formulate hypotheses of the formation of worlds
not in order to portray their true history but in order to reveal their
nature. "Let us begin," he says in a symptomatic statement, "by
eliminating all the facts." This does not mean, however, that the
state of nature did not exist, but that his description of it is not
based on any document. His description is nevertheless justifiable
since, like attraction in celestial mechanics, "no other system can be
formulated which will provide the same results." It is true, then,
that Rousseau is aware of a historical evolution which profoundly
affects the conditions of human life. "The human species of one
age," he writes in his conclusion, "is not the human species of
another age. . . . Through imperceptible alterations the soul and
human passions undergo what might be called a change of nature . . . ; as the original man gradually disappears, in the eyes of
the sage society becomes nothing more than an assemblage of artificial men and unnatural passions which are the product of all these
new relations and have no true foundation in nature."

In the state of nature man has a unique relationship with things,
and he takes the fixity and constancy of these things as a model. He
always has the possibility of breaking away from them since he is a
free agent, capable of deviating from instinct and the rule of nature,
but he would never have done so "without the fortuitous concurrence of several alien causes which might never have occurred"—for

instance, barren years, long winters, and hot summers which force him, in order to subsist, to enter into partnership with other men. This gives birth to the state of savagery which, though quite different from the state of nature, is still not the civil state; first there are transitory bands of hunters, then floods and earthquakes force men to establish permanent unions, with the result that there is a change of morals; jealousy, discord, vanity, and contempt make their appearance in assemblies; the state has no laws, however, and fear of revenge is the only force that restrains man. The savage state, still observable, "was the least subject to revolutions, the best for man, who was obliged to emerge from it only by some dire peril."

It is in fact only by an "extraordinary circumstance" that the use of fire, necessary for agriculture and consequently for any civil state, was discovered. This was the origin of the civilization of Europe, the country in which iron and wheat are most abundant. This agricultural civilization depended, along with the foresight and labor which it presupposed, on the division of land, on property based on continuity of work and possession. Thus inequality, based initially on strength and skill, became more and more perceptible. The division of society into the rich and the poor would have given rise to excessive brigandage at the expense of the rich if they had not reached an agreement among themselves to consolidate their situation by instituting general regulation for maintaining the peace: "That was the beginning of society and the laws that provide new shackles for the weak and strength for the rich, destroy natural liberty forever, establish the law of property and inequality."

On the whole, *The Discourse on the Origin of Inequality* is a solution to the problem of evil: "Men are evil . . . ; yet man is naturally good . . . ; what, then, can have depraved him to this point except the changes that have befallen his constitution, the progress that he has made, the knowledge that he has acquired?" (note *i*). Man's degradation is due, moreover, to accidental reasons and not to an inexorable law. Here we see the complete Rousseau, the author of The *Confessions*: craving solitude, the simple life, guileless friendship, on every hand he encounters conventions, prejudice, hatred. The problem of his philosophy was the problem of his life: an attempt to rediscover in social depravation a state of innocence and purity.

The reflections set down in his article on "Political Economy" in the *Encyclopedia* and in the second chapter of *Political Institutions* show that he became increasingly more conscious of his disagreement with the Philosophes. In a recent work,[2] René Hubert showed that the *Encyclopedia* contained five different doctrines on the origin of society: the traditional theory which attributes it to the will of God, the theory of familial and patriarchal origin, the theory of a natural instinct of sociability or sympathy, the theory of deliberate personal interest, and the theory of the contract (referring to the contract which gave birth to government—for instance, the pact between the king and the people which established the Frankish monarchy). Each one of these theories is explicitly criticized by Rousseau. Religion is not the origin of society, for the common people will never have anything but "gods as insane as they are," and the institutions of religion entail "carnage more often than harmony and peace." The family, in which "the duties of the father are dictated by natural sentiments," is quite different from a political society, in which the chief, without any interest in the welfare of individuals, "often seeks his own in their wretchedness." The instinct of sociability is explicitly denied; man's only reason for entering into partnership with others is that "the help of his fellow-creatures becomes a necessity to him." The idea of the unison of deliberate egotism and the social bond, as presented by Diderot in his article on "Natural Law," is criticized by Rousseau. "It is not true," he writes, "that in the state of independence reason persuades us to contribute to the common good with a view to our own interest. Far from there being an alliance between private interest and the common good, they are mutually exclusive in the natural order of things; and social laws are a yoke which each would like to impose

[2] *Les sciences sociales dans l'Encyclopédie* (Paris, 1923).

on the others without imposing it upon himself." [3] As for the contract, Rousseau had shown, beginning with *The Discourse on the Origin of Inequality,* the invalidity of a pact which is binding on only one of the parties and which detracts not only from the liberty of the one who enters into it but also from the liberty of his descendants.

## III   *The Doctrine of the Social Contract*

Rousseau, however, was persuaded to posit a wholly new and different problem: Since the social state is necessary inasmuch as man can no longer dispense with the help of others, and since this state is unnatural and based on conventions, how can one design a pact which will combine the certain advantages of the social state with those of the state of nature? This is the central problem in *The Social Contract or Principles of Political Law,* a work difficult of interpretation. The work has been said to contradict *The Discourse on the Origin of Inequality,* but this is not true. The *Discourse* depicts a social state which destroys all the qualities of man in the state of nature; the *Contract* claims to find an origin of the social state which preserves these qualities. Here we find no more contradiction than between the bad system of education condemned in *Émile* and the new principles which he wishes to substitute for it. *Émile* and the *Contract* are closely related: they study two aspects of the same problem. Émile, Rousseau's pupil, must live in society, but a system of education must be found to permit him to retain all the innocence and virtues of the natural state, all the innate goodness of man.[4] Similarly, men must associate with each other, but a form of association must be found to preserve for individuals the equality and liberty which they had by nature.

Rousseau stressed these relations in *Émile.* In the state of nature man depends only on things and not on other men, and this depend-

---

[3] *Œuvres,* ed. Musset-Pathey, V, 447–51; *Encyclopédie,* Article "Economie politique."
[4] *Émile,* Book IV.

ence does not jeopardize his liberty. How can this advantage be preserved in the social state? The answer is to be found in "substituting law for the individual and arming the general will with a real strength beyond the power of any individual will. If the laws of nations, like the laws of nature, could never be broken by any human power, dependence on men would become dependence on things; all the advantages of a state of nature would be combined with all the advantages of civil life in the commonwealth, and the liberty which preserves a man from vice would be united with the morality which raises him to virtue." [5] Émile's tutor arranged everything so that his pupil would be instructed only by the "power of things," and would obey only because he was compelled to obey, in the sense that he was compelled by nature to act according to the principle of self-preservation. It is in this sense that the social man is to be governed by law: Rousseau thought that he had found the secret of a society which would eliminate direct relations between one individual and another, along with all the passions and conflicts engendered by these relations, and replace them by the common bond of a law as impersonal and stable as a thing. This may explain Voltaire's quip, "The social contract is an unsocial contract." [6]

In Diderot's article on "Natural Law" in the *Encyclopedia* (which Rousseau criticized), Rousseau found the idea of the general will which is "in each individual a pure act of an intellect reasoning in the silence of the passions." It is "always good," has never been and will never be deceptive, and should "set the limits of all our duties." Rousseau says exactly the same thing: the general will, setting aside all particular wills, always follows the common interest; therefore it is always right and can never err. "Remove from these particular wills the extremes which cancel each other, and the sum of the remaining differences is the general will" (Book II, chap. iii). Furthermore, it was before he had considered the idea of a contract that he developed, both in the article on "Political Economy" and in the manuscript of his *Political Institutions,* the idea of the general will and law, "this salutary organ of the collective will which re-establishes equality among men . . . , this celestial voice which dictates to each citizen the precepts of public rationality." In the second book of *The Social Contract* every chapter on the general will can be interpreted without the slightest reference to the theory of the contract.

How, then, did he evolve the celebrated theory responsible for the title of the whole work? We need only recall what he criticizes in Diderot's article on "Natural Law": not the idea of the general will but the idea that the general will can be imposed through the simple effects of reflective egotism. This question then arises: How can the general will be made effective and active? The theory of the contract is the answer to this question. "If there were no different interests," Rousseau writes in a note, "one would hardly be conscious of the common interest, which would never encounter obstacles; everything would go along by itself and politics would cease to be an art" (II, iii). Thus the obstacles posed by egotism need only be removed in order to give free rein to the general will, just as, in religion, the will itself needs only give way in order for grace to flow freely. Now the contract, as it is understood by Rousseau, ought precisely to remove these obstacles. It is quite different from the social contract of Locke and the Encyclopedists, which simply reinforced pre-existing social bonds; quite different from the ordinary contract in which the will of each party to the contract is affirmed even as it is restricted and defined. Through the social contract the individual will disavows itself; indeed, "total alienation of each associate, with all his rights, from the whole community" (I, vi) is the only clause in the contract. Unlike alienation for the benefit of an already existing being—a master or a despot—this alienation gives being and power to the general will for whose benefit it is effected; by putting our whole person and our power "under the supreme direction of the general will," the contract re-moves the obstacles that originate in our particular wills, creates the social body, and gives it an identity of its own.

This act of renunciation is a veritable conversion of the individual.

In reality, however, at the very moment when it seems that everything is taken from him, everything is given to him, for law and morality begin with social living. Law and morality exist only when there are universal rules; there is no universal rule when there is no general will, that is, before the contract, when each individual follows his own will. Thus the individual renounces himself as a sensible being only in order to assert himself as a rational, moral being.

Here an obvious difficulty arises. How can reason and morality issue from the contract when they seem also to be its necessary condition? How could each individual silence his egotism in order to participate in this solemn contract if he had no presentiment of his duty and his rights?

The last three books of *The Social Contract* are intended to show the general will in action. In a society, according to Rousseau, the sovereign and the subjects are the same civil body, viewed from two angles—as legislators when they are taken as a whole, as subjects when each is taken separately. This is the definition of absolute democracy, typified not by ancient democracy with its turbulent assemblies which acted through personal decrees instead of laws, but by Genevan democracy, already praised by Rousseau in the preface to his *Discourse on the Origin of Inequality,* with its plebiscites in which each individual in the silence of his passions made his decision concerning laws proposed by magistrates. Rousseau's state is small and it "ought to be limited to a single town at most," he wrote in the first draft of his manuscript. Such was the state of Geneva, founded on May 13, 1387, by Prince-bishop Adhémar Fabri, on the idea that the sovereignty of the people is inalienable and can never be prescribed.

It must be noted that to Rousseau law, the expression of the general will, is not purely conventional and arbitrary: "That which is good and fitting is such through the nature of things and independently of human conventions." But the general will, which is always right, is not always enlightened. Thus Rousseau does not in any way attribute to the common people, a blind multitude, the enlightenment indispensable to the making of a good law. Such enlightenment can pertain only to a legislator—an exceptional man who is neither magistrate nor sovereign, who has no legislative rights but who is the interpreter of the general will in the editing of laws which he must subsequently propose and submit to the people. To the author of *The Social Contract* Calvin was such a legislator, and for the Poles and the Corsicans he wanted to be such a legislator.

To join the enlightenment of the legislator and the direct will of the people is not enough; there also must be a government. "Laws are made for Titus and Cassius," said Hobbes, "and not for the body of the state." [7] Taking the opposite view, Rousseau holds that laws emanate from the body politic and must apply equally to each individual subject. Measures for executing laws, as soon as they concern individuals, are no longer laws but decrees which cannot emanate from the legislative body. Hence the necessity for an executive power or government. This is not the re-establishment of the theory of Montesquieu, according to whom the two powers are not only distinct but also independent, to such a degree that each has a different historical origin. Rousseau, who sharply criticized Montesquieu's theory, holds that they are distinct but not independent; a democratic, aristocratic, or monarchic government exists only because it is instituted by the people. That a difficulty is inherent in this dependency is obvious, but there would be no such difficulty if the "general will"—something on the order of Malebranche's God—could be the only social force and determine every detail solely in terms of the universal order; if this is not the case, the governmental will, which is particular, tends to oppose the general will. Balance of powers, as in the days of the National Assembly, and absorption of the executive power by the legislative powers, as in the days of the Convention—such were the two issues of which Rousseau had a presentiment and which he wished to set aside.

Rousseau wished from the beginning to eliminate the individual as such from the state. But the individual reappears of necessity in

[7] *De cive*, 12.

the legislator and in the government, and Rousseau is unable to integrate him into a system from which he is excluded. It is from this angle that the religious problem appears in the chapter on civil religion (iv, 8): the object is to eliminate from religion everything which could confer on the individual an independent life isolated from civil life; that is why Rousseau condemns Christianity or the priestly religion which separates the theological system from the political system; for "everything that destroys social unity is worthless; all institutions that set man against himself are worthless." Moultou wrote that "the Christian approved by Rousseau is more of a cosmopolite than a patriot," for he has no civic attachments. Still, Rousseau does not believe, like Bayle, that a society composed of atheists is possible: "No state has ever had anything but religion as its foundation." What can we do but determine the dogmas that are indispensable to civil life and impose them as laws, thereby banishing from the state "not as impious but as unsociable" anyone who does not believe in them? These dogmas are the dogmas of natural religion: the existence of God and of providence, rewards and punishments in a future life for conduct in this life, the sanctity of the social contract and laws. These dogmas, since they emanate solely from the general will, exclude intolerance.

## iv  *The Savoyard Vicar's Profession of Faith*

The state of innocence, forfeiture, and restoration; innocence in the state of nature, forfeiture in the social state, restoration through the social contract; state of nature through man's obedience to his natural instincts, social state issuing from the conflict between particular passions and wills, social contract or man's obedience to the general will—such are the three aspects of man studied, with momentous consequences, by Rousseau. In *The Savoyard Vicar's Profession of Faith,* which contains all the elements of Rousseau's religious philosophy, we find the characteristic rhythm of his thought —a rhythm perhaps even more sentimental than intellectual. Here his enterprise differs strikingly from "natural religion," not in the details of his arguments, perhaps, but certainly in their spiritual overtones. The positive, dry, completely rational arguments of the advocates of natural religion contrast sharply with the vicar's attempt to escape from the painful state of doubt or from the arrogant negations of the materialists; only a sincere heart possesses enlightened reason, and the vicar decides to follow the rule of "accepting as evident all propositions from which, in the sincerity of my heart, I cannot withhold my consent." His sentimental attitude implies the negation of the thesis, then common, that all knowledge derives from the senses. This thesis, as interpreted by Rousseau, holds that any opinion is imposed as rigorously as a sensation; but "if my judgments depend on and are dictated by the impressions I receive, I am futilely exhausting myself in these pursuits; they will or will not be accomplished independently, without my trying to direct them." Thus the *self* that compares and judges must be completely separated from the senses; the feeling "of being hurled into this vast universe, lost, drowned in the immensity of beings" must be eliminated. Confidence of the self in itself, in turn, can be affirmed only through knowledge of the existence of God—the strong, wise will which is the principle of the motion of the universe just as I am the principle of my actions, and which orders the universe according to the relation of means to ends, revealed to us in the spectacle of nature. The vicar finds support for the self in his God: "The rapture of my mind, the charm of my weakness," he says to God, "is to be overwhelmed by your grandeur."

But this confidence, in turn, is shaken by the existence of evil. Rousseau poses the problem of the theodicy in terms of sentiment: How can I put my trust in the Providence of a God who is the author of a world filled with evil? How can I "resolve this incongruity"? In resolving the incongruity Rousseau drew much of his inspiration from his Malebranchist models. He sees the justification of evil only in human liberty, which has two alternatives: it can follow or not follow "the laws of order" and justice. Human liberty is incapable, however, of "disturbing the general order," for its re-establishment and maintenance are assured by the sanctions imposed after death.

The inner feeling that leads us to this reassuring view of the universe is also our only moral guide, for "few of these cadaverous souls have become insensitive, apart from self-interest, to everything just and good." To Rousseau the practical rule is, before all else, to return to the immediate dictates of conscience, which never err: "Whatever I feel to be evil is evil; the best possible casuist is my conscience." Rousseau harshly reproves Condillac, in a note, for saying that reflection is prior to instinct and even that it is the author of the instinctive act. We need only recall his celebrated apostrophe: "Conscience! Conscience! Conscience! Divine instinct, immortal, celestial voice, sure guide of a mean, ignorant being. . . ." Rousseau has complete confidence in the original goodness of the human heart; all vices are acquired, and there is not one vice "whose mode and manner of entrance cannot be explained." It is reason which is naturally egotistical and "which relates everything to the self." But it must be clearly understood that instinct is "love of order," that by instinct "I yield to the order established by God," and that consequently instinct, in its innermost nature, is linked to reason. Notwithstanding appearances, our conscience cannot be a purely objective feeling, for it establishes a relation between us and the universal order.

Thus the profession of a faith ends with the same theme as *The Social Contract* and all the rest of Rousseau's works: the attempt to find for the individual a less deceptive support than that provided by other men and external nature. That is why, here again, he is hostile to Christianity, that is, to a revelation of God who could not dispense with men as interpreters—in short; the religion of the priests. The vicar's apostrophe "How many men stand between God and me!" expresses the same sentiment that caused him to seek, beyond the social state, a state of nature in which he would be in direct contact with things and, beyond existing institutions, a social contract in which an individual will would no longer find expression. While all around him mind was being dissolved into sensible impressions, nature into isolated facts, morality into passional relations, society into individual wills, and religion into a human invention, Rousseau was restoring the essential reality of mind, conscience, the universal will, God. It must be added—and perhaps this accounts for both the weakness of his thought and the strength of its influence—that he restored them without criticism, by an appeal to immediate awareness, to inner evidence, to the "sincerity of the heart." Condillac and D'Holbach had at times vaguely sensed the insufficiency and barrenness of their system. Hume especially, the greatest critic of his era, had clearly indicated the points where thought, faltering, ought to yield to nature and imagination. Rousseau's work fulfilled a need of his era.

Beginning around 1775, philosophical thought became thoroughly imbued with Rousseau's distrust of pure analysis. Some philosophers, following Rousseau's method of purification, tried to identify truth by sentiment and intuition; at the same time, however, the philosophy of Kant was beginning to take shape. It, too, was a restoration of spiritual values, but by a bold reversal it established these values on the basis of criticism itself.

# BIBLIOGRAPHY

## Texts

Rousseau, Jean-Jacques. *Œuvres complètes,* ed. V. D. Musset-Pathey. Paris, 1818–20.

――――. *Œuvres complètes.* 13 vols. Paris, 1910.

――――. *Œuvres complètes de J.-J. Rousseau.* Collection Pléiade, vol. 1. Paris, 1959.

――――. *Correspondance générale de J.-J. Rousseau,* ed. T. Dufour and P. P. Plan. 20 vols. Paris, 1924–34.

――――. *Le Contrat social, édition comprenant, avec le texte définitif, les versions primitives de l'ouvrage collationnées sur les manuscrits autographes de Genève et de Neuchâtel,* ed. E. Dreyfus-Brisac. Paris, 1916.

――――. *Du contrat social,* with an introduction and notes by G. Beaulavon. 5th ed. Paris, 1938.

――――. *Profession de foi du Vicaire savoyard,* ed. P.-M. Masson. 1943.

――――. *Profession de foi du Vicaire savoyard,* ed. G. Beaulavon. 1937.

――――. *The Political Writings of Jean-Jacques Rousseau,* ed. C. E. Vaughan. 2 vols. Cambridge, 1915.

――――. *J.-J. Rousseau: Political Writings,* trans. F. C. Green. London, 1941.

――――. *The Social Contract and Discourses,* trans. G. D. H. Cole. London, 1913.

――――. *Citizen of Geneva: Selections from the Letters of J.-J. Rousseau,* ed. C. W. Hendel. New York and London, 1937.

## Bibliographies

Sénelier, J. *Bibliographie générale des œuvres de J.-J. Rousseau.* Paris, 1949.

## Studies

Babbitt, I. *Rousseau and Romanticism.* New York and Boston, 1919.

Baldensperger, F. *et al. J.-J. Rousseau, leçons faites à l'École des hautes études sociales.* Paris, 1912.

Barth, K. *Protestant Thought from Rousseau to Ritschl,* ch. 11. New York, 1959.

Boutroux, E. *et al.,* in *Revue de métaphysique et de morale,* XX, 1912.

Bouvier, B. *J.-J. Rousseau.* Geneva, 1912.

171

Burgelin, P. *La philosophie de l'existence de Jean-Jacques Rousseau*. Paris, 1951.

Cassirer, E. *The Question of Jean-Jacques Rousseau*. New York, 1954. 2d ed. Bloomington, Indiana, 1960.

———. *Rousseau, Kant and Goethe*. Princeton, 1947. 2d ed. New York, 1963.

Faguet, E. *Rousseau penseur*. Paris, 1912.

Green, F. C. *Jean-Jacques Rousseau: A Study of His Life and Writings*. Cambridge, 1955.

Guéhenno, J. *J.-J. Rousseau*. Vol. 3, *Grandeur et misère d'un esprit (1758–78)*. Paris, 1952.

Guillemin, H. *Les philosophes contre Rousseau*. Paris, 1942.

Hendel, C. W. *Jean-Jacques Rousseau: Moralist*. 2 vols. New York and London, 1934. 2d ed. 1960.

Hoffding, H. *J.-J. Rousseau and His Philosophy*, trans. W. Richards and L. E. Saidla. New Haven, 1930.

Hubert, R. *Rousseau et l'Encyclopédie: Essai sur la formation des idées politiques de Rousseau (1742–56)*. Paris, 1928.

Janet, P. *Histoire de la science politique*. 2 vols. 3d ed. Paris, 1883.

Lemaître, J. *J.-J. Rousseau*. Paris, 1907.

Masson, P. M. *La religion de J.-J. Rousseau*. Paris, 1916.

Morel, J. *Recherches sur les sources du discours de J.-J. Rousseau sur l'origine et les fondements de l'inégalité*. Lausanne, 1910.

Proal, L. *La psychologie de J.-J. Rousseau*. Paris, 1923.

Starobinsky, J. *J.-J. Rousseau: la transparence et l'obstacle*. Paris, 1958.

Touchard, J. *Histoire des idées politiques*, vol. 2. Paris, 1959. 2d ed. 1962.

Vuy, J. *Origine des idées politiques de J.-J. Rousseau*, 2d ed. Geneva and Paris, 1889.

Werner, Ch. *Études de philosophie morale*. Geneva, 1917.

*Annales de la Société J.-J. Rousseau*. Geneva, 1905 and following.

# THIRD PERIOD
## 1775–1800

# SENTIMENT AND
# PRE-ROMANTICISM

### 1 *Mysticism and Illuminism: Saint-Martin*

That there was, around 1775, a gradual diffusion throughout
Europe of the distaste for critical, destructive analysis and a return
to sentiment and immediate intuition, is attested by the popularity
of Rousseau's works. Fanciful musing was cultivated for its own
sake: "If all my dreams had been realized," Rousseau wrote to
Malesherbes in 1762, "I would still have been dissatisfied; I would
have imagined, desired, dreamed, desired again. I found within me
an inexplicable void which nothing could have filled, a certain aspiration after another source of enjoyment which I had not yet
envisioned but which I sensed to be indispensable. Well! *That in
itself was sheer delight,* for through me surged a strong emotion and
an enticing sadness which I would not have wished to miss." This
feeling finally surpassed anything known to exist: "My heart, con-
fined within the limits of beings, found them too narrow; I was
suffocating in the universe and longed to leap into infinity."

The thesis that knowledge can discover its object, its measure, and
its justification only through sentiment was prevalent long before
this time. "Let those who have never loved," wrote Duclos, "be assured that notwithstanding their intellectual superiority, there are
numberless ideas—apt ideas, I say—that they cannot attain and that
are reserved to sentiment alone. . . . It can be said that the heart has

175

ideas of its own." That idea was common to all the English senti-mentalists. As early as 1719, Jean Baptiste Du Bos (*Critical Reflections on Poetry and Painting*) attributed knowledge of the beautiful to no other source. "Reason must intervene in judgment only in order to justify the decision of sentiment; the heart asserts itself independently, prior to any deliberation." In England his opinion was shared by Addison, Hutcheson, and Burke.[1] In ethics, also, there were attempts to find in sentiment and conscience an organ of truth inaccessible to doubt; whoever reasoned was already a skeptic; quite different from reason was conscience, "this separate faculty of the soul," this "moral instinct which discerns good and evil through a kind of sensation and taste," this sentiment which is a "sure, enlightened guide, a gentle bond between hearts."[2] A belief that satisfies sentiment passes for a well founded and justified belief; according to Maupertuis, it is the desire to be happy, more universal still than the natural light, which engenders our belief in God, nature, and man, which are "objects that surpass all our ideas and all our intellectual powers." Jean Ray (*Existence and Wisdom of God,* 1714) goes even further: "If the existence of God were unfounded, we would still find it advantageous." This anticipates the Savoyard Vicar, with his comforting illusions: "I would be corrupted less by following my own illusions than by surrendering" to the "lies" of the philosophers. We have already observed just such confusion of the useful and the true in La Mettrie, D'Holbach, and Helvétius, who defended their "materialistic" theses by showing that they were useful or at least harmless.

During the period under consideration, two themes overlap: Truth is attained through a kind of intuition, sentimental in nature; truth must be proportionate to its utility to the receiver. The joining of these two traits gave rise to the illuminism and esoterism

---

[1] V. Basch, *L'Esthétique de Kant,* "Introduction."

[2] Passages from Formey, *De la conscience,* 1754; Burlamaqui, *Principes de droit naturel,* 1747; G. de Biliena, *Le Triomphe du sentiment,* 1750. As quoted by Masson, *La Religion de Rousseau,* I, 237.

characteristic of the end of the eighteenth century.[3] Occultists like Cagliostro sometimes reduced them to charlatanism, but men like Lessing and Herder raised them to a conception of the universe distinct from that of the philosophers of the Enlightenment. For in Kant's view *Schwärmerei* or illuminism, about which he often complained, includes Platonic mysticism as well as Swedenborg's visions. Whereas Voltaire, following Locke, believed there was an exact, natural relation between our faculties and our needs, here we see a contrast between the transcendental faculties, which are the lot of a small number of men, and common sense. A line of demarcation has been drawn between initiates and outsiders.

In contrast to the philosophy of the Encyclopedists, doctrines linked to Mme. Guyon and Jakob Böhme were elaborated in Masonic circles and in mystical and theosophical societies. Joseph de Maistre, himself an initiate, reports that the lodges of Lyons taught "the exalted Christianity which in Germany is called transcendental Christianity—a mixture of Platonism, Origenism, and Hermetic philosophy, superimposed on Christianity." At issue was the mystical story, inspired by Böhme, which recounts the creation of man, his fall, and his final restoration: the return to God, which must be accompanied by the radical separation of good and evil and by the destruction of matter. These mystical doctrines then were opposed to natural religion founded on reason; their exponents, however, adopted the tone and manners of the Philosophes. The idea of the continuity of reality or the great chain of being, an idea that dominated the philosophy of the century, also asserted itself here: "If the system presented to you, regardless of its source, provides you with a chain of which all the links are in place and present to you a total pattern which explains and demonstrates to your mind the whole intellectual and physical universe," the Mason Villermoz, of Lyons, wrote to Joseph de Maistre in 1779, "if it demonstrates to you your own existence as a man with all the ties

---

[3] Cf. Auguste Viatte, *Les Sources occultes du romantisme, illuminisme, théosophie,* Vol. I, *Le Préromantisme* (Paris, 1928).

that bind you as a man to the rest of the universe and its maker, admit that it will fulfil everything promised by truth and that a being endowed with reason and a fondness for truth cannot long refuse to adopt it." [4] This image of the universal chain appeared in a mystical form in Proclus and Berkeley; it took on a philosophical cast in Leibniz, and naturalists and ideologists gave it a positive slant; theosophists also wished to make it the sign of the rational character of their doctrine. To the image of the chain of living beings is linked the image of the universal force that pervades it. For example, it is the universal fluid, forever in motion, through which Mesmer explains the phenomenon of animal magnetism, a phenomenon which reveals the intimate, sympathetic interrelations between all things. It is the world system of Restif de la Bretonne, who took up Buffon's cosmogonic hypothesis and imagined a center from which the sun emanates; the planets break away from the sun; each planet (as André Chénier also remarked concerning the earth) is a living individual—one which gives birth to species which in turn give birth to other species until finally, after thousands of centuries, the result is man; then through a reverse motion of reabsorption, all beings return to the center.

There we have the essential images of the great metaphysical and philosophical systems of nature that succeeded each other until the middle of the nineteenth century. They are merely distortions of ideas current among philosophers like Diderot and D'Holbach, but they are imbued with a religious quality and suggest a superior revelation. This accounts for the hostility between those who fashioned them and the Philosophes. The words "natural" and "religion" are mutually exclusive, wrote Dutoit-Membrini in *Divine Philosophy* (1793); and Villermoz' object is not to accommodate all creeds and promote tolerance—than is, indifference—by extracting in the name of natural religion whatever is common to all beliefs, but to restore a primitive Christianity whose dogmas have been lost. At a general meeting in 1782, the Masons explicitly proscribed the philosophy of the century and the tendency of certain members to base

[4] As quoted by Dermenghem, *Joseph de Maistre mystique,* p. 59.

a new religion on this philosophy. In Prussia Frederick William II expelled the rationalist philosopher Nicolai and sought, according to Lavater, "to slaughter the monster of unbelief, Socinianism, and irreligion." In fact, in 1788 he reestablished censure of deism and rationalism. Fabre d'Olivet, in his *Philosophical History of the Human Race,* sets the illuminists against "the abomination of philosophical systems," "hideous deism," "the *Encyclopedia* which serves to overturn everything, the friend of destruction." Even when Fessler, an impassioned disciple of Kant, revised the statutes of the Royal-York Lodge in Berlin in 1797 (the lodge with which Fichte became affiliated in 1799), he was careful to state that "no one would ever be allowed to include as one of its aims or resoures that which is called the propagation of enlightenment." [5] Of course Kantian criticism—practical logic and postulates—is remote from *Aufklärung.* These illuminists, even when Protestant by birth, were sympathetic to Catholicism. There were famous conversions like that of Schlegel; Fabre d'Olivet, a Protestant by birth, was disposed to accept a pope; Novalis envisioned the restoration of a militia of Jesuits; and the celebrated Lavater, though he maintained that a universal religion was as impossible as a universal monarchy and added that faith was individual and peculiar to each person, nevertheless believed that a basis for a unitary faith existed because of the continuity of beings and because "each nature is a copy of other natures." In other instances this image of the universal chain of living beings and their unity culminated in the revolutionary idea of fraternity and equality, and Bonneville, who in *The Spirit of Religions* (1792) classes "the atheist a little above the orangutan but not among men" adopted integral communism. The whole idea of the rights and independence of the individual was dissolved in the image of the world as a "great animal" whose soul was God.

The Marquis Louis Claude de Saint-Martin (1743–1803), "the unknown philosopher," gave some consistency to these muddled ideas. Hostile toward occult practices and apocalyptical visions, he found his model in the speculative mysticism of Böhme, with

[5] Xavier Léon, *Fichte et son temps* (Paris, 1924), II, 17.

whom he became acquainted in 1788 and whose *Aurora, or the Rising of the Dawn* he translated. In his work we find the central idea taken up later in Lamennais' *Outline of a Philosophy*: the creature is to God as God the Word (conceived, spoken, manifested) is to God the Father (conceiving, speaking, opining. Everything is an image: "We swim under a shadow in an atmosphere of images." From this idea issued his entire criticism of the philosophy of the century, which viewed languages, societies, and the sciences as the reflective creation of human reason working with the data of experience. Languages have their origin in a primitive revelation; if philosophers think otherwise, this is because "for them languages are only an aggregate instead of being the expression and fact of life itself." Societies and governments take shape by themselves; they are natural products; a contract cannot create a society, for man cannot give himself rights which he does not have. The sciences originate in a common tradition whose remnants are reflected in our thoughts and in the thoughts of people everywhere. It is absurd to say that the sciences are based on experience, for "facts merely confirm intelligence and are rightly given only second place." The French Revolution, though it issued from these false principles, nevertheless has a providential significance; by provoking the fall of the "Church that previously existed," it announces a spiritual Christianity; as for its victims, they are "victims of an expiation necessitated by original sin." In short, Martinism contains the essential elements of the counterrevolutionary ideas developed by Maistre and Bonald.

## II  Lessing, Herder

German philosophy, in this period, gradually broke away from the ideal of the Enlightenment. The ideas of Lessing and of the young Goethe, the doctrines of Herder and Jacobi, and the criticism of Kant all combined to show that the rational intellect constructed on the basis of Locke's analysis and Newton's science did not penetrate to the heart of reality.

Lessing (1729–81), whose most important writings belong to this period (*Wolffenbüttler Fragmente,* 1774–77, and *Die Erziehung des Menschengeschlechts,* 1780), was indeed, in many respects, the continuation of the French and English freethinkers. In the *Fragmente* he published anonymously a work by Reimarus who, like many others, called attention to the weakness of orthodoxy in the face of biblical and evangelical criticism, and who asserted in particular that Jesus was the author of the dogma of ransom and salvation. In the bitter dispute forced upon him on this occasion by Goeze, as well as in his other writings, he nevertheless exhibited a variety of free thought quite different from that of men like Voltaire and Toland. This difference is traceable to his profound intuition of the evolution and transformation of beliefs. "It is not possession of truth that accounts for its worth," he says, "for man does not succeed in his quest, nor does he believe that he will; it is not in possession but in pursuit of truth that his strength develops." The Christian religion, then, is not judged false and rejected as such, but it is one phase in the discovery of truth, a phase that must be surmounted. A good Mason, Lessing was acquainted with "truths that should be kept secret" (he is known to have believed in transmigration of souls) because the mind is not sufficiently mature to receive them as well as with truths which, at a given moment in history, are transmitted to the mind as revelations and which later become demonstrated truths: "God allows simple truths of reason to be taught as revealed truths for a time in order to spread them more quickly and make them substantial." [6] The pure, rational religion that he envisions stands clearly apart, then, from the natural religion advocated by freethinkers opposed to orthodoxy, for it transcends and absorbs revelation. Thus it provides the fundamental ideas for Hegel's philosophy of religion, clearly revealed in his discussion of Leibniz. "Leibniz freely set aside his system," he says, "and tried to guide each individual along the path of truth on which he found himself." It follows that so-called truths are never anything except fleeting forms of a truth which is revealed only in its progression. Furthermore, Lessing often insists on the

[6] *The Education of the Human Race,* sec. 70.

purely practical character which his religious beliefs must have in order to be effective: "It is one thing to believe in the immortality of the soul as a philosophical speculation, another to use this belief as a basis for instituting internal and external beliefs."

Herder (1744–1803) followed the trend of his time and intensified it by musing at length on nature and on history which apprehends our present life as a pulsation within the whole of things. In all of his works he was careful to express his intuitive awareness of the unity of the divine plan. He shows a singular predilection for indulging in reveries concerning the past—the earliest stages in which he pretends to discover human qualities in their natural state. This accounts for his *Origin of Language* (1772): "It is as natural for man to invent language as it is for him to be a man," for language, which might have been invented by a recluse, is not based on any social convention. Language is nature itself finding expression in the mind of man: "If rustling leaves shower their freshness upon the poor hermit, if a brook murmurs in passing, if a rippling breeze cools his cheeks, he is inspired to acquaint himself with these beneficial things and to name them in his soul, without having recourse to his eyes or his tongue. The tree will be called the rustling thing, the breeze the rippling thing, the spring the murmuring thing. Here we have a little dictionary, already fashioned, expectant." This accounts for his works on popular poetry, on Pseudo-Ossian, in which he sees the realization of man's original gifts for seeing things intuitively. Finally, this accounts for his great work, *Outlines of a Philosophy of the History of Man* (1784–91), which is diametrically opposed in spirit to the works in which the successors of the philosophers of the Enlightenment—in particular, Iselin (*On the History of Man,* 1764) and, later, Condorcet—tried to show the progress of mankind. Whereas these philosophers determined the successive stages through which man progressed in knowledge and perfection, Herder takes an entirely different course and seeks to identify not the sequence of events but the ideal types around which everything in nature and history seems to oscillate. Nature and history are not a web of casually interconnected events but an organic whole embracing different outlines: first in nature, "where, from stones to crystals, from crystals to metals, from metals to the vegetable kingdom, from plants to animals, we see the form of the organism arising"; then in history, which shows us all races and types of civilization, culminating in the European civilization, which is "a civilization of men as they were and as they wished to be."

The dominant idea is the idea of the continuity of forms, beginning with an original type. His philosophy reappears in the youthful meditations of Goethe (born in 1749), with whom he was closely associated at Strasbourg in 1770, then at Weimar after 1776. Both of them imagine a universe in which nature passes from one form to another in a smooth, unbroken transition. This is no longer the Leibnizian axiom of the "plenum of forms" which states that all compossible forms must actually be realized, for to them nature is an evolutionary force which produces new forms within the limits adopted for each type; it is even further removed from the theory of the patterning of germs according to which manifested forms pre-existed on a miniature scale, for nature is creative, and Goethe explicitly contrasts the theory of pre-existence with the theory of epigenesis, which implies a true metamorphosis in which there is a gradual transformation of one form into another—the transformation, for instance, of the brain of the fish into the brain of man, revealed in the schematic drawings of the physiologist Camper, or the transformation of the leaf into all the organs of the plant, demonstrated by Goethe himself in his *Metamorphosis of Plants* (1790).[7]

An intellect that thinks by fixed concepts, superficial experience, the analytical reasoning of men like Locke or Newton—all are insufficient and must be replaced by intuitive knowledge closely related to sentiment and art: direct insight into the very operation of nature.

[7] René Berthelot, "Lamarck et Goethe," *Revue de Métaphysique et de morale* (1929), p. 299 ff.

III *Jacobi versus Mendelssohn; Hemsterhuis*

No less inimical to the rationalism of the philosophy of the Enlightenment, at approximately the same time but in a wholly different sense, is the philosophy of Jacobi (1743–1819). His main theme is the impossibility of rational religion and the necessity of faith (*Glauben*). Any consistent rationalism leads to atheism or Spinozism, which is the same thing, since rationalism consists in thinking according to the principle of sufficient reason: nothing comes from nothing. Drawing support from Wolff's critique,[8] Jacobi shows that Spinozism entails the conclusion that everything else is but a mode of one universal substance; as soon as we envision God as being prior to the world or conceive of a world as existing apart from God, or of free persons, we break away from the principle of sufficient reason. Leibniz, if he were consistent, would have to be a Spinozist. We must therefore accept faith as a source of certainty, independent of reason, and make this certainty the necessary condition of rational certainty, for it alone is immediate, since it excludes any proof, and should provide the premises of any mediate certainty, such as rational certainty ought to be. Any proof implies something already proven on the basis of revelation. Jacobi again takes up Pascal's theory of principles and cites this thought: "We have an idea of truth which can withstand any attack by Pyrrhonism." The existence of my body and of other bodies and other thinking beings outside me—these are objects of true revelation, "which nature compels each and every one of us to believe and to accept." For man, faith is as inevitable a milieu as society: "We are all born in the faith and obliged to remain in the faith, just as we are all born in society and obliged to remain in society."

This is radically opposed to the philosophy of the Enlightenment. The intellect does not govern the will but "develops by means of

---

[8] Cf. especially *Ueber die Lehre des Spinoza,* 1785. Revised by H. Scholz, *Die Hauptsschriften zum Pantheismusstreit zwischen Jacobi und Mendelssohn.*

the will, which is a spark shot forth from the pure, eternal light";
man's thought depends on his conduct; "the way that leads to
knowledge is not syllogistical or mechanical." Thus Jacobi arrives
at the relativist theory of truth advanced by Lessing: "Each age
has its own truth . . . , its own living philosophy, which expounds
the dominant mode of action of this age as it progresses."

The dispute over Lessing that took place in 1785 between Jacobi
and Mendelssohn (1729–86), the defender of natural religion and
the philosophy of the Enlightenment, casts light on the nature of
the currents of thought of this era. Jacobi claimed that Lessing
was a pantheist because he assumed that all things are interconnected, that God's idea of a thing exhausts its essence, and finally
that the world as a whole is identical to the Son of God, to God's
conception of himself. Mendelssohn, a friend of Lessing, defended
him against this charge as early as 1754. But their debate became
more intense and centered on the notion of faith itself. Mendelssohn,
who remained faithful all his life to Judaism, the faith of his parents,
recognized only one possible faith—faith in historical truths, such
as the facts on which the ritual of Judaism is founded. He held
that the existence and omnipotence of God are known through
reason, that Judaism is not a revealed religion but a revealed law,
and that revelation prescribes acts (this is Spinoza's point of view)
without augmenting our knowledge. In his view, the truths of religion involve very simple reasoning which is accessible to good
sense and which philosophy simply provides with a firmer basis.
Thus neither Jacobi, the defender of faith, nor Mendelssohn the
champion of reason, seemed to grasp intellectual intuition as it was
adumbrated in Lessing, brought into sharp focus in Herder or
Goethe, and, in spite of Kant, posited as the central idea of German
philosophy.

With the views of Jacobi are associated those of his friend, the
Dutch philosopher Hemsterhuis (1720–90), an excellent but neglected writer of French prose. His common themes are atheism,
based on the unlimited investigation of causes, and the existence
of two kinds of convictions—those arising from an inner, ineffable

feeling and those traceable to reason and unable to subsist without the first. "If on occasion a healthy man expresses a longing for the best, the future, perfection," he writes, "this is more than a geo-metrical demonstration of the nature of the divinity." [9]

## iv *The Philosophy of Thomas Reid*

Notwithstanding the difference in atmosphere, similar preoccu-pations are reflected in the doctrine of the Scotsman Thomas Reid (1710–96), professor at the University of Glasgow in 1763. A trait common to all theories of knowledge from Descartes to Hume is the thesis which Locke's adversaries called "idealism": we have no immediate knowledge of things but only of our ideas. A whole series of problems resulted from the attempt to determine how, starting from our ideas, we can arrive at affirmations about things and then justify these affirmations. Following attempts that led to the most extraordinary doctrines (innatism, seeing all things in God), Berkeley and Hume, each in his own way, finally declared the problem insoluble—the first by denying any reality to things distinct from ideas, the second by refusing to attribute any value other than that of a spontaneous belief to affirmations that transcend the content of ideas. Thus there was an insuperable gap between philosophy and common sense.

Instead of resolving these problems, Reid went back to the only thesis which shed light on them: the thesis that we know only through ideas. This thesis, according to him, is grounded on a commonplace misunderstanding: it is said that a thing cannot act or suffer in a place where it is not present, and that, consequently, the mind can perceive its own modifications but not external bodies to which it is not present. The mistake is in thinking that in per-ception a body acts on the mind, for one being acts on another only if there emanates from the first a force which produces a change in the second: "however, an object, in being perceived, does

---

[9] Aristée, in *Œuvres philosophiques* (Paris, 1809), II, 102.

not act at all. . . . To be perceived, is what logicians call an external denomination, which implies neither action nor quality in the object perceived." [10] Commenting on Reid, Hamilton calls attention to the fact that he borrowed from Gassendi the idea and the term extrinsic denomination, or perception which was probably suggested to Gassendi by the Ockhamist nominalists, notably Biel. This common-sense tradition, contrary to Cartesianism, refuses to put something from the mind into the object perceived immediately.[11]

As Reid himself admitted, however, denunciation of this prejudice is the sum and substance of his philosophy. The result is a justification of sorts not only of immediate perception of external objects of sense but also of immediate perception of the truth of common sense. To him common sense does not mean—as it had to Beattie before him—a spontaneous, natural belief common to all men and opposed to reason or the faculty of discovering unknown relations through known relations; it embraces reason—as it had for Buffier, whom he regards as a predecessor. "The same degree of understanding that makes a man capable of acting with common prudence in the conduct of life, makes him capable of discovering what is true and what is false in matters that are self-evident, and which he distinctly apprehends." Thus to him common sense means, in the words of Dugald Steward, the "fundamental laws" of belief: rules which are immediate, irreducible, original, natural, necessary, and universal, and which can be discovered only through an indispensable analysis.[12] Moreover, common sense implies no passivity of the mind, and he observes that by the word "sense" philosophers mean a simple receptive faculty and in this way are forced to separate judgment from perception, but that in

---

[10] *Essays on the Intellectual Powers of Man,* in *The Works of Thomas Reid,* ed. Hamilton (Edinburgh, 1880), I, 301.

[11] *Ibid.,* II, 970.

[12] Cf. Dugald-Stewart, *Elements of the Philosophy of the Human Mind* (in *The Collected Works of* . . . , ed. Sir William Hamilton, Edinburgh, 1877, Vol. II), 50 ff. and 108 ff.; cf. also Dugald-Stewart's "Account of the Life and Writings of Thomas Reid," in *The Works of Thomas Reid,* I, 22.

ordinary speech the word often implies judgment ("good sense," "nonsense," "sensing").[13]

The principle of immediate perception transforms the philosophy of mind: the idealists reduced all mental faculties to consciousness or thought, since their sole object was the idea; but if consciousness is the immediate perception of present modifications, it should be separated from external perception (immediate perception of external objects), from memory (immediate perception of the past), and more especially from all mediate knowledge. Reid therefore substituted description and classification of psychological faculties for so-called physiological explanations, in vogue from Descartes to Hartley, and for attempts to achieve a reduction to unity, as in Condillac. Thus psychology became descriptive, classificatory, and prudently inductive.

We can be sure that this return to the immediate, this shackling of the power of analysis, this failure to proceed beyond given, irreducible realities which the intellect could manipulate only from the outside through comparison and classification corresponds to a general trait of the period.

[13] Reid, *On the Intellectual Powers of Man*, VI, ii (*The Works of* . . . , I, 421–6).

BIBLIOGRAPHY

## Histories and Studies of Eighteenth Century Thought

Ayraut, R. *La genèse du romantisme allemand, situation spirituelle de l'Allemagne dans la deuxième moitié du XVIIIe siècle.* 2 vols. Paris, 1961.

Berthelot, R. "Lamarck et Goethe," *Revue de Métaphysique et de Morale,* 1929.

Franck, A. *La philosophie mystique en France au XVIIIe siècle.* Paris, 1868.

Gagnepin, B. *Burlamaque et le droit naturel.* Geneva, 1944.

Hansen, A. *Goethes Metamorphose der Pflanzen, Geschichte einer botanischen Hypothese.* Giessen, 1907.

Monglond, A. *Histoire intérieure du préromantisme français de l'abbé Prévost à Joubert.* Grenoble, 1929.

Saint-Martin, C. de. *Mon portrait historique et philosophique,* ed. R. Amadou. Paris, 1961.

Schneider, F. J. *Die Freimaurerei und ihr Einfluss über geistige Kultur in Deutschland am Ende des XVIIIten Jahrhunderts.* Prague, 1909.

Viatte, A. *Les sources occultes du romantisme: Illuminisme, théosophie (1770–1820).* Vol. 1, *Le Préromantisme.* Paris, 1928.

## Works

Lessing, Gotthold E. *Sämmtliche Schriften.* 23 vols. Stuttgart, 1886–1924.
———. *Laokoon,* trans. E. A. McCormack. New York, 1962.
———. *Lessing's Theological Works,* trans. H. Chadwick. Stanford, 1957.

## Studies

Aner, K. *Die Theologie der Lessingzeit.* Halle, 1929.

Barth, K. *Protestant Thought from Rousseau to Ritschl,* chap. 3. New York, 1959.

Danzel and Guhrauer. *Lessings Leben und Werke. Leipzig,* 1850–54. 3d ed. Berlin, 1880–81.

Dilthey, G. E. *Das Erlebniss und die Dichtung,* chap. 2. Leipzig, 1905. 4th ed. 1912.

Fittbogen, G. *Die Religion Lessings.* Halle, 1915.

Garland, H. B. *Lessing, the Founder of Modern Germany Literature.* London, 1937.

Gombrich, E. H. "Lecture on a Master Mind," *Proceedings of the British Academy*, XLIII (1957), 133–56.
Kretzschmar, E. *Lessing und die Aüfklarung*. Leipzig, 1905.
Leisegang, H. *Lessings Weltanschauung*. Leipzig, 1931.
Lorenz, P. *Lessings Philosophie*. Leipzig, 1909.

## Texts

Herder, Johann G. *Sämmtliche Werke*. Ed. B. Sulphan *et al.* 33 vols. Berlin, 1877–1913.
——. *Treatise upon the Origin of Language*, translator unknown. London, 1827.
——. *Outlines of a Philosophy of the History of Man*, trans. T. Churchill. 2d ed. London, 1803.
——. *The Spirit of Hebrew Poetry*, trans. J. Marsh. 2 vols. Burlington, Vermont, 1832.
——. *God: Some Conversations*, trans. F. H. Burkhardt. 2d ed. New York, 1949.
——. *Textes choisis*, ed. É. Bréhier. Paris, 1925.

## Studies

Andress, J. M. *J. G. Herder as an Educator*. New York, 1916.
Clark, R. T., Jr. *Herder, His Life and Thought*. New York, 1963.
Gillies, A. *Herder*. Oxford, 1945.
Haym, J. *Herder nach seinem Leben und seinen Werken*. 2 vols. 1877–85.
McEachran, F. *The Life and Philosophy of J. G. Herder*. Oxford, 1929.

## Texts

Jacobi, Friedrich H. *Werke*, ed. F. Roth. 6 vols. Leipzig, 1812–25.
——. *Aus F. H. Jacobis Nachlass*, ed. by R. Zöpporitz. 2 vols. Leipzig, 1869.
——. *Auserlesener Briefwechsel*, ed. F. Roth. 2 vols. Leipzig, 1825–27.
——. *Briefwechsel zwischen Goethe und F. H. Jacobi*, ed. M. Jacobi. Leipzig, 1846.
——. *Briefe an Bouterwek aus den Jahrn 1800–1819*, ed. W. Meyer. Göttingen, 1868.

## Studies

Haraens, O. F. *Jacobi und der Sturm und Drang*. Heidelberg, 1928.
Lévy-Bruhl, L. *La philosophie de Jacobi*. Paris, 1894.
Thilo, C. A. *Jacobis: Religions, philosophie*. Langensalza, 1905.
Weiller, von and Thiersch. *Jacobi's Leben, Lehre und Wirken*. München, 1918.

## Texts

Mendelssohn, Moses. *Werke,* ed. G. B. Mendelssohn. 7 vols. Leipzig, 1843–44.
———. *Gesammelte Schriften.* ed. J. Elbogen, J. Guttman, and M. Mittwoch. Berlin, 1929—.

## Studies

Ritter, J. H. *Mendelssohn und Lessing.* 2d ed. Berlin, 1886.
Scholz, H. *Die Hauptschriften zum Pantheismusstreit zwischen Jacobi und Mendelssohn.* Berlin, 1916.

## Texts

Hemsterhuis, François. *Œuvres philosophiques.* Paris, 1809.

## Studies

Boulan, E. *François Hemsterhuis: Le Socrate hollandais.* Groningen and Paris, 1924.

## Texts

Reid, Thomas. *Works,* ed. Sir William Hamilton. 2 vols. Edinburgh, 1895.

## Studies

Fraser, A. C. *Thomas Reid.* Edinburgh and London, 1898.
Grave, S. A. *The Scottish Philosophy of Common Sense.* Oxford, 1960.
Pringle-Pattison, A. S. *Scottish Philosophy: A Comparison of the Scottish and German Answers to Hume.* London and Edinburgh, 1885.
Woozley, A. D. *Reid's Essay on the Intellectual Powers of Man.* London, 1941.

# THE PERSISTENCE OF
# RATIONALISM

## 1 *The Economists*

Though there was a continuation of rationalism in France and
England, there was a singular retraction of its field of application.
That reason should contribute to the happiness of all had been
repeated so often, and the practical aspect of the Enlightenment
had been stressed so often that the Philosophes, leaving to dreamers
grandiose speculations concerning the universe and the destiny of
man, concentrated their efforts on discovering means of putting
science to use in improving human life. The characteristic creation
of the second half of the eighteenth century was political economy,
founded in France by Quesnay (1694-1774) and in Britain by
Adam Smith. The new sciences stemmed from the attempt to
remove from the arbitrary control of governments general measures
relating to the wealth of nations and to identify the laws—natural,
necessary, and independent of the human will—on which they
should be based. Notwithstanding the profound divergence between the physiocrats, who were disciples of Quesnay, and the English economists, the two schools have one common trait: their indifference, or even their hostility at times, to the great liberal movement founded on the idea of human rights. Bent on determining
through reason the conditions under which society exists and progresses, they deduced laws whose scientific precision, according to

the physiocrats, should take the form of a legal despotism which functions in the name of evidence: "Euclid," said one of them, "was truly a despot, and the geometrical truths which he has transmitted to us are truly despotic laws." Once an advocate of the liberalism of Montesquieu, Mirabeau—the father of the revolutionary—was converted to Quesnay's ideas in 1757 and in his *Letters on Legislation* (1775) declared his hostility to representative government as well as to privileged bodies and families.[1]

Countering the doctrine of the physiocrats, who looked upon agriculture as the source of all wealth and condemned luxury industries, was the political economy of Adam Smith, who sought to justify the division of labor and the industrial development of England through natural law, and to show that the interests of producers and consumers are identical when the government does not intervene but allows full freedom of operation to the natural law of division of labor and to the natural law that depends on it—the law of supply and demand (*The Wealth of Nations,* 1776). Neither the freedom of industry championed by Smith, nor the freedom of commerce in grains championed by the French physiocrats, nor simple nonintervention on the part of the government had anything to do with the juridical notion of the rights of man.

English utilitarianism, closely tied in its development to political economy, advanced under the influence of Bentham (1748-1832) toward the rational precision which, in ethics and legislation, makes possible the formulation of absolute decisions, without recourse to a juridical ideal. Élie Halévy[2] has observed that the utilitarians had no part in the advancement of the democratic ideas which shook England between 1776 and 1785; Priestly in his *Essay on the First Principles of Government* (1768) says that, in great states, the general interest cannot be assured unless severe restrictions are placed on political liberty. As for Bentham, he concedes with Smith that

---

[1] E. Carcassone, *Montesquieu et le problème de la constitution française au XVIIIe siècle* (Paris, 1927), pp. 311–325.

[2] *La Formation du radicalisme philosophique,* Vol. I, *La Jeunesse de Bentham,* pp. 231 ff.

harmony of interests is realized spontaneously in the development of wealth, but he believes that in civil and political matters it can be achieved only through a system of representative legislation which gives man a motive for subjecting his self-interest to the utility of all; the notion of human rights is absent. It has been judiciously observed[3] that Bentham's theory, like Adam Smith's, is founded rather on a belief which is almost religious in character: Man lives under conditions which preclude the attainment of pleasure except at the price of suffering and work; if there were an abundance of goods political economy would be useless, and so would legislation and ethics if the pursuit of immediate pleasure always led to the greatest possible pleasure.

## II  *Theoreticians of Progress*

Scientific rationalism, which gradually replaced juridical rationalism, indicates to man not so much the ideal which he is to follow as the necessary conditions of his conduct. It is reflected in the general views of the French theoreticians of progress, Turgot and Condorcet.

Condorcet's treatment of history is quite different from Voltaire's. A disciple of the physiocrats, Condorcet (1743–94) believed that "a good law should be good for all men as a proposition is true for all men,"[4] supported (before 1789) a strong national monarchy, and condemned privileged bodies. His celebrated *Sketch for a Historical Picture of the Progress of the Human Mind* (1794) is not comparable in any way to the historical relativism of Lessing and Herder; to him there is one absolute, one permanent human nature. For example, he notes that the "resemblance between the moral precepts of all sects of philosophy prove that they possess a truth independent of the dogmas of these religions and the principles of these sects; that the basis of his obligations and the origin of his

---

[3] *Ibid.*, pp. 218–19.

[4] "Observations inédites de Condorcet sur le 29ᵉ livre de *l'Esprit des Lois*," at the end of Destutt de Tracy, *Commentaire sur l'Esprit des Lois*, 1819.

ideas of justice and virtue must be sought in the moral constitution of man." Furthermore, his *Sketch* is less the history of an immanent development of the human mind than an appraisal the ten epochs which he identifies on the basis of their orientation (or temporary regressions, as in the Middle Ages) toward the only intellectual and ethical culture susceptible of unlimited progress, without regression—to wit, cultivation of the sciences, inaugurated in the sixteenth century, and the concurrent evolution of rational techniques. The vast gains made by the cultivation of the sciences, according to him, insures both the possibility and the necessity of man's unlimited progress; for, unlike Diderot, who thought that mathematics had reached its limits during his epoch, Condorcet takes pains to show (and this is the most important part of his *Sketch*) that infinity is inherent in sciences such as physics and mathematics. "No one," he says at the outset, "has ever thought that the mind could exhaust all the facts of nature or ultimate means of precision in the measurement and analysis of these facts . . . ; relative magnitudes alone, combinations of this idea alone, quantity or extension constitute a system which is already so vast that the human mind can never apprehend it entirely." [5] From this it must not be concluded that the mind, with its limited power, will encounter a term beyond which it cannot go, for progress is not accomplished through juxtaposition: "In proportion as we identify more multiple relations among a larger number of objects, we succeed in . . . subsuming them under simpler expressions, in presenting them in configurations that allow us to apprehend a larger number of them even though we may possess only the same brain power." In a word, unlimited progress is made possible by the generalization of methods, which allows us to pass from arithmetic to algebra, for example, or from computations involving rational numbers to computations involving irrational numbers. The same indefinite progress applies to techniques that depend on these sciences and to the moral sciences, in which the application of com-

[5] *Esquisse,* "Dixième époque."

binatorial computation to moral facts (a question with which Condorcet was personally preoccupied), the development of a more precise language, and the elaboration of laws to destroy the apparent opposition between the interest of the individual and the common interest are all fields open to indefinite progress.

This indefinite character of scientific knowledge runs counter to the narrow, precise limits of any religious dogma. For example, to insure progress Condorcet relies less on an inexorable law than on a well-oriented education which protects man from prejudices that close and restrict his mind; his draft decree for the organization of public instruction (1792) advocates the division of high schools into four classes: three for the sciences (mathematical and physical sciences, moral and political sciences, scientific technology) and one for the study of living and dead languages.

The tendency of the philosophy of the Enlightenment is clear: To show that knowledge of the physical and moral sciences is indispensable to man's pursuit of happiness. "Through the law of his sensibility," wrote Volney (1757–1820), one of the most typical representatives of the Enlightenment, "man tends as invincibly to become happy as fire tends to rise. . . . His obstacle is his ignorance, which misleads him concerning means and deceives him concerning effects and causes." [6] For philosophy, then, our instruction is not an end, for our end is imposed by nature. That is why Volney, in his *Ruins* (1791), recapitulated all the arguments of his century against religions, each of which claimed to impose an end upon men, and showed that, following the tradition passed from Fontenelle to Auguste Comte, they embodied before all else a false system of physics in which physical forces, deified, gave rise to the astrological cult from which all other cults were derived. He attacked mainly the dogmatism of religions, the trait that made them hostile to progress. "My book," he wrote to Dr. Priestly, "generally reflects a spirit of doubt and uncertainty, which seem to me to be most in keeping with the weakness of the human understanding

[6] *Les Ruines,* chap. xiii: "L'humanité s'améliorerait-elle?"

and most appropriate to its improvement . . . , whereas dogmatism and the spirit of certainty, by limiting our progress to an initial received opinion, make us victims of chance, but without putting us back under the yoke of error and deceit." [7]

[7] *Œuvres choisies* (1833), p. 576.

BIBLIOGRAPHY

## Texts

Condorcet, Marquis de. *Œuvres complètes,* ed. Mme. Condorcet *et al.* 21 vols. Paris, 1801–4.
———. *Œuvres,* ed. A. Condorcet O'Connor and M. F. Arago. 12 vols. Paris, 1847–49.
———. *Sketch for a Historical Picture of the Progress of the Human Mind,* trans. J. Barraclough. London, 1955.

## Studies

Alengry, F. *Condorcet, guide de la révolution française.* Paris, 1904.
Frazer, J. G. *Condorcet on the Progress of the Human Mind.* Oxford, 1933.
Granger, G. G. *La mathématique sociale du marquis de Condorcet.* Paris, 1956.

## Other Works and Studies

Chevalier, M. *Étude sur Adam Smith et sur la fondation de la science économique.* Paris, 1874.
Foucault, M. *Folie et déraison: Histoire de la folie à l'âge classique.* Paris, 1961.
Gaulmier, J. *L'idéologue Volney.* Beirut, 1951.
James, E. *Histoire des théories économiques.* Paris, 1950.
———. *Histoire sommaire de la pensée économique.* 2d ed. Paris, 1959.
Martin, K. *Rise of French Liberal Thought in the 18th Century.* 2d ed. New York, 1954.
Schelle, G. *Turgot, œuvres et documents avec biographie et notes.* Paris, 1913.
Weulersse, G. *Le mouvement physiocratique.* 2 vols. Paris, 1910.
———. *La physiocratie à la fin du règne de Louis XV.* Paris, 1959.
———. *François Quesnay et al Physiocratie.* Paris, 1958.

# KANT

## I  Life and Works

The literary production of Kant embraces a period of fifty years (1794–99). Born at Königsberg in 1724, he came from a family of very small means. In 1732 he attended the Collegium Fridericianum, then under the direction of Albert Schultz, a supporter of the Pietist sect founded at Frankfurt in 1670 by the Alsatian Spencer (1935–1705), who preached inner regeneration through personal meditation on Scripture. In 1740 he entered the University of Königsberg, where he studied under Martin Knutzen, who was both a Pietist and a disciple of Wolff. Between 1746 and 1755 he was a private tutor. In 1755 his *Dissertation on Fire* won him an appointment as lecturer at the University; during the same year he completed the requirements for his doctor's degree by publishing two theses: *New Explanation of the First Principles of Metaphysical Knowledge* and *On the Use of Metaphysics Combined with Physics in Philosophy, or Physical Monadology*. In 1770, upon submitting his inaugural dissertation *De mundi sensibilis atque intelligibilis forma et principiis*, he was appointed professor. He spent his whole career at the University of Königsberg and did not abandon teaching until 1796. He died in 1804.

By 1770 he had already written many short works on physics (*Thoughts on the True Estimation of Living Forces*, 1747; *New Conception of Motion and Rest*, 1758); on geography (*On Changes in the Rotational Motion of the Earth,* 1754; *The Aging of the Earth,* 1754; *On Earthquakes and Winds,* 1756 and 1757); on astronomy (*General History of Nature and Theory of the Heavens,* 1755); and on philosophy (*Views on Optimism,* 1759; *False Subtlety of the Four Syllogistic Figures,* 1762; *The Only Possible Ground of Proof for a Demonstration of God's Existence,* 1763; *Attempt to Introduce the Concept of Negative Quality into Philosophy,* 1763; *Observations concerning the Sense of the Beautiful and the Sublime,* 1764; *Inquiry into the Distinctness of the Principles of Natural Theology and Morals,* 1764; *Dreams of a Spirit-Seer, Explained through the Dreams of Metaphysics,* 1766).

Thus he had behind him a considerable number of works when he published his *Critique of Pure Reason* in 1781 (second edition, 1787). He had been able to read Hume's *Philosophical Essays* as early as 1755, when they were translated into German, and had found in Hume's writings the inspiration for his first critical investigations. In 1783 he published his *Prolegomena to Any Future Metaphysics,* in which he changed only the mode of exposition of ideas. In 1788 he published the second critical work, *Critique of Practical Reason,* and in 1790 the third, *Critique of Judgment.*

In addition to the three critical works, he published a large number of works closely related to them. Besides his works on geography and general history (*Idea for a Universal History from the Cosmopolitan Point of View,* 1784; review of Herder's *Ideas,* 1785; *Definition of the Concept of the Human Race,* 1785; *Conjectures concerning the Beginning of the History of Mankind,* 1786), he completed those related to his *Critique of Pure Reason* (*First Metaphysical Principles of the Science of Nature,* 1786; *On the Failure of All Attempts of Philosophers in the Matter of Theodicies,* 1791) and to morals (*Foundations of the Metaphysics of Morals,* 1785; *Concerning Hufeland's Principle of Natural Law,* 1786; *Religion within the Bounds of Mere Reason,* 1793; *On Perpetual Peace,* 1795; *Metaphysics of Morals,* including *First Metaphysical Principles of the Doctrine of Law and First Metaphysical Principles of the Doctrine of Virtue,* 1797; *Conflict of the Faculties,* 1798; and a short treatise, *On the Use of Teleological Principles in Philosophy*.

To this list of publications must be added the lectures and notes which were published posthumously.

## II  *Precritical Period*

From the end of the eighteenth century until today almost all philosophical speculation has issued, directly or indirectly, from meditation on the Kantian doctrine, with the result that there has often been a tendency to consider criticism not as a momentary episode in the history of ideas but as a definitive discovery which radically separated the past and the future. By indicating the permanent conditions to be imposed on any knowledge which is to be effective, Kant is supposed to have written, in keeping with the title of one of his books, the preface to any future metaphysics and to have circumscribed with rigorous preciseness the field of possibilities open to the human mind. Far from their being universally accepted, however, as early as the end of the nineteenth century there was a sharp reaction against the results of criticism. Since everything depends on the background against which criticism is viewed, to appreciate its historical importance we must be careful to disregard the use to which it was later put and the disputes which it engendered.

The genesis of the critical doctrine dates from the decade 1770–80. In the twenty-year period that preceded its elaboration, Kant wrote a number of treatises on physics and philosophy; in them he broke away from the doctrines of Leibniz and Wolff and followed instead the intellectual trend of his time—a kind of rationalistic empiricism which had issued from meditation on the work of Newton and which was very suspicious of apriorism. In his philosophy of nature, in *Thoughts on the True Estimation of Living Forces* (1749), he attributed to each body an active force independent of extension; then in his *Physical Monadology* (1756) he reached a dynamism which was halfway between Leibniz' and Newton's, and which has many points in common with the dynamism advocated by Boscovich during the same period. Here Leibniz' representative monad becomes a center of attractive and repulsive force which, in turn, fills a finite space not because of the plurality of its parts but by virtue of its relations to other monads. Here, as in his *First Ground of the Difference between the Regions of Space* (1768) Kant, like Newton, posits an absolute space to accommodate these monads, which exert a physical influence on each other. This dynamism, which attributes substantial reality only to force, is a permanent trait in the thought of Kant, who incorporated it into his critical doctrine.

His philosophical treatises contain a discussion of the fundamental conceptions of Wolffian rationalism. His *New Explanation of the First Principles of Metaphysical Knowledge* (1755) brings to light the difficulties inherent in the notion of contingency in Leibniz' doctrine. Hypothetical necessity had an important role in this notion, but Kant finds the distinction between absolute necessity and hypothetical necessity nonsensical; and since there cannot be two kinds of determinism, freedom must be treated as an aspect of determinism—and this is another nonsensical affirmation.

*The Only Possible Ground of Proof for a Demonstration of God's Existence* (1763) contests, in principle, the ontological proof which conceives existence as an enrichment of essence or a realization of a possibility (*complementum possibilitatis*). The argument that a perfect being which by definition has the fullest essence must therefore exist would prove too much, since it would prove the existence of any being perfect in its own class—a perfect world, for example; but in reality it proves nothing, for it is based on the false idea that existence, when attributed to a thing, enriches the concept of this thing in some way; the content of the concept is the same afterward as before, with the result that existence can never be found analytically in a concept conceived as possible. Here Kant attacks the vulnerable point of rationalism: the impossibility of demonstrating an existence rationally. The new proof that he introduces does not descend from the possible or essence as the principle to the existence of God as the consequence; it ascends from the possible as the consequence to the existence of God as the principle. The possible can be conceived as such only in relation to an existing being—a necessary (since without it the possible would become impossible), simple, immutable, eternal being.

The same difficulty is examined in Kant's *Essay on the Introduction of the Concept of Negative Quantity in Philosophy.* Wolff had tried to reduce the principle of sufficient reason to the principle of contradiction and, consequently, truths of fact to truths of reason. Kant holds that this reduction is grounded on a misunderstanding and that there are in fact two kinds of opposition: logical opposition between a term and the negation of this term, and real opposition between two equally positive terms, such as two forces in equilibrium (for instance, two weights which keep the beam in a vertical position when placed on the scales of a balance)—in short, two terms each of which offsets the effect of the other. The rationalists, confusing these two kinds of opposition, wrongly believed that the assertion of one fact logically implied or denied the assertion of another fact. Logically, one can posit an affirmation and from it infer the negation of its negation, but if two terms are positive, "how, because something exists, can I infer that something else comes into existence or ceases to be?" This is what happens when we use words like cause and effect, force and action, which seem to imply that one fact is included in another.

Still more explicit are *Dreams of a Spirit-Seer Illustrated by the Dreams of Metaphysics* (1766). The spirit-seer is Emanuel Swedenborg, who maintained that he had developed his own inner sense—a faculty common to all men but one of which other men were unaware—and could communicate directly with the world of spirits. Kant shows that the metaphysicist who chooses to speak of spiritual realities should have direct experience or, barring this, simply state negative predicates and admit that he knows nothing about them; in the first case, however, he is no different from the fantasts and spirit-seers whom he pretends to scorn; in the second case, metaphysics becomes what it should be—the science of the limits of the human mind. Rationalism, then, is visionary or critical, and this alternative obviously implies that all knowledge is founded on experience; it follows that everything said about causes, forces, or actions should be drawn from experience, yet spiritual phenomena—for example, the way in which my will moves my arm or what thought would be like independently of the body—do not fall within the realm of experience.

Kant also reassures those who link our moral destiny to the affirmations of spiritualist metaphysics. This page, written twenty years before the *Critique of Practical Reason,* merits citation: "It is ordinarily assumed that a rational theory of the spirituality of the soul is necessary if we are to believe in its existence after death, and that the latter is the necessary basis for a virtuous life. . . . But is it good to be virtuous only because there is another world? Would not actions be rewarded simply because they are good and virtuous in themselves? . . . It seems more consistent with human nature and the purity of morals to found the expectation of the world to come upon the sentiments of a virtuous soul than to found virtue upon the hope of another world. Such is *moral* faith, which in its simplicity can dispense with the subtlety of reason and which alone is appropriate to man in his actual state, leading him directly to his true end." In these words we hear an echo of the meditations of Rousseau and, before him, Hume—two thinkers who led Kant away from the rationalism of Wolff.

In *An Inquiry into the Distinctness of the Fundamental Principles of Natural Theology and Morals* (1764) Kant, obviously contradicting the Wolffians, had stressed the danger of following the method of mathematics in philosophy. Whereas the mathematician begins with simple definitions of which he has complete knowledge, since he is their author, philosophy must begin with the data of experience, which are often vague and indistinct—the definite concept of a trillion, for example, in contrast to the ill-defined philosophical concept of liberty; mathematicians, then, can follow a synthetic, constructive method grounded upon a firm basis, but philosophers cannot, through analysis, arrive at concepts which permit such a construction.

Up to this point it seems that Kant contrasts the empiricism which then held sway with Wolff's rationalism. This is his pre-critical period, which is not at all rationalistic, as it is often said to be, but empirical. During this period German philosophers tended generally to turn away from Leibniz and Wolff. For example Creuz (*Essays on the Soul,* Frankfurt, 1754), though inclined toward mystical views concerning the world of spirits, nevertheless denounced the universal illusionism that issued from Leibniz' theory: "According to him, everything we think, everything we imagine when a body is present to our consciousness is only a phenomenon, an illusion, a phantasmagoria—in short, nature seems to us to be a deceitful Circe." This period witnessed the collapse of the Leibnizian edifice, the rupture of the equilibrium, established with such great care, between religion and ethics. Eberhard (*New Apology of Socrates,* 1772) maintained that ethics was independent of Christian beliefs. Edelmann (*The Divinity of Reason,* 1741) and others went back beyond Leibniz to Spinoza or, like Ploucquet, who supported occasionalism, to Malebranche. The celebrated Mendelssohn, in turn, rejected the relationship seen by Wolffians between metaphysics dealing with realities and mathematics dealing with possible concepts from which no reality can be inferred (*On Distinctness in Metaphysical Sciences,* 1764). Lossius (*Physical Grounds of Truth,* 1775), a resolute empiricist, found that "the theory of reason is a part of the theory of the soul and is related to it as metaphysics is related to experimental physics. . . . The theory of the origin of concepts should be considered more useful than theories of logic." Finally, Tetens—whose *Philosophical Investigation of Human Nature* (1777) may have been influenced by Kant's dissertation of 1770—abandoned associationist empiricism; instead of returning to Leibniz, however, he attributed knowledge to a synthesis of passive impressions, a synthesis which is "a spontaneous activity of the understanding"; ideas constructed in this way "are prior to experience; we do not apprehend them by abstraction, nor do we weaken their connections by repeated exercise."

## III  *The Dissertation of 1770*

Up to this point Kant was merely a participant in the general movement of his time. The situation changed abruptly in 1770, when he published, in Latin, his *Dissertation on the Form and Principles of the Sensible and Intelligible World*. It may be that the reading of *New Essays,* which had appeared in 1765, encouraged his return to rationalism, for though his hostility toward Wolff was no less obvious than before, the plan of his discussion changed. The fundamental idea of his *Dissertation* is that a pure intellectual notion cannot be reduced to a passive sense impression (contrary to the contentions of empiricists) and that sensation cannot be reduced to an indistinct notion (contrary to what Leibniz and Wolff had said). For the most part, it is to the latter deduction that Kant attributes the decline of philosophy: "I fear," he writes, "that Wolff, by this distinction—which to him is merely a logical distinction—between sensible and intellectual things (as between distinctness and indistinctness), may have done great harm to philosophy by abolishing the noblest part of ancient philosophy, the part that discussed the character of phenomena and noumena, and may have caused minds to turn from this pursuit to the minutiae of logic."

The very principles of Leibnizian monadology were at issue: Leibniz had started from the intellectual axiom that composite implies simple and that the universe is constituted by the synthesis of simple elements. This axiom is inapplicable, however, when we are dealing with the sensible reality and trying to accomplish *in concreto* the operations that it implies; we never reach the simple element because of infinite division, which is never accomplished; we never accomplish a synthesis because of the perpetual unfolding of the universe in time. But does this not point up a contradiction since the axiom clearly seems to have an absolute value?

If we consider the intellectual notions that figure in the axiom— the notions of whole, simple, composite as well as the notions used by Leibniz in his *Monadology* (possibility, existence, necessity, substance, cause)—we see "that they never enter as parts in any sensible representation, and that they cannot have been deduced from any sensible representation." Leibniz made the mistake of treating sensible things as if they were intelligible things; it follows that the difficulty lies not in the intellectual concept but in the conditions of sensible intuition. For through sense we are affected only by the presence of an object, with the result that sensation extends only to things as they appear, as phenomena; the understanding, on the contrary, apprehends things as they are. Kant's distinction between passive sensory affections and intellectual concepts is of capital importance; it introduces into our faculties a division quite different from those previously known; the particular, the contingent, the obscure, the truth of fact were assigned to sense and the universal; the necessary, the distinct, the truth of reason to the understanding. But if sensation is an affection, there is nothing to prevent us from attributing to sense a universal, necessary, and distinct element, for our capacity to be affected has a determinate structure, and this structure is a form or inherent law according to which the mind co-ordinates its impressions. Space and time are forms of the mind; they are not an order of successive, co-existing things (as Leibniz thought) but are a priori forms of sense, of ways in which we are affected. Thus there are sciences which pertain to sensible things and which nevertheless are universal—for instance geometry, the science of space.

In short, the ideas in the *Dissertation* and the ideas in the *Critique of Pure Reason* do not fit into the same scheme. The *Dissertation* reveals the principles of transcendental aesthetics—that is, the distinction between sense and understanding, and the a priori forms of sense; but we should note that here the distinction results from the impossibility of applying intellectual concepts to sensible things, and from the contradiction that would arise if these things were not essentially different from the objects of the understanding. Thus the critical thought of Kant evolved initially in the atmosphere of what was later called antinomy, or the enigma of a world which should be a whole but cannot.

But such a clear-cut distinction raised new difficulties, with which Kant was preoccupied in his *Letters to Marcus Herz,* the only document that casts light on his thought during the ten years of reflection that preceded the *Critique.* Indeed, we may understand how a sensible representation can have a corresponding object inasmuch as the representation is based on the attachment of the mind to the object, but it is much more difficult for us to understand how a notion of the understanding can have an object. How can I affirm the real existence of substances, causes, or objects in general that correspond to the concepts of the understanding? For these objects are not, as in the case of the senses, causes of representations; nor is our understanding an *intellectus archetypus,* which, like the divine understanding, produces its own objects. How is it that these notions which appear as products of my mind in its isolation (*sich isolierenden*) provide laws for objects? For "merely to say that a superior being has wisely implanted these particular concepts and principles in us is to subvert philosophy." [1]

## IV  *The Critical Point of View*

How can an object correspond to a concept of the understanding? This is the question that gave birth to the revolution in criticism. For there are in fact philosophical sciences or disciplines which proceed by utilizing intellectual concepts, apart from any experience or any sensible impression, and which pretend to know their object a priori: for example, mathematics, metaphysics, ethics, and even, according to some critics, aesthetics, which provides the laws of taste. Each of these disciplines presents the same problem to the mind; as early as 1771 Kant had grasped the link between them and determined to deal with metaphysics, the theory of taste, and ethics in the work which he was then preparing under the title *The Bounds of Sense and Reason.* Of course, according to prevailing conceptions, the a priori character of these sciences was easily explained. These sciences, to the degree that they were pure and

[1] Letter of February 20, 1772.

not empirical, were supposed to depend solely on analysis of given concepts and not on any principle other than the principle of contradiction; mathematics was an extension of logic for both Hume and Leibniz; as for metaphysics and ethics, they imitated the method of mathematics in all things (according to Wolff's school) or (according to Hume) were not reducible to mathematics and therefore lost every trace of their a priori character, leaving skepticism as the only possible outcome.

The Leibnizian solution is only apparent, however, for by analysis of a concept knowledge already possessed can be made explicit, but new knowledge cannot be acquired, contrary to the pretensions of mathematicians and metaphysicians; to say what the concept contains is not to provide the concept with an object. Moreover, this solution laid the basis for the skepticism of Hume, who proved conclusively, according to Kant, that the principle "whatever happens has a cause" was not analytically demonstrable; consequently the only recourse was to derive it from experience and to attribute its necessity (which actually means to deny it) to a subjective practice. Any a priori proposition is analytical (that is, the attribute is implicitly included in the subject); any synthetic proposition— that is, a proposition in which the attribute is not included in the subject ("Gold melts at 1,100 degrees," for example)—is a posteriori or grounded on experience; this is true, in Kant's language, of the thesis of Leibniz who, in essence, refused to attribute any object to the understanding and in consequence denied the problem of criticism.

The problem arises only if there are synthetic a priori problems, that is, propositions which extend our knowledge without drawing support from experience—for instance, the propositions of mathematics, pure physics, or metaphysics. A proposition such as $7 + 5 = 12$ assumes the synthetic act by which we construct the number 12 with the units included in the numbers 7 and 5, and an axiom such as "A straight line is the shortest distance between two points" must be a synthesis since the notion of quantity (the shortest distance) is not included analytically in the purely qualitative impression of the straightness of a line. The principle of causality (this is the Humean thesis which, by Kant's own admission, aroused his interest) is a synthesis. Finally, it is evident that metaphysics claims to extend our knowledge of the mind, the world, and God without recourse to experience, and that ethics prescribes laws which are not grounded on simple analysis of human nature. But all such syntheses are a priori since they are universal and necessary, whereas experience yields nothing but particular and contingent data. The understanding (here, the faculty associated with a priori knowledge) therefore has not only a logical use, governed by the principle of contradiction, but also a real use.

How can this use be justified or, putting it another way, how are synthetic a priori judgments possible? This is the question studied in the *Critique of Pure Reason,* in which different a priori syntheses—in mathematics, pure physics, and metaphysics—are subjected to critical examination.

## v *The Critique of Pure Reason: The Transcendental Aesthetic*

It seems certain that Kant took as the paradigm of knowledge the aspect of knowledge made familiar by Newton's physics: on the one hand a number of scattered experiences acquired independently of each other, on the other a concept or a law which the mind discovers and which harmonizes or unifies these experiences.

If we wish to describe the general structure of this aspect of knowledge and to determine its bounds, we may begin with a pure abstraction of a passive datum dispersed as pure diversity, of the active understanding, and of the synthesis of this diversity by the understanding; here we have an approximation of the essential elements of the Transcendental Aesthetic and the Transcendental Analytic, that is, of the first two parts of the *Critique of Pure Reason.* Kant tried to justify, to set forth as the very essence of knowledge, to raise to the highest possible degree that aspect of knowledge that had been in vogue since the seventeenth century.

Hence the transcendental and nonpsychological character of his investigation. Transcendental means that the functions of the understanding are studied, not by themselves, but in relation to a priori knowledge made possible through them. Sensibility is not knowledge of sensible things—no more than understanding is intellectual knowledge of ideas; sensibility is the faculty which provides us with the manifold or diversity, dispersed in space and time, whereas understanding is the faculty which relates and synthesizes this manifold. The understanding and sensibility do not have exclusive objects occupying distinct planes; each contributes in its own way to our knowledge of objects.

Consequently his work is divided into the Transcendental Aesthetic which studies the a priori and universal characteristics of the manifold given to us through sensibility, and the Transcendental Analytic which studies, in its purest and most abstract form, the operation of the understanding which gives it unity.

We can gain an understanding of the transcendental aesthetic by imagining the dispersion of the manifold given to us through sensibility after we remove every sensible quality that might particularize it; we then have left the forms according to which the manifold is dispersed, namely space and time. Space is the form of the outer sense according to which the manifold is juxtaposed; time is the form of the inner sense according to which the manifold forms a succession. These definitions apply to pure time and pure space— to time and space divested not only of any content provided them by the matter of sensibility but also of any unity, which can be conferred on them only by the understanding. It follows that to conceive of dimensions in space is no longer to conceive of pure space, for these dimensions can be apprehended only through a synthetic operation of the understanding which gives a certain unity to the manifold of space. Apart from matter and the unification of the understanding, space and time appear to us to be a priori forms of sensibility, which are the necessary conditions of any sensible intuition.

This manifold, taken by itself and in the abstract, has no internal tendency toward unification. Kantian time is pure diversity; it differs completely from Platonic time, which is an image of eternity, a diversity patterned on the motions of the planets. Kantian space differs completely from the universal web in which, according to Aristotle, things have their places marked out; it is the completely homogeneous manifold of geometry and mechanics. This rigorous dispersion, which has a necessary place in Kant's thought, is what he calls the ideality of time and space. Ideality means unreality if reality applies to things in themselves, which necessarily contain their own unity, independently of the operation of the understanding; if space and time are pure diversity, they become phenomena. This theory of the ideality of space is joined artificially to the thesis, often elaborated by skeptics, that we know things only by the impressions that they produce on our minds—that is, we do not know things in themselves but only appearances. In short, by virtue of empirical matter the sense manifold, which the understanding must unify in order to create knowledge, contains sensible impressions, and by virtue of transcendental conditions it contains the pure forms of space and time. Kant's phenomenalism or idealism consists in the affirmation that in its unifying work the understanding acts only on the manifold of sensible intuition, that is, on phenomena. It is obvious that in his theory of knowledge phenomenalism (and with it the purely intuitive, nonconceptual character of time and space) is an indispensable element without which the active, unifying role of the understanding would disappear, and that this phenomenalism is based solely on the transcendental aesthetic and not, as it is erroneously stated at times, on the transcendental analytic.

## vi  *The Critique of Pure Reason: The Transcendental Analytic*

In the Transcendental Analytic, Kant studies the acquisition of knowledge of objects through the unifying power of the understanding. Focusing on the transcendental deduction of the concepts of the understanding, he proves that there could never be an object of experience without an a priori synthesis of the sense manifold by the understanding itself. Everything else is merely preparatory or consequential, with the result that what is essential sometimes risks being hidden under a complicated mass of developments.

First, the preparatory developments. The understanding is the faculty of concepts, and the function of a concept is to draw together and unify intuitions. By imagining this unifying function as abstractly as possible—apart from any empirical matter to which it can apply itself—we obtain the a priori concept of the understanding as a universal and necessary condition of the unifying operation. But here we find a particular difficulty which necessitates the preliminaries under discussion: there are several a priori concepts or categories. The understanding does not connect sense impressions in general; it connects them on the basis of a particular a priori concept. For example, in determining the length of a line, it connects the manifold of space on the basis of the concept of a quantity; in determining the intensity of heat, it connects the data of sensibility on the basis of the concept of quality; in apprehending the necessary succession of phenomena, it makes use of the concept of causality. In each instance it connects sense impressions, but the connections differ in nature. Transcendental deduction shows clearly the necessity of synthetic unity in general, according to Kant, but it does not have to discover the concepts according to which connections are made. This does not mean, however, that we are to follow the example of Aristotle in relying on mere empiricism in the discovery of categories; instead, we must find a clue which will enable us to accomplish a complete enumeration a priori. Kant thinks that he has found the right clue in the following observation: the judgments studied by logicians have a logical form which allows us to classify them in four groups of three—judgments of quantity (universal, particular, singular), of quality (affirmative, negative, infinite), of relation (categorical, hypothetical, disjunctive), and of modality (problematic, assertoric, apodeictic). This list shows all the functions of the understanding in its logical use; each function unifies the representations which enter into judgments. If we imagine the same function of unification applying itself to the manifold of intuition, we obtain an equal number of universal concepts of objects or categories—the categories of quantity (unity, plurality, totality), of quality (reality, negation, limitation), of relation (substance and accident, cause and effect, reciprocal connection), and of modality (possibility, existence, necessity).

Regardless of the worth of this classification of categories (the artificiality of the table of judgments and especially of their correspondence to categories has often been pointed out), the central part of the Transcendental Analytic—the transcendental deduction —is independent; the former can be modified or eliminated without changing a word of the latter. Kant gave two completely different versions of the Transcendental Deduction, one in the first edition (1781) and the other in the second (1788).

An experience is a whole (*ein Ganzes*) and cannot exist where there are isolated representations; but sensibility yields only unorganized diversity, with the result that an experience is possible only if a spontaneous activity unites this diversity, and if we consider the a priori diversity of sensibility (space and time), the spontaneity of the understanding as it applies itself (according to categories) to this a priori diversity will yield a priori the conditions of any experience: such is the central idea of the Transcendental Deduction.

In the first edition Kant thought that he could explain his theory only by drawing a parallel between the psychological conditions or phases of our knowledge of objects and its transcendental conditions. To gain knowledge of a whole whose parts follow one another in time, we must apprehend all these successive parts together (synthesis of apprehension); for us every object is composed of parts which are actually given and of parts which are not given but have been connected to them in our past experience; consequently, to know an object the imagination must pass from what is given to what is not given and reproduce the latter (reproductive synthesis of the imagination); these different elements still do not constitute a single object, however, unless they are apprehended as one concept—"some gold," "a house," etc. (synthesis of recognition in the concept). Now suppose that instead of considering the matter of sensible representations we picture to ourselves only the a priori diversity of time which is its necessary condition; then, with respect to the diversity of time, we have an equal number of transcendental syntheses, which are the condition of the empirical syntheses which we have examined: a transcendental reproductive synthesis of imagination which, at each instant in time, reproduces past moments (for instance, if I draw a line, this line exists for me only if, at each point, I reproduce in my imagination the parts which I have already drawn); finally, a transcendental synthesis of recognition in the concept—a synthesis which, because it was presented somewhat obscurely in the first edition, must have caused Kant to revise it in the second edition, in which he retained its essentials and even went so far as to make it the basis for all deduction.

For in the second edition Kant discarded completely the psychological scaffolding which he had judged indispensable in the first edition. The second exposition begins precisely where the first one ended; he did not think that a preface was necessary, however, and he was no longer concerned with the diverse phases of synthesis. But one preliminary observation is indispensable to the understanding of the work: Kant's aim is to show the necessity of using categories as the unifying principle of the sense manifold in providing an object of experience. It might be assumed that this aim is achieved by showing that, thanks to the use of categories, the sense manifold—which is scattered and disorderly, and which is "nothing but a blind interplay of representations, less than a dream"—causes our affections to occur one after the other, in a universal and necessary order, an order which in a strict sense constitutes their objectivity; for example, the concept of a cause is that of a necessary synthesis of what follows and what precedes. This is still not deduction, however, for a category is not justified by the factual role it plays; deduction poses a question of law, not a question of fact.

A category or an a priori concept is not in fact the highest point of departure of knowledge. It is a union, and this implies a prior unity; furthermore, "it is by attaching itself to the representation of the manifold that unity makes possible the concept of union." Before my representations are joined, they must first be mine: "Consequently it should be possible for the 'I think' to accompany all of my representations; otherwise there would be in me something represented and not thought—in other words, something of which the representation would be impossible or at least would be nothing for me." The "I think" is a spontaneous act which precedes all acts of the understanding; it is a pure, originating apperception which accompanies all our empirical perceptions; the unity of self-knowledge, which can be called the transcendental unity since it is the ground of all knowledge, is expressed in the "I think," across all representations. But particular stress must be placed on the fact that the unity of the "I think" across all our representations is an analytical, and even an identical proposition. The deduction properly consists in showing that this identical proposition is the ground for the necessity of synthetic a priori unions according to categories, for the unity of consciousness disappears unless the manifold of intuition is synthesized as concepts of objects. In a simple succession of affections, the "I think" is not identical in each affection: it is identical in successive representations only if there is in this succession a universal and necessary—that is, objective—union, and this union is in turn impossible unless it is accomplished according to the a priori concepts of the understanding. Thus there is no unity of consciousness without unity of its object or rather (since the object is essentially one) without an object; as Kant puts it, "all sensible intuitions are subjected to the categories, which are the only conditions under which the manifold of intuition can be united as consciousness." As soon as the manifold of intuition is presented to the mind, the unity of the "I think" entails, through logical necessity, the construction of objective reality. Thus the necessity of syntheses is deduced analytically, and this deduction constitutes a veritable demonstration.

The transcendental deduction outlines a dialectical movement which was characteristic of the German mind and which, largely through the influence of Kant's meditations in the *Critique,* was reintroduced to later metaphysicists: the unity of self-knowledge would be lost in the manifold of intuition if it did not accomplish the synthesis of this manifold with the help of the categories. Furthermore, all these acts and operations of the understanding must be interpreted transcendentally, that is, as being prior to the experience of which they are the condition; the *Ich* which affirms is not the empirical ego known through time—the form of inner sense —but the transcendental ego—its stable, permanent condition—and pure acts of the understanding are not accomplished on the basis of objects known through experience but are the constitutive acts of experiential objects.

After showing why the spontaneity of the understanding synthesizes the sense manifold, Kant must show how the union is accomplished, or how the manifold of intuition is subsumed under a priori concepts. The rest of the Transcendental Analytic—the theory of transcendental judgment (for judgment consists in apprehending an object of intuition as a particular instance of a concept)—deals with that issue.

Here Kant encounters one particular difficulty which focuses attention on the transcendental point of view. In effective knowledge, to know whether an object of intuition is a particular instance of a concept one must determine whether the characteristics of the concept reappear in the object; for example, terrestrial gravity, tides, the movement of the stars are found to be particular instances of universal attraction. But Kant, pursuing this type of knowledge to the limit, isolated on the one hand the pure concept of unity with no intuitive content and on the other pure intuition—scattered diversity which has nothing reminiscent of the concept, nothing suggestive of the intellectual act. Thus it seems that the heterogeneity of the understanding and of sensibility makes it impossible for him to solve a problem which the transcendental deduction directs him to solve. Kant provides a solution through transcendental schematism. A *schema* is a rule according to which the images that correspond to a concept can be constructed—for example, the schema of circumference is the constructive rule governing every possible circumference; the schema is neither an intellectual concept nor a sensible image but the intermediary between the two, the product of the imagination. The problem therefore can be resolved only by discovering, between pure understanding and pure intuition, an equally pure or transcendental schema.

What is this schema? Its most obvious characteristic is the role played in it by time: according to the Transcendental Aesthetic, time, like space, is pure a priori diversity; it is the form of the inner sense just as space is the form of the outer sense. Time nevertheless takes precedence over space; the apprehension of an object in space can be effected only by the successive synthesis of its parts, with the result that time becomes the universal prerequisite to the apprehension of objects in space. Time allows us to apprehend a spatial magnitude by adding one unit to another and thus providing an object for the category of quantity, and this example should reveal to us the nature of the transcendental schema—a rule in the successive apprehension of the manifold of intuition. Thus number, which is the successive addition of one and one, is the schema of the category of quantity; time is the schema of reality when filled with sensation and the schema of negation when devoid of sensation; the persistence of the real in time is the schema of substance; constant succession is the schema of causality, regular simultaneity that of reciprocity. The schema of the categories of modality is, for possibility, concurrence with the actual conditions of that which fills time (the real excludes the simultaneous existence of its opposite); for reality, the existence of an object in a determinate time; and for necessity, existence throughout time.

The schematism reveals the possibility of objects of pure understanding in sensible intuition. The logical analysis of principles, which comes next, shows the necessity of these objects as conditions of any possible experience; following the thread of the categories, Kant then shows that we can know objects by experience only if our intuitions are extensive quantities (axioms of intuition), only if the real has for us an intensive quantity (anticipations of perception), only if we imagine a necessary connection between our perceptions (analogies of experience, which show that substance persists, that changes occur according to the law of causes and effects, and that all substances act reciprocally), and only if we imagine things as being possible, real, or necessary (postulates of empirical thought). The principle of these demonstrations is the principle that pervades the *Critique:* It is impossible for us to know a thing through a pure category, which is the empty thought of an object; we must also call upon sensible intuition.

In short, principles express what the "I think" requires of intuition in order to retain its identity. Here, for example, are the main points of the demonstration of the second experiential analogy concerning the principle of causality; there is in me a subjective succession of phenomena which, since it is subjective, is fully indeterminate, completely arbitrary, and devoid of any unifying principle; it is not thinkable and would be so only if it could be deduced from an objective succession of phenomena—that is, from a succession in which each change succeeds the preceding change according to a rule, with the result that the position of each event in time is fixed in a universal and necessary manner.

But if the whole Analytic consists of demonstrating in this way the conditions under which sensible intuition insures the unity of the "I think," does it explain the infinite docility of intuition in submitting to the demands of the understanding? Kant admits that this is not necessarily true: "Phenomena might well be such that the understanding would not find them consistent with the conditions of its unity," he writes, "and everything would be in disorder; for example, there might be nothing in a succession of phenomena which would make possible the rule of synthesis and correspond to the concepts of cause and effect, with the result that this concept would be completely empty, null, and meaningless." Kant probably thought that the transcendental deduction had decisively warded off the danger by grounding the necessity of syntheses on an identical proposition. But this necessity is at bottom merely hypothetical: a thinkable world may be a world in which intuition is subjected to categories, but why should there be a thinkable world? It might always be said, of course, that intuition offers to thought simple, unorganized, infinitely malleable diversity, and this is exactly what Kant means when he keeps on repeating that we know only phenomena and not things in themselves—that is, things which have a structure and a reality, independent of the manner in which the mind is affected. But if we consider the last part of the Analytic, namely the schematism and logical analysis of principles, we see that Kant is forced by the difficulties which he encounters to attribute to sensible a priori intuitions the structure which the Aesthetic, with its pure dispersion, seems to withhold from them. Take the singular role of time: in the schematism it is linked more closely to thought than is space, and purely intuitive characteristics —constant succession, simultaneity—provide a schema for a concept which, nevertheless, has had no part in their production. In the logical analysis of principles Kant establishes a distinction between the first two groups of principles—those relating to the mathematical structure of things and to the characteristics that enable us to imagine their dimensions—and the last two groups, which enable us to apprehend a dynamic relation in things. The first two groups are called constitutive principles because they tell what things are; the last two are called regulative principles because they inform us of the rules according to which things attain existence or continue to exist. Now this distinction is grounded solely on a characteristic of time. This characteristic, disregarded in the constitutive principles but not in the regulative principles, is the irreversibility of the course of time. In mathematical principles time intervenes only in the successive apprehension of co-existing things, and that is why the irreversibility of time is not taken into account in the determination of these things; in the dynamic or regulative principles change (or permanence) in time imposes on them an order of succession completely independent of the fact of their being thought. Consequently Kant cannot maintain to the end his own abstract notion of discovering the structure of things in thought alone and its materials in intuition alone; such an undertaking is impossible, since these materials have a structure of their own.

Thus the "I think" asserts itself only by constituting an objective reality. That is how Kant makes a radical distinction between his idealism and the idealism which he refutes at the end of the Analytic, in the second edition of the *Critique*—Berkeley's idealism, which he had been accused of reviving. According to him, Berkeley (like Descartes, in that phase of his philosophy which might be described as problematic idealism—that is, after he had posited the *Cogito* but still doubted the existence of the outer world) was wrong in thinking that he could posit the inner sense, his consciousness of his own existence, without positing at the same time the existence of objects in space outside himself. In pure time everything flees, everything escapes, everything vanishes, and my awareness of my existence would disappear if I did not perceive outside myself a permanent reality, which is the necessary condition of the determination of my existence in time. Kant exhibits one constant and noteworthy trait: his reflections on the "I think" and the inner sense do not culminate in contemplation of a thought which seeks to possess itself in all its purity; they serve only to make the mind rebound toward an object, revealing in the object a condition permitting thought and not an obstacle to thought.

It is in this sense that his idealism is transcendental (that is, that it finds in thought not so much thought itself as the a priori conditions of an object) and not subjective. It is not an idealism which merely reduces the objective to the subjective; thus in a sense it is a realism, an "empirical realism" which assumes the reality of objects as objects of experience—that is, it assumes the universality and necessity of the relations through which they are constituted.

This realism confronts Kant with a difficult problem, that of things in themselves. We have already seen how the reality of the objects of knowledge is the reality of phenomena: things as they are in themselves are outside the realm of possible experience. Kant nevertheless assumes the existence of unknowable things, and his assumption is based on two distinct courses of reasoning: a thing in itself is at the outset the unknowable *x* which is the counterpart and foundation of phenomena, but it is also a *noumenon* or an intelligible—that is, a reality known only through the intellect. To understand the significance of the word "noumenon," we must recall that categories are concepts of objects in general, and that it is only in our human mode of knowing that these concepts are empty and require sensible intuition in order to find an object. It follows that our understanding is of use only in relation to possible objects of experience or phenomena. An intuitive understanding which used concepts like ours and knew its object simply by thinking a concept would know noumena—for instance, a substance which would not be simply a permanent reality in time or a cause which would not be merely an event followed by another event in time in accordance with a rule; but we could have only purely negative knowledge of such a substance or cause.

Since it is a critique, the Analytic determines only the general principles of our knowledge of objects. But it is oriented entirely toward a metaphysics of nature, that is, toward a discipline designed to reveal everything that can be known a priori about objects. In *Metaphysical Foundations of Natural Science* (1786) Kant indicates what the scope of this knowledge can and should be. His basic principle is that matter not only "occupies" but also "fills" space—that is, it resists any other matter tending to occupy space. It cannot fill a space, however, unless it is assumed to have a repulsive force which tends to separate its parts, and it will necessarily be dissipated in space if it endowed only with this force; consequently this repulsive force must be offset by a force of attraction capable of stopping dissipation or of containing it within certain limits; this force of attraction, in turn, cannot be the sole property of matter, for if it were, matter would be reduced to a point. Finally, one cannot suppose that these forces of attraction and repulsion involve corpuscles which are given and already existing, for this would simply extend the problem and raise another question: How does a corpuscle fill space? If matter is continuous, we must not say that it is endowed with these two forces but that it is "constructed" from them, and that intrinsically it is nothing but the reciprocal limitation of attraction and repulsion.

## VII  *The Critique of Pure Reason: The Transcendental Dialectic*

If metaphysics purports to be knowledge of things in themselves and of noumena, it would seem that the Analytic and the Aesthetic, by showing that things in themselves are unknowable, constitute an effective critique of metaphysics and supersede the last section of the *Critique,* the Transcendental Dialectic, in which Kant examines in turn the three parts of Wolffian metaphysics—psychology, cosmology, and rational theology.

In fact, this section of his work is highly composite. The principle of his critique is not always the same, and in his critique of rational psychology he shows that metaphysicists' statements concerning the soul as a substance are due to ignorance of the Analytic, whereas the critiques of cosmology and theology would subsist even if no one knew anything about the Analytic. Related to this anomaly is the following historical circumstance: It would seem that Kant had long acknowledged the worth of rational psychology, which he was still expounding in his courses between 1775 and 1779, and that as a consequence his critique of rational psychology is subsequent to the discoveries of the Analytic, whereas his critiques of cosmology and theology are, in essence, merely reproductions of tracts prepared long before his precritical period.

If Kant gave such a place to the dialectic, the reason is that, without it, the exposition of the pretentions of reason would be incomplete. What Kant criticizes under the name of metaphysics are not doctrines which have had a historical existence; on the contrary, he believes that the statements of metaphysicists are not derived from experience, inner feeling, or any accidental factor such as the state of the sciences, but that they form a system which proceeds from the very nature of reason, which is universal and necessary, and which can and must be constructed a priori. There can be no doubt about the positive significance and historical importance of this thesis concerning the nature of metaphysics—a thesis which survived his critique of metaphysics.

How did reason produce metaphysics? The understanding is the faculty of concepts, judgment subsumes an intuition under a concept, and reason, thanks to the middle term, reveals the condition that validates the subsumption. Thus reason proceeds from the conditioned to the condition. But is it possible for us to find a stopping point—to reach an ultimate condition which, in its turn, is no longer conditioned? Such is the pretension of *reason* which, in the special sense in which the word is used throughout the Dialectic, usually signifies, not the faculty of knowing a priori, but the faculty of apprehending a priori the unconditioned; the conditioned would never discover the integral explanation required by reason if regression continued indefinitely. It is also easy to draw up a priori a table of all the unconditioned principles or Ideas of reason. Since Reason relates conditioned objects to a condition, the three categories of relation enable us to apprehend a priori every possible form of relation; an accident is related to a substance (categorical relation), one event to another (hypothetical relation). There follow three unconditioned principles: a thinking substance or subject which is only a subject and no longer an attribute; the world, a complete synthesis of events; and God, who is the absolutely unconditioned, the condition of all objects in general. Finally comes the division of metaphysics into its three parts, traditional since Wolff: psychology, cosmology, theology. Their essential and common rule is that of deducing their affirmations solely from reason.

First, rational psychology. Descartes had deduced from the *Cogito* the substantiality of the soul, its spirituality, its unity. This Cartesian spiritualism is essentially the basis of rational psychology as it is understood by Kant. He himself attached great importance to the "I think," especially in the second edition of the Analytic, in which the *Ich* appears as a unique subject that retains its identity across all representations and remains distinct from all other things. From this the metaphysicist concludes that it is a simple substance with the identity of a person and an existence distinct from the existence of the body. Thus he commits a paralogism: the conditions under which a substance is conceivable are known to include the manifold of sensible intuition and a unifying category; the *Ich denke* is posited as pure thought, however, and therefore cannot be known as a substance. The paralogism consists in confusing the formal, a priori condition of all knowledge with an object of knowledge and consequently in making into a substance something which is only the condition through which we know a substance.

Kant completely eliminates from questions of rational psychology any data provided by the inner sense. The ego known to itself through the inner sense is a purely phenomenal ego which apprehends itself, in the realm of experience, across the a priori form of time and according to categories; the transcendental ego, the a priori condition of any objective knowledge, is not a datum provided by the inner sense. This situation is nothing short of paradoxical and proves embarrassing to Kant. The *Ich denke* is not easily treated as the simple result of analysis since it is a spontaneous act which posits itself as existing. Kant himself twice repeats that the "I think" is an "empirical proposition," and that it contains existence analytically. Do we not have here an example of a datum which is not subjected to the conditions of all data, an existence not subsumed under the a priori concept or category of existence? Kant tells us, of course, that this spontaneous act would not occur if matter were not given intuitively to the "I think," and that its perception of its own existence is always conditioned by the empirical intuition which, no matter what else it may be, is its basis; the fact remains, however, that the "I think" is apprehended by abstraction as a separate existence. The reason is that the *Ich* is not only a "logical subject"—the term of a proposition—but also an act and a principle.

We saw earlier that Kant's first work—the *Dissertation* of 1770, in which his critique was first announced—had as its theme the notion of the world. Even at this early stage Kant had noticed that reason attributed to sensible things considered in their totality—that is, to the world—contradictory assertions which seemed equally legitimate. This antinomy of Pure Reason and the contradictions in which Pure Reason becomes entangled persist in the *Critique* and cause Kant to declare that any rational cosmology is vain. A rational cosmology views the world as an absolute and unconditioned totality, that is, as a total series of things. Indeed, for Kant the cosmos is not the static, harmonious order originally designated by the word—an order in which the idea of the whole precedes and determines the idea of the parts; it is a whole achieved by adding things, a whole composed on the one hand of simultaneous things which we apprehend successively according to the law of our knowledge, and on the other of things which actually succeed one another. In both instances the world for us is a complete temporal series, but the unity of the series—this bears repeating—is not prior but subsequent to the completion of the series and results from the addition of its parts. Metaphysics asks what can be said a priori of this totality.

The cosmological Idea is the only one of the three Ideas of pure reason in which the unconditioned appears as a series, and that is why, according to Kant, it is the only idea that takes the form of an antinomy; a series has only two possible a priori predicates—it is either finite or infinite. Thus the whole of cosmology is reduced to the question of determining whether the world is a finite totality or an infinite totality, and each aspect of the totality will be reflected in the question. The world is a totality of things in space, and it is a succession of things in time, so we ask at the outset whether it is limited in space and had a beginning in time or whether, on the contrary, it is unlimited and had no beginning. The world is the sum of its parts, so we ask whether the division into parts culminates in simple, indivisible parts or continues to infinity. The world is a series of events joined by a relation of cause and effect, so we ask whether regression leads us to a free first cause or continues indefinitely. We see that the possibility of one event depends on another event which is itself contingent, so we ask whether contingent events depend on an absolutely necessary term or whether no such being exists.

These four questions are the only questions that may be asked concerning the unconditioned totality, for according to the list of categories, the only possible series are the series of increasing or decreasing magnitudes, the dynamic series of causes and effects, and the series of contingency and necessity.

It also seems that each question poses alternatives and that reason is forced in each instance to choose between the two terms. This is not true, however, since each of the four questions engenders four conflicts in which the finite thesis is demonstrated by reason no less rigorously than the infinite antithesis. It is easy for us to examine the principle without going into the details of Kant's demonstration of each thesis and antithesis. The finite principle begins with what is actually given, goes back through the series of conditions, and shows that regression cannot continue to infinity since this would mean than the conditions would never be given in their totality; consequently the actual moment must lead to the first moment, actual space to a limit (first antinomy), a compound to simple parts (second antinomy), an actual effect to a free cause (third antinomy), contingency to necessity (fourth antinomy). The infinite antithesis begins with the limit posited by the finite thesis and demonstrates that the existence of this limit is contrary to the conditions of knowledge; the position of an event in time is always relative to that of another event which has preceded it, the place of an object to the place of other objects around it (first antinomy); the compound posited as the limit in the process of decomposition is a compound only if it is in space and, in consequence, divisible (second antinomy); a free cause breaks the causal series if it is not itself the effect of another cause (third antinomy); the absolutely necessary being whose existence is posited cannot exist either in the world or outside it (fourth antinomy).

In the demonstration of his theses as in the demonstration of his antitheses, Kant considers the operation of the understanding through which we fashion the idea of the unconditioned totality of a series. Reason prescribes the formation of an idea of the whole, but the understanding—that is, the faculty which operates through additive synthesis—willingly responds to the demands of reason. But the antinomy is resolved by this very expedient: reason delegates to the understanding a task which it cannot perform.

To understand this important point, we must return to historical circumstances which Kant systematically avoids mentioning. We saw that Newton had freed physics from the notion of universe by considering, instead of the total system of things, the elementary law connecting the different parts of matter; the position and motion of a particle at a given moment are determined, not by a detail in the general design, but by the relation, according to the law of attraction, between it and all other particles; thus the elementary law applies to any quantity of matter whatsoever. We also saw that Kant had pushed to the limit the type of knowledge assumed by Newtonian physics, for transcendental apperception introduces unity and conjunction into the unlimited diversity provided by sensibility. Following this is the antinomy which starts precisely from the inverse supposition—from the supposition that, prior to any action on the part of the understanding, the sense manifold constitutes an absolute totality, a universe which is discovered simply by the understanding. It is clear that in order to adopt this hypothesis as a basis for his argument, Kant had to forget everything he had written in the Analytic.

The introduction of the Analytic immediately robs the demonstrations of his theses of any plausibility, since the objects of our experience, if they are not things in themselves but phenomena, have no reality until the understanding confers reality upon them in thinking them. When the finite thesis seeks to stop the process of regression from one condition to another, it is "too limited" for an understanding which can posit a phenomenon only by connecting it to an antecedent condition; and when the infinite antithesis requires the process of synthesis to continue to infinity, it is "too long" for an understanding which has never accomplished its synthesis. Thus the hope of finding the bounds of the world, the ultimate constituents of matter, free causes, or the necessary being supporting contingent reality is annihilated, while the insoluble task of penetrating things to infinity is abandoned as senseless. It would seem, then, that the antinomy is an indirect confirmation of the Analytic, since it shows the contradictions encountered as soon as phenomena are treated as if they were things in themselves.

But the antinomy also has a positive value. That no human faculty is useless if only its legitimate use can be found is an implicit axiom of Kantianism. Consequently cosmological Ideas, even if they are not constituitive principles which help us to understand the nature of objects, at least serve a regulative function by showing us "how we must institute empirical regression" from one condition to another. The understanding seeks to discover a condition for an unconditioned principle; reason prescribes that the search must not be abandoned until the totality of conditions has been discovered, indicates the direction the search must take, and stimulates the understanding by presenting as a "heuristic fiction" the totality from which the idea must orient its activity.

The Antinomy has one other positive result: it reveals one possible solution of the ancient opposition between freedom and determinism.

The universe is a quantitative aggregate in space, and it is viewed as such in the first two antinomies, which are called the mathematical antinomies. The universe is also a dynamic conjunction of causes and effects, and it is viewed as such in the last two antinomies, the "dynamic antinomies." The notion of quantitative aggregate in space applies only to phenomena, however, with the result that whatever is said about the dimensions of the universe as a thing in itself—both the thesis and the antithesis—is false. The same is not true of the notion of cause. We recall that the category, taken by itself, designates an object in general; it is solely by virtue of the nature of our faculty of knowing that it determines for us only one possible experiential object in time; the necessary succession of causes and effects in experience alone can provide the category of cause with an object of knowledge; it does not follow that there is no free cause—that is, a cause whose existence is not determined by an antecedent cause; to an intuitive understanding capable of knowing noumena, a cause outside any temporal condition would seem to be free. Thus nothing would prevent one and the same being from being a free cause as a noumenon and a determined cause as a phenomenon which is manifested to itself in time; for example, the series of our voluntary acts, determined by motives and incentives that derive all their power from our character, could be the phenomenal appearance of an "intelligible character," a completely free act, transcending temporal relations. In this way both the thesis and the antithesis of the third antinomy would be true: the thesis which affirms that there are free causes would be true of noumena, and the thesis which affirms that everything is determined would be true of phenomena.

That much ingenuity was required to link the problem of freedom to the antinomy is obvious. What was Kant trying to demonstrate? In tracing causes in a series to their effects, we must eventually discover a first phenomenon. But what does this first term, which is a spontaneous phenomenon, have in common with the noumenal cause revealed in the phenomenon? Why is the only cause which is regarded as free the cause which, in the phenomenon, appears to me to be my empirical ego and my will? Finally, why should we not treat mathematical antinomies and dynamic antinomies in the same way? For whatever was said about the concept of cause and its relation to phenomenal determinism could be repeated, *mutatis mutandis,* with reference to the category of quantity and its relation to mathematical dimensions, and a theory of ideal numbers corresponding to the theory of intelligible character could easily be formulated.

Yet these rather laborious developments yield one extremely important result (found in its entirety in the Analytic and in no way dependent on the Dialectic): the uniquely phenomenal value of determinism. Determinism is a law of our knowledge, not a law of being; it applies to reality as we know it and not to reality as it is; consequently, if through the inner sense we know ourselves only phenomenally, the determinism of our actions is no proof against our real freedom.

The notion of God, like the notions of the soul and of the world, is a necessary product of human reason. As early as 1763, Kant showed how we could not conceive a being as possible without grounding this possibility on a necessary being. But whereas he then believed that a proof of the existence of God had emerged from his demonstration, in the *Critique* he sees that demonstration only as the process by which reason fashions the notion of God. "All diversity is but a multifarious way of limiting the notion of the supreme reality which is the common substratum of things, just as all figures are but diverse ways of limiting infinite space." Thus the possibility of things finds its ground in an *ens realissimum* which is the model or prototype of that of which they are defective copies—in an Ideal of Pure Reason. Each thing that exists is "completely determined," and this means that if we take every possible pair of contradictory predicates, one predicate in each pair will belong to it by necessity; it is clear, therefore, that we can conceive each thing with its complete determination only in relation to a being that contains every possible positive reality, in somewhat the same way that we determine the positive or negative attributes of a man only through comparison with an ideal of humanity which contains every possible human perfection.

Does this *ens realissimum* exist? The ontological proof attempted to establish that it does: the most real being, according to the ontological proof, is at the same time a necessary being; if you take away its existence, you take away a positive reality and can no longer say that it is the most real being. To deny this proof, Kant falls back upon the argument advanced in his *Treatise* of 1763: Existence adds nothing to the fulness of essence that can be possessed by a being; a hundred possible thalers have the same predicates as a hundred real thalers. A possible God plays, as the ideal of pure reason, the same role as an existing God; his possibility does not necessitate his existence.

The cosmological proof or the proof *a contingentia mundi* attempts in its turn to establish the existence of God by showing that the contingent character of things known to us through experience assumes, beyond them, a necessary being to serve as their foundation. This was the proof familiar to the English theists who, it will be recalled, also completed it by showing that this necessary being could only be God. These are also the two steps which Kant recognizes in the cosmological proof: first, if something exists a necessary being exists; second, the necessary being is God. If the first assumption is granted, it still must be proved that the necessary being whose existence has been demonstrated in no way resembles matter or the God that the pantheists envisaged but is a personal, creative God. This requires that there be no necessary being other than the *ens realissimum,* but without the ontological proof—which teaches us that it exists by virtue of our notion of it—how can we know the *ens realissimum?* The cosmological proof must be completed by the ontological proof, and the vanity of the latter has been demonstrated.

There remains the most popular of the proofs—the proof which Kant treats with all the tenderness exhibited by his era, the physico-theological proof or proof by final causes. Beginning with the harmonious arrangement perceived in things, one can apprehend the contingent character of this order and arrive at the idea of a sage who regulates all things. But, Kant asks, is this wise, providential being the omnipotent being and creator called God? To regulate things is not to create them, and the physico-theological proof would lead only to the existence of a being with very great but finite power if there were no reason to conclude, on the basis of the contingent character of the things he regulates, that he is their creator. Thus the physico-theological proof must be grounded on the cosmological proof which must in turn draw its support from the ontological proof.

Kant's critique of speculative theology consists in showing that an argument founded on experiential knowledge of the universe can never lead us to the existence of God unless the very notion which we have of God includes his existence; but pure thought is no more conclusive than experience; even in privileged instances where it possesses the notion of the *ens realissimum,* pure thought can never establish an existence without sensible intuition, which is totally lacking here.

The *Critique of Pure Reason* provides a complete answer to the question, "How can an object correspond to a concept?" or "How are synthetic a priori judgments possible?" An object can correspond to a concept if—like figure and number—it is constructed a priori in the sensible intuition of space and time; this is true of the objects of mathematics, and this is why the synthetic a priori judgments of mathematics are possible. A concept can also have an object when it provides an a priori rule according to which the manifold of sense intuition is united to make possible an object of experience—for instance, the concepts of substance and cause, and the synthetic judgments of physics, which are possible a priori. But the synthetic a priori judgments of metaphysics meet neither of these conditions; their objects—the soul, the world, or God—cannot be exposed through sense intuition and they are not conditions of a possible experience; this means that they cannot lay claim to any objective value. Thus metaphysical affirmations or *dogmata* clash interminably in a futile struggle while *mathemata* progress victoriously.

## VIII  *Practical Reason*

Does reason, which has a place and a role in our knowledge of objects, also have a role in ethics? Is there a pure practical reason just as there is a pure speculative reason? Demonstration of the existence of a pure practical reason is the subject of *Foundations of the Metaphysics of Morals,* which studies the a priori elements in our rules of conduct. Whereas there are pure sciences—mathematics, the pure part of physics, metaphysics—which show in detail the theoretical application of reason, human conduct contains such a bewildering mixture of motives and incentives that the pure rational element, if it exists, must first be isolated.

To obtain this pure rational element, Kant starts with moral judgments, which are produced spontaneously in all men. There is nothing to which an absolute value is attributed, he observes, except a *good will*. Consider everything commonly called goods— talent, wealth, power; they cease to be goods as soon as they are made to serve a bad will. But again, when is a will good? It is on this point that moralists begin to disagree among themselves: Is a good will one that conforms to a certain order of perfection known intuitively through reason (as in Malebranche)? One that acts through benevolence or through love of one's neighbor? One that seeks through reflection its own utility or the utility of society? Kant holds that all doctrines prevalent during his time erred by going against popular opinion and relating the will to something other than its own inner disposition; knowledge of orders of perfection, knowledge of the utility of others or of one's self are in no way dependent on the will. Rousseau had condemned the pretention common to the whole philosophy of the Enlightenment of identifying the good with the advancement of knowledge; he posited as the only good purity of heart and obedience to conscience. Here Kant sides with Rousseau, against the Enlightenment. Though he does not concur in Rousseau's criticism of the way the human mind is progressing in speculation, he maintains that this does not entail progress in morals, and that man's worth is independent of such progress. He rediscovers with Rousseau a current of thought which had been almost totally neglected by philosophy through the ages and which sought through the study of human nature to lay a theoretical foundation for practical rules. In this profoundly vital current of thought Kant sees "popular moral philosophy," which judges man not by referring to some end outside his will but solely by the inner attitude of his will.

It is true that such a view seems at first to contradict rationalism and to be ill suited to the role of directing Kant toward the discovery of the rational elements of conduct, and his distinctive contribution is the transition from popular moral philosophy to rationalism.

A good will is the will to accomplish one's duty. Duty is accomplished not only when an act conforms to duty but also when it is performed through duty; in fact, one can accomplish acts that conform to duty (abstaining from lying, helping a neighbor) for reasons completely unrelated to duty (from self-interest or pity, for example), but such acts are not morally good. Kant is a rigorist: since the disposition of the will alone matters, mere material conformity of an act to duty is of little consequences; the presence of any motive other than duty, no matter how slight, is enough to divest the act of any merit. We should also note that, in his rigorism, Kant is more of an analyst than a moralist. Here he does not offer advice or try to persuade; he seeks to apprehend morality in its pure state. Even if this state is a fiction and no act has ever been accomplished through pure duty, Kant's ethical doctrine loses none of its rigorism, for it is grounded on the rigor of thought. If we are somewhat disturbed by the thought of divesting pity, devotion, and affection of any value, we must agree that the wholly subjective judgments by which we attach praise to them are not truly related to moral merit.

The technical part of Kantian ethics is in his interpretation of this sacred character of duty: like something immutable at the heart of constantly changing circumstances and interests, it stands as a kind of absolute, resisting all the promptings of cunning and prudence. Rousseau explains it by a "divine instinct." To Kant, however, universality means rationality; if duty commands universally, this is because it is essentially rational. Here we find the most vulnerable section in the *Metaphysics of Morals,* for if we consider the whole array of motives of human conduct which are analyzed and the inner discussions that precede decisions, duty seems to be not rational but purely irrational—a final order which puts an end to any discussion. Rousseau saw a divine instinct and called attention to the unique, heterogeneous character of the moral conscience. Later Schopenhauer attacked the wholly irrational character of an order which did not reveal its reasons and compared Kantian duty to Jehovah, too jealous of his power to justify the laws he imposed.

What does the rationality of duty mean to Kant? We should note at the outset that when conduct which has "its reasons" is contrasted with irrational duty, the rationality under consideration here is purely speculative or theoretical. Cunning or prudence consists in employing theoretical reason in the pursuit of our interests; reason in itself, then, is not a motive for acting but simply contributes its light, whereas the moving cause is in pleasure, perfection, or some similar end. According to Kant, on the other hand, the universality of duty springs from reason, a faculty of the universal law, and as such it commands imperatively; reason itself is practical and compels our will.

What can practical reason command? Nothing except the rationality or universality of our actions, which means, not that an action is rational by virtue of its conformity to an end posed from without, but that the maxim or rule which we follow in an action has the characteristic of not being subordinated to a particular end but of being able to become a universal law: "Act only according to that maxim by which you can at the same time will that it should become a universal law." Such is the formulation of the celebrated categorical imperative or moral law—the law of reason which commands through pure rationality or the pure form of legality. The categorical character of this imperative contrasts sharply with all the hypothetical imperatives of cunning—those whose nature can be inferred from what was said earlier, and which command us to act as if we were pursuing a particular end. Why, for example, is the restitution of a thing placed in trust a duty? Not because it corresponds to a variable interest but by virtue of an intrinsic characteristic of the maxim which commands us to make restitution—the characteristic of being potentially a universal law. If the reverse were true—if the rule concerning the restitution of something placed in trust were arbitrary, fallible, adaptable to circumstances—then the very notion of a deposit for safekeeping would be meaningless; in short, a rule is self-contradictory unless it is universal.

Once it has been shown that the authority of duty is the same as that of pure practical reason, a reversal, similar to that described in Rousseau's *Social Contract,* occurs in the perspective from which moral life is examined. The reversal is similar to that described in Rousseau's *Social Contract,* in which we saw man giving himself completely to society even while obeying only himself. Similarly, in Kant the authority of duty is that of reason, but man is ruled by the faculty through which he is a man. Respect for reason is therefore respect for the humanity which is present in others and in himself, with the result that the categorical imperative can be stated in this way: "So act as to treat humanity, whether in your own person or in another, always as an end, and never as only a means." Furthermore, if our reason commands and provides laws, we actually obey only our rational will which, as such, is the universal legislator. The discovery of practical reason, then, is also the discovery of the absolute worth of the person and its autonomy in the moral life. All other moral doctrines are necessarily doctrines of "heteronomy" since they subordinate human action to an end distinct from its own nature. But because man is reason, duty, far from uprooting him and sacrificing him to some transcendent, inexplicable end (as first impressions might suggest), confers on him dignity and autonomy.

Rigorism in judging the moral value of actions, formalism in stating a moral law which is not subordinated to any end, autonomy making the will the universal legislator—these are three inseparable aspects of moral rationalism.

Thus Kant discovered, along with the categorical imperative, the rational, a priori elements of ethics. The critique of this new apriorism—pure practical reason—could not be patterned on the critique of pure theoretical reason, in which he had justified a priori syntheses on the basis of their being a priori conditions of our sense intuitions or of the possibility of experential objects. The moral law does not have to be justified, however, for it is categorical. It is totally impossible for us to understand why and how pure reason is impractical, but the absolute character of its commands makes us understand why it is incomprehensible to us. A doctrine which sought to deduce the moral law as the a priori condition of human action, just as the principles in the Analytic are the condition of experience, would be unfaithful to both the letter and the spirit of Kantianism.

The *Critique of Practical Reason* therefore reverses the procedure of the *Critique of Pure Reason*. It teaches us what things should be in order for the universality and necessity of the moral law to be safeguarded. It does not justify the moral law because it makes things possible; it justifies our affirmations concerning things because they make the moral law possible.

The moral law implies at the outset that the human will is a free cause, for duty requires us to make decisions on the basis of a purely rational motive—one not contaminated by motives associated with sensibility—and this is the very definition of freedom. Through duty, then, man knows that he is not only what he appears to be—that is, a part of the sensible world, a fragment of universal determinism—but that he is also a thing in himself, a source of his own determinations. Practical reason therefore justifies what theoretical reason made us conceive as possible in the third antinomy: the conciliation of the freedom which we possess as noumena with the necessity of our actions as experential objects in the world of appearances.

The opposition between man as a phenomenon and man as a noumenon must not be confused with the traditional opposition between the sensible life which is enslaved to the passions and the free, moral life which follows reason, for everything that man is in the phenomenal world—whether this be good or bad—simply expresses his intelligible character. Man's entrance into the sensible world is not, as in Plato, a descent of the soul; there is no trace of myth in Kant. Consequently, it is not a question of an extension of knowledge—an extension resolutely condemned in the *Critique of Pure Reason*. Kant does not want the discovery of practical reason to be the occasion for a new mystique which would admit us to a world closed to the metaphysicist. To know that we are a free cause, that is, that we are free of phenomenal determinism, is not to know ourselves as a free cause. The concept of cause is a universal category which, in itself, is no more applicable to phenomena than to noumena, and the moral law requires us to possess a causality independent of phenomena.

Man has both sensibility and reason. Just as knowledge is possible only through the concurrence of sense intuition and concepts, so our actions—even our moral actions—should spring from an incentive present in sensibility, for the pure concept of duty could not act in its capacity as a concept. But this incentive would divest the moral act of any value if it sprang from our own nature; an act consistent with duty would still be possible, but not an act accomplished through duty. The moral law, if it can be executed, thus requires sensibility to be determined a priori by a feeling that corresponds exclusively to it: the feeling of respect (*Achtung*) experienced only in the presence of the sanctity of the moral law. This feeling, which is incomparably superior to any other feeling, constitutes the moral incentive.

Practical reason, like speculative reason, has its dialectic. It seeks to realize the supreme good, virtue; but since man is a being endowed with reason, it seeks to satisfy his sensibility—that is, it seeks to make him happy to the degree that he is worthy of happiness. Since the supreme good is the perfect harmony of virtue and happiness, happiness depends on natural conditions which appear to be totally alien to morality; consequently it seems that one must seek only happiness, like the Epicureans, or only virtue, like the Stoics, who looked indifferently on all sensible satisfactions. This antinomy ought to be resolved if duty has meaning—that is, we should postulate a reality such that nature would finally yield to the demands of the moral law. These *postulates of practical reason* are the immortality of the soul and the existence of God. The immortality of the person signifies belief in a future life in which nature will be consistent with the law of justice, and belief in God is belief in a supreme being who is the creator of nature as well as the author of the moral law which, consequently, must contain the ground of the final agreement between virtue and happiness. These postulates are the object of a *moral faith completely* different from speculative faith—faith in realities that exist in our eyes only as conditions of the moral life. Moral faith does not require, as many authors of natural religions wrongly believed, that these truths be demonstrated by speculative reason which, on the contrary, neither can nor should demonstrate them. That it cannot was shown in the *Critique of Pure Reason*; and it should not because the constitution of our faculties does not allow the accomplishment of our duty to depend in any way on demonstrations which are not easily understood, for this would affect the categorical character of the imperative. Practical reason therefore does not have to enlist the support of speculative reason; the *primacy of practical reason,* according to Kant's formulation, means that speculative reason should accept the beliefs required by practical reason if only they are possible; the transcendental dialectic has expressly reserved the possibility of a free will, an immortal soul, and an omnipotent God.

In short, in the second *Critique* as in the first, Kant reversed the usual order of the problems. Determination of our duty no longer depends on knowledge of our destiny; because duty is imposed as an absolute, we know that we have a destiny ruled by an omnipotent and completely just being. In this "Copernican revolution" the object of speculative reason is determined as an object of possible experience, and the object of practical reason as an object of faith. The idea of our destiny is at bottom only belief in the perenniality of the conditions which make possible our progress toward the moral perfection which the moral law commands us to attain; and, by an understandable ambiguity, the immortality of the soul, in making possible an equitable distribution of happiness, ought above all to be the occasion of a new moral effort.

## IX  *Religion*

The reversal of problems, characteristic of criticism, revived a host of religious, legal, and political questions. Meditation on these questions engrossed Kant after the *Critique of Practical Reason.* Rousseau said that the great mistake of his predecessors had been in separating the political problem from the moral problem. This is the crucial idea in Kant's criticism; he banishes the idea that religion, law, and political constitution depend on inelectable historical or geographical conditions that man ought passively to accept, and he is antipathetic not only toward the idea of a religion or a constitution based on a historical tradition but also to the idea of an absolute social reality that would use persons as means or as instruments. He infuses all these questions with a spirit of freedom and a faith in the possible renovation of man through the use of his freedom, which explain his well-known enthusiasm for the beginnings of the French Revolution.

*Religion within the Limits of Reason Alone* (1793) offers this definition: "Every religion is based on the premise that, with respect to all of our duties, God is the legislator to be revered." The moral act, from the religious point of view, is the act which is pleasing to God and by virtue of which we can enter the kingdom of God. Hence a natural religion, identical at bottom to the Christian religion, and predicated on the stable will to accomplish our duties in order to please God. All difficulties spring from the clash between this natural religion and a historical, dogmatic, and "statutory" religion such as the religion of the Protestant churches. First, in the case of dogma, Kant's postulate of the immortality of the soul and of the God of righteousness is quite different from the Protestant dogma of the God of vengeance; anguish resulting from failure or from ignorance (failing to satisfy God and never knowing, through ignorance of one's own sins, whether God has been satisfied), obsession with the original and irremediable corruption of human nature, fear of eternal damnation—all this casts gloom over the theological dogma and sets it apart from the Kantian postulate which expresses, along with the idea of divine equity, the indefinite possibility of regeneration. Closely linked to this transformation of dogma into a postulate is the transformation of the dogma of original sin into the theory of radical evil, which he defines as a will that is intrinsically imperfect to the extent of being subject to the passions given to each man at birth. In dogma, however, radical evil is also inherent in all humanity and is transmitted naturally as a defilement which man himself is incapable of ever remedying; to Kant it is "the most personal of all faults" and expresses, in the sensible realm and in an inexplicable way, a decision on our part in our capacity as intelligible beings. Thus radical evil, far from having the depressing effect of the dogma of original sin, serves both as a point of departure and a stimulus to the moral life.

Secondly, in the case of the church, the Kantian idea of the kingdom of God transforms the notion of a historical church which is founded on the revelation of a Holy Bible and teaches rituals which, indifferent in themselves, are pleasing to God and assure the faithful of salvation. The universal church (here Kant agrees with Luther) includes all men of good will, all men animated by a pure faith; but "a particular weakness of human nature is responsible for the fact that we must never make this pure faith, no matter how meritorious it is, the sole basis of a church. Hence the necessity of established churches. But these churches are always human inventions which do not draw their authority from God; they not only have no right to impose beliefs, but they seek to find rational justification on the basis that they are approximations of a universal church. "Insofar as they concern religion," Kant writes in *The Conflict of the Faculties* (1798), "all interpretations of Scripture should follow the principle of morality, which is the end of revelation; otherwise they are practically void or even thwart the pursuit of the good."

## x  *Law*

Kant infuses the same new spirit into political and legal problems. He does not believe in the inexorable progress of mankind. "How is history possible a priori? Reply: If a prophet prepares and institutes the events he announces in advance."[2] Even in 1798, the French Revolution, despite the cruelty of the Reign of Terror, seemed to

---

[2] *Streit der Facultäten* (ed. Reclam), p. 99.

him to testify to the existence of a moral disposition in mankind, for it expressed the feeling a whole nation had of its right and its duty: its right to adopt a political constitution of its choice, its duty to choose a constitution which, in principle, would rule out foreign wars—in other words, a republican constitution.

True progress, according to Kant, then is juridical and ethical progress—tasks which are imposed on the will. In particular, in his treatise on *Perpetual Peace* (1795), he challenged the notion, enshrined in the Christian philosophy of history, that war is inevitable. Eliminating secret treaties directed against other nations, prohibiting whole countries from being treated as properties to be exchanged, abolishing permanent armies, securing complete political independence for each country, outlawing odious types of warfare such as assassination or poisoning—these seem to him to be the preliminary measures which should make possible definitive articles to insure perpetual peace. The articles themselves are essentially the adoption by all countries of a republican constitution which alone can guarantee all rights, the creation of a society of nations (*Völkerbund*) which should not be a superstate (*Völkerstaat*) but a federation capable of creating international law (*Völkerrecht*). The dominant idea of his celebrated tract is obvious: to substitute the rule of law for the rule of nations and the moral state for the natural state, relying solely on understanding and good will.

Between the transcendent conception of absolute, immutable law rooted in theology (its immutability could come only from an order established by God) and the subjectivistic conception which attributes law to the conventions that men establish among themselves to satisfy their needs, Kant introduces the critical conception of law as a consequence of practical reason. "So act as to treat humanity always as an end, and never as only a means," says the imperative. Hence the deduction of the general principle of law: "So act outwardly as to enable the free exercise of your will to coexist with the freedom of each according to a general law"—a maxim which explains at once the outer restraint which the state, as the organ of law, should exercise on individuals, the right of the individual to resist the state, and the right of property which gives to each a sphere for the exercise of his freedom.

## xi  *Judgment*

Kant planned to write a critique of taste—the a priori elements that enter into aesthetic judgment—when he set out to write his other two critiques, but it was not published until 1790. It makes up the first part of the *Critique of Judgment,* which also includes an introduction explaining the connection between the study of finality in nature and the study of the beautiful, and—in the second part—his critique of judgments of finality.

This introduction, written after the rest of the work, represents the strongest attempt ever made by Kant to forge a link between the different parts of philosophy; and the third *Critique* as a whole can be considered as the result of an attempt to achieve unification. The first two *Critiques* established an unbridgeable moat between nature and freedom: nature, the knowable and the phenomenal or rather that which is knowable because it is phenomenal; freedom, the unknowable and the noumenal, the sphere of moral action or duty, which requires a pure attitude of the will. On the one hand is the understanding whose concepts unify sense intuition and provide an a priori outline of the structure of nature, on the other hand reason which commands by an absolute, unconditional law.

The deep moat separating nature and freedom poses a problem: nature and freedom are not equal realities since one is phenomenal while the other is a property of things in themselves; and determinism of nature, far from being the negation of the freedom of the will, is grounded on this freedom; moral action brings us into contact with reality, which we can know only through phenomena. How the phenomenal depends on the noumenal is the question which Plato thought he had resolved through his theory of participation and intermediaries, and which the *Critique* proved to be insoluble by showing that the noumenal is unknowable; but that the phenomenal depends on the noumenal is certain. Hence there is a place in criticism for a theory which will play, *mutatis mutandis,* the role of the theory of intermediaries in the Platonic dogmatism. A critical doctrine of intermediaries between the intelligible and the sensible is the distinctive contribution of the *Critique of Judgment*. To Kant judgment is what δόξα is to Plato in the *Theaetetus* —the faculty that subsumes the particular under the universal and links sense intuition to concepts. The only difference is that the Platonic dogmatism recognizes but one kind of judgment, the determining judgment (*die bestimmende Urteilskraft*) in which both the universal and the particular are objects of knowledge, with the result that the particular is determined as an instance of a universal law or rule. If particular instances are given while the universal is not given and cannot be given, and if we nevertheless know that the particular instances depend on an unkowable universal, we must still exercise our faculty of judgment and discover the universal principle which will account for them; in this case we are dealing with a reflective judgment (*die reflectirende Urteilskraft*) which does not determine an object of knowledge as the determining judgment does, but which provides us with a universal principle for reflection upon the empirical instances presented by nature. To understand the role of reflective judgment, we should recall that the unity of possible experience, accomplished through the transcendental analytic, leaves completely indeterminate the empirical content of the sense manifold. We know that there are laws, but we do not know what these laws are. It is possible for us to discover empirical laws and fit them into a single law (as in Newton's physics) only by virtue of a unity which is to empirical diversity what transcendental apperception is to the a priori manifold of intuition. In this case nature is seen as the execution of a design inherent in the concept of nature, that is, as something determined by ends, for a final cause is merely the determination of an effect by the concept of this effect.

It is clear that we have no concept of such a unity. If we had one, there would be no room for empirical knowledge, and our apprehension of the universe would be complete a priori. Complete apprehension pertains only to an intuitive understanding, which determines an object through its concept; there still remains the mental tendency toward systematizing experience under fewer and fewer laws, and that is the characteristic role of reflective judgment. The function of reflective judgment is to discover the lines which converge toward an imaginary center which is for us the supreme intelligence and creator of the universe. Even though reflective judgment does not enable us to determine any new object, it does provide us with an indispensable rule without which we could not reflect upon the universe.

It was before he prepared his introduction that Kant discovered the role of finality in aesthetics. Beauty is the object of disinterested pleasure (pleasure linked neither to a sensible interest such as delight nor to a moral interest such as the good) and this pleasure is a basis for a judgment of taste which lays claim to universality. There we have an enigma which empirical aestheticians tried vainly to resolve by reducing the beautiful to the delightful or useful and stressing the diversity of tastes; what could be the source, they reasoned, of a pleasure that corresponds to no need or of a universality for which there is no obvious a priori principle? From these two characteristics Kant deduces a third: man experiences pleasure when he discovers that an object conforms exactly to the end for which it was made and displeasure when he discovers that it does not; in other words, he experiences either the pleasure of perfection or the pain of imperfection. The faculties involved in this pleasure are imagination which schematizes objects according to their concepts, and the understanding which provides the concept according to which an object is judged; and it is judgment which links the schemata of imagination to concepts. Now suppose that no concept is given but that the object which is given is such that the imagination can freely schematize, not in order to represent a particular concept but as it does when it represents a concept; then the action of imagination conforms to the conditions of unity of the understanding but without representing a concept. There is finality in the representation of an object since there is an agreement between the imagination and the understanding, but it is *finality without an end* since the imagination does not subject itself to any concept. The free play of the imagination spontaneously conforming to the conditions of the understanding, produces pleasure since there is finality; the pleasure is disinterested since this finality is free of any concept; and the pleasure has universal value since it derives from a priori conditions of the exercise of the faculty of judging—the concurrence of the imagination and the understanding; here, however, we are dealing with reflective judgment, which is not determined by a concept. The beautiful, therefore, has no objective reality but is nevertheless universal because it derives from a relation between objects and our faculties.

There were many formalistic aesthetic doctrines before Kant—doctrines which ascribed beauty not to a particular or general impression but to certain formal relations such as propriety, harmony, and unity within variety—but Kant's critical formalism seeks to discover in our faculties the ground of these formal relations and of the pleasure which they cause in us. By this criticism he did much to free aesthetics from the absurd pretention of providing rules for the fine arts—rules which assume concepts to which objects must subject themselves and thus suppress entirely the free play of imagination. But he assigns genius to its proper place—that is, to the inner disposition, created by nature, by means of which "nature supplies rules for art." The fine arts are the product of genius, and a critique of taste cannot pretend to do anything except to show the a priori conditions of its fertility. Kantian formalism, here as elsewhere, is not a superficial scheme but a point of departure, an indication of an infinite task to be accomplished.

His formalism encounters a difficulty in the sublime, which was beginning to play the important role we know it took in the development of romanticism. The sublime stirs the soul while contemplation of the beautiful calms it. Kant is aware, in fact, that in the sublime—either the "mathematical" sublimity of greatness or the "dynamic" of moral or physical power—imagination remains inferior to its task, and the soul is painfully aware of the immensity that surpasses it on all sides. Yet the sublime pleases us and provides us with material for aesthetic judgments. The reason is that the sublime stands in approximately the same relation to the beautiful, according to Kant, as the Ideas of reason do to the concepts of the understanding. In the beautiful the imagination has a finite, limited task, which it accomplishes; in the sublime it experiences the infinity of an inexhaustible task; hence the mixture of pain, which stems from the awareness of its weakness, and pleasure, which stems from the fact that it is destined by nature to tend toward the Idea which surpasses it.

The notion of finality has a legitimate place in the conception of nature only by virtue of our faculty of judgment and not by virtue of objective reality. We have already seen that Kant uses the notion of finality in the determination of the system of empirical laws, but it has a special place in the science of organic beings. In fact, an organic being is a being whose parts can be apprehended only if they are related to the idea of the whole considered as the cause of their possibility—that is, to a final cause. Here, obviously, his explanation clashes with mechanism; indeed, the transcendental analytic suggests that the mechanical explanation should be exhaustive since its laws determine the place of each phenomenon in time; consequently one solution would be to consider the mechanical explanation as being the only definitive explanation and finalism, as being a wholly subjective, provisional way of thinking. This is not Kant's point of view; he considers finalism to be an explanation which will always be indispensable even though it does not teach us anything about reality. Kant holds that we can view nature only as a work of art executed in accordance with certain ends, but that this explanation does not serve to determine nature as an object. There would be something incomprehensible in this attitude if determination through final causes did not provide man with a substitute for knowledge which eludes him. In fact, if we assume an intuitive understanding—an understanding whose concepts immediately determine objects—neither a mechanical explanation nor a teleological explanation is in order, for nature would appear directly before the understanding. If we now consider our discursive faculty of knowing and refer to the idea of an intuitive understanding, we see that determination of the objective reality of nature by the application of categories to sense intuitions reveals to us nothing concerning the inner constitution of nature, and we understand the necessity of adopting the teleological point of view—not, of course, in order to determine nature as the object of knowledge, but in order to apprehend nature as constituting the phenomenon of a reality that eludes them. On the other hand, if practical reason revealed to us the existence of God the Creator, we can easily see how the conception of purposiveness finds a place between knowledge of determinism and moral faith and provides a unifying link between nature and freedom. Thus the *Critique of Judgment* introduces the idea of an intuitivist metaphysic which Kant considered impossible of achievement but which his successors, using his idea as a point of departure, carefully elaborated.

## XII *Conclusion*

On the whole, Kant's criticism represents a restoration of the spiritual values which had been compromised by mid-eighteenth century skepticism and materialism: science, ethics, law, religion, and art were all validated by reason. But the price was exorbitant. It was not through intuition or the rational discovery of a transcendent reality, for such a reality forever eludes us; it was because these values were revealed to be the indispensable conditions of the most humble and most elementary exercise of the human faculties. What does the *Critique of Pure Reason* demonstrate? That the perception of an object already includes all the mental functions involved in the most complex sciences, and that science is therefore validated. Moral values spring immediately from the practical character of reason, beauty and finality from the necessary conditions of activity of imagination and the understanding. Only metaphysics, which related all these values to things in themselves, is rejected.

But two facets, which perhaps are irreconcilable, are discernible in this validation. On one hand, criticism brings into the foreground activity, spontaneity, freedom. An object of knowledge is not a limit but a product of the mind; freedom is the sole condition of moral life; art and beauty depend on the free play of imagination. On the other hand, this activity somehow transcends our actual life and experience: in our perception we apprehend only the results of the synthetic activity which has constituted our knowledge; and with respect to freedom, we know only the consequences of an intemporal decision. From the first point of view Kant's criticism then was and still is a stimulus to thought, a doctrine which transforms the "given" into tasks for this activity, a philosophy of spiritual work; it gave birth in the nineteenth century to all the doctrines which treat reality as an operation to be accomplished rather than as a thing to be verified. But from the second point of view his criticism seems to be an implacable validation of the given. He has a static conception of science, which he subjects to conditions surpassed long ago by the sciences; a rigoristic conception of ethics, which he places outside the real conditions of human activity; a formalistic conception of art, which he comes close to emptying of all its content. Everywhere, then, the mind is forced to follow paths already laid out, and the Kantian a priori represents both its domination and its subjugation.

## XIII  Kantians and Anti-Kantians at the End of the Eighteenth Century

Beginning around 1786, Kantian criticism became the subject of much discussion in Germany. It was at this time that C. E. Schmid published his *Summary of the Critique of Pure Reason*; that L. H. Jakob, in his *Study of Mendelssohn's Morgenstunden,* criticized from the Kantian point of view Mendelssohn's proofs of the existence of God; and that Tittle wrote *On the Reformation of Ethics in Kant.* In 1788 Weishaupt, a theologian, published his *Doubts concerning the Kantian Concepts of Space and Time.* Moreover, Reinhold, a professor at Jena, boasted that he had gone to the heart of Kantianism in his *Essay on a New Theory of the Repre-*

*sentative Faculties of Man* (1789) and in his *Letters on the Philosophy of Kant* (1790).

Reinhold finds that the dualism established by Kant between sensibility and the understanding does not provide a solution but that it poses a problem: Why is the understanding always linked to matter provided by sensibility? The explanation offered is that otherwise experience is not possible, but that is not an answer to the question. Reinhold therefore attempts to preface the critique by an elementary theory in which he goes beyond the three faculties recognized by Kant (sensibility, understanding, and reason) and studies the element common to all three—representation (*Verstellung*). When he shows that any representation implies a subject which represents and an object which is represented—in other words, it has a given substance or matter which it receives and a form or structure which it produces—Reinhold is simply describing in a more abstract manner. but without explaining it, the Kantian distinction between the manifold of sensibility and the unity of perception. Furthermore, Reinhold did not remain faithful to his generalized scheme of Kantianism. Because the Kantian theory of ethical postulates did not satisfy the needs of the religious man who longed for a more real God whom he might worship, Reinhold turned toward the ideas of Jacobi and concluded that the divine could be perceived by a means not accessible to the faculty of knowing. Later, under the influence of Bardili, he was inclined to connect criticism and ontology, and to see in human reason a faculty capable of discovering the unconditioned.

The year 1790 also saw the publication of Salomon Maimon's *Essay on Transcendental Philosophy,* which later was completed by his *Essay on Logic, or Theory of Thought* (1794) and his *Philosophical Dictionary* (1791). Maimon contests both the demonstration given by Kant of the apriority of syntheses (inasmuch as, by nature, the sense manifold does not in any way require unification through the understanding) and the very fact of this apriority, which is shown to be an illusion by Hume's subjective constraint. There is nevertheless a transcendental philosophy which permits the a priori determination of objects. To discover it, Maimon relies on general logic: the relation between genus (line) and specific difference (straight line or curve) is the same as the relation between a determinable and a determination; moreover, any determination contains a priori the notion of one and only one determinable ("straight" implies "line"), even though the reverse is not true ("line" does not imply "straight"); consequently there is a unilateral synthesis between the determinable and the determination. It must be added that, in Maimon's view, knowledge of this synthesis nevertheless transcends general logic because the latter, which considers only form can arbitrarily take any term as the subject or predicate, whereas transcendental logic claims to make a distinction between the true subject and the true predicate. It is nonetheless true that Maimon's unilateral synthesis bears a close resemblance to what Kant called analysis, for the predicate (straight) contains the notion of the subject (line). It seems that the transposition of a problem of general logic is also to be seen in Maimon's speculation concerning the infinite understanding and differentials. Aristotle, of course, found the problem of the determination of essence—that is, the union of genus and specific difference—to be insoluble. Maimon poses the same problem when he states that a unilateral synthesis cannot be the ground either of its own intelligibility or of the intelligibility of the relations which it establishes; in other words, these relations still contain a pure datum, a pure juxtaposition of difference and identity—reality with its diversity transcends logic founded solely on the principle of identity. The infinite understanding (also called "originating consciousness" or "absolute Ego") must unite, even while keeping them distinct, identity and difference, logic and reality. Thus he indicates the bounds of an aspiration based on reason: "Reason requires us to consider what is given (diversity, juxtaposition) not as something immutable by nature, but as a consequence of the limitation of our faculty of knowing, which would disappear in an infinitely superior intellect. In this way reason searches for an infinite advancement characterized by a continuous increase in what is thought and a decrease to the infinitesimal in what is given."[3] This advancement represents the transition from the given to the law of production of the given—a law of production which plays the same generative role with respect to the given as the differential with respect to the curve. In brief, Maimon's doctrine assumes the ultimate disappearance of the distinction between intuition and concepts, and the determination of the real through concepts alone—that is, the intuitive understanding discussed by Kant in the *Critique of Judgment*.

In 1792 Schulze published anonymously his *Anesidemus*, in which he defended skepticism against the pretentions of the *Critique of Pure Reason*. We can conceive things only in accordance with the principles of substance, causality, and so on; *therefore* these principles are true of things. This, according to Schulze, is the heart of the argument put forward by Kant, who did not actually answer Hume's contention that a principle must be found to explain the agreement between our representations of objects and the objects themselves; it is clear that the impossibility of conceiving them otherwise is not such a principle. Schulze also indicates veritable contradictions in Kantianism, notably the idea that a thing in itself affects sensibility. This idea, which provides the foundation of his whole *Critique,* is nevertheless impossible according to the same *Critique,* for the thing in itself is posited as a reality and as a cause—that is, it is subjugated to categories which should be applied only to sensible things.

In 1794 Fichte published *The Theory of Science,* in which he attempted to continue and advance Kant's work. Although Kant disavowed the attempt, Schelling in his early works—*The Ego as the Principle of Philosophy* (1795) and *Philosophical Letters on Dogmatism and Criticism* (1795)—used Fichte's ideas to revive Spinozism.

J. S. Beck, in *The Sole Point of View from Which Critical Philosophy Should Be Judged* (1796), answers the attacks made by Schulze and Jacobi on things in themselves but gives an interpretation of Kant which occasionally runs into difficulties. It is true that

[3] *Philosophischer Wörterbuch,* p. 169. As quoted by M. Guéroult, *La Philosophie de S. Maïmon* (Paris, 1929)

the notion of a thing in itself is contradictory since it should produce the materials for our sense intuitions even as it exists outside time and space, being subjugated to no category, but such a notion is not traceable to Kant, for every passage in the *Critique* in which it seems to appear can be explained by the fact that the work was written with the dogmatic reader in mind. Thus Beck turns Kant's philosophy toward pure phenomenalism.

The dominant thesis of transcendental logic is contested by Bardili in his *Summary of Logic, Purified of the Errors of Prior Logic, Particularly Those of Kant* (1800). To Kant pure logic, grounded on the principle of contradiction, included only analytical judgments, which neither extend our knowledge nor determine reality; hence the necessity of a transcendental logic concerning a priori knowledge of objects. Bardili, on the other hand, would have logic itself posit real objects. Logical thought is wholly in the principle of identity $A = A$, which posits only the pure, empty unity of a thought which is repeated to infinity. How could this principle give rise to duality, and with duality, the multiple variety of objects? Bardili's answer is based on the argument that the unifying function and oneness are by nature the same, and in this way he rediscovers the old Neo-Platonic thesis of the One as the cause of being. To exercise its unifying function, oneness must posit, outside itself, matter which is pure diversity, simple exteriority, and plurality— a limit which it imposes on itself as the condition of its determination. In short, by giving oneness the function that Kant gives to the "I think," he makes critical idealism a kind of rational realism.

All these commentaries or critiques came from philosophers intent upon modifying or replacing Kantianism, but by following a similar course of thought. The reverse is true of Herder's *Metakritik* and *Kalligone.* Kant, Herder's former teacher, had been antipathetical toward *Outlines of a Philosophy of the History of Man,* which he criticized sharply, first in a literary journal *Allgemeine Literarische Zeitschrift,* 1784), then in an article "On the Beginning of History" (1788). Few theories could have been more distateful to Kant, for whereas Herder dissolved man in nature, he stressed the freedom of man in evolving an ethic in which nature has no part. Herder's appeal to transcendence—the idea that reason, the distinctly human possession, is introduced into history by the influence of superior beings—was no less displeasing to him. When Fichte, speaking as Kant's disciple, declared that reason soon would be the sole religion, Herder understood the import of Kant's attacks, and he wrote the two works in which he attempted to refute first the *Critique of Pure Reason* and then the *Critique of Judgment*. Herder had a profound sense of the unity and continuity of all things, and he was constantly dismayed by the divisions and separations introduced by Kant. "Splitting Human Nature," "Separating the Faculties of Knowing," "The Division of Universal Nature," "The Division of Reason Itself"—these titles of the final chapters in his *Metakritik* suggest the tone of the whole work. The truth is that these divisions between sensibility and the understanding, between phenomena and things in themselves, and between theoretical reason and practical reason offended not only Herder but many others. Post-Kantian metaphysics was concerned exclusively with the problem of transcending Kantianism by re-establishing the unity of mind which his *Critique* had torn asunder.

# BIBLIOGRAPHY

## Texts

Kant, Immanuel. *Gesammelte Schriften.* 22 vols. Berlin, 1902–42.
———. *Immanuel Kants Werke,* ed. E. Cassirer. 11 vols. Berlin, 1912–18.
———. *Kant's Cosmogony,* trans. W. Hastie. Glasgow, 1900.
———. *Dreams of a Spirit–Seer Illustrated by the Dreams of Metaphysics,* trans. E. F. Goerwitz, ed. F. Sewall. New York, 1900.
———. *Inaugural Dissertation and Early Writings on Space,* trans. J. Handyside. Chicago, 1929.
———. *Critique of Pure Reason,* trans. N. K. Smith. 2d ed. London, 1933.
———. *Critique of Pure Reason,* trans. J. M. D. Meiklejohn. London, 1934.
———. *Critique of Pure Reason,* trans. Max Müller. New York, 1896.
———. *Prolegomena to Any Future Metaphysic,* trans. J. P. Mahaffy and J. H. Bernard. London, 1889.
———. *Prolegomena to Any Future Metaphysic,* trans. P. P. Carus. New York, 1950.
———. *Prolegomena to Any Future Metaphysics,* trans. and ed. P. G. Lucas. Manchester, 1953.
———. *Immanuel Kant: Critique of Practical Reason and Other Writings in Moral Philosophy,* trans. and ed. L. W. Beck. Chicago, 1949.
———. *Kant's Critique of Practical Reason and Other Works on the Theory of Ethics,* trans. T. K. Abbott. 6th ed. London, 1909.
———. *The Metaphysics of Ethics,* trans J. W. Semple. 3d ed. Edinburgh, 1886.
———. *The Moral Law; or, Kant's Groundwork of the Metaphysics of Morals,* trans. H. J. Paton. London, 1950.
———. *Kant's Lectures on Ethics,* trans. L. Infield. London, 1930.
———. *Critique of Judgment,* trans. J. H. Bernard. 2d ed. London, 1931.
———. *Religion within the Limits of Reason Alone,* trans. T. M. Greene and H. H. Hudson. Glasgow, 1934.
———. *Perpetual Peace: A Philosophical Essay,* trans. M. C. Smith. London, 1903.
———. *Kant: Selections,* ed. T. M. Greene. London and New York, 1929.

## Bibliographies

Dickes, E. A. *Bibliography of Writings by and on Kant.* First published as supplements to *The Philosophical Review.* Boston, 1893– .
Eisler, R. *Kant-Lexicon.* Berlin, 1930.

256

*Studies*

Basch, V. *Essai sur l'esthétique de Kant.* 2d ed. Paris, 1927.

Beck, L. W. *A Commentary on Kant's Critique of Practical Reason.* Chicago, 1960.

Beck, L. W. *Studies in the Philosophy of Kant.* New York, 1965.

Bohatec, J. *Die Religionsphilosophie Kants.* Hamburg, 1938.

Borrics, K. *Kant als Politiker.* Leipzig, 1928.

Boutroux, E. *La philosophie de Kant.* Paris, 1926.

Caird, E. *The Critical Philosophy of Immanuel Kant.* 2 vols. 2d ed. London, 1909.

Campo, M. *La genesi del criticism Kantiano.* 2 vols. Varese, 1953.

Cassirer, H. W. *A Commentary on Kant's Critique of Judgment.* London, 1938.

———. *Kant's First Critique: an Appraisal of the Permanent.* London and New York, 1954.

———. *Significance of Kant's Critique of Pure Reason.* London, 1955.

Cohen, H. *Kommentar zu Kants Kritik der reinen Vernunft.* 2d ed. Leipzig, 1917.

Coninck, A. de. *L'analytique de Kant,* part 1. Louvain, 1955.

Cresson, A. *Kant, sa vie, son œuvre. Avec un exposé de sa philosophie.* 2d ed. Paris, 1955.

Daval, R. *La métaphysique de Kant: Perspectives sur la métaphysique de Kant d'après la théorie du schématisme.* Paris, 1951.

Delbos, V. "Les harmonies de la pensée kantienne d'après la Critique de la faculté de juger," *Revue de Métaphysique et de Morale,* XII, 1904.

———. *La philosophie pratique de Kant.* Paris, 1905.

Duncan, A. R. C. *Practical Reason and Morality.* Edinburgh, 1957.

———. *Practical Rule and Morality: A Study of Immanuel Kant's Foundations for the Metaphysics of Ethics.* London and Edinburgh, 1957.

Dussort, H. "Husserl juge de Kant," *Revue philosophique.* October–December, 1959, pp. 527–44.

England, F. E. *Kant's Conception of God.* London, 1929.

Ewing, A. C. *Kant's Treatment of Causality.* London, 1924.

———. *A Short Commentary on Kant's Critique of Pure Reason.* London, 1938.

Friedrich, C. J. *Inevitable Peace.* Cambridge, Mass., 1948.

Garnett, C. B. *The Kantian Philosophy of Space.* New York, 1939.

Goldmann, L. *Mensch, Gemeinschaft und Welt in der Philosophie Kants.* Zürich, 1945.

Gregor, M. J. *The Laws of Freedom.* Oxford, 1964.

Heidegger, M. *Kant und das Problem der Metaphysik.* Bonn, 1929.

Heimsoeth, H. *Studien zur Philosophie Kants.* Cologne, 1956.

Jones, W. T. *Morality and Freedom in the Philosophy of Immanuel Kant.* Oxford, 1940.

Körner, S. *Kant*. Baltimore, 1955.

Kroner, R. *Kant's Weltanschauung,* trans. J. E. Smith. Chicago, 1956.

Lachièze-Rey, P. *L'idéalisme kantien.* 2d ed. Paris, 1950.

Lindsay, A. D. *Kant.* London, 1934.

Lotz, B. S. J. *Deitor, Kant und die Scholastik heute.* Munich, 1955.

Maréchal, J. *Le point de départ de la métaphysique.* 5 vols. Bruges, 1923–46.

Martin, G. *Kant's Metaphysics and Theory of Science,* trans. P. G. Lucas. Manchester, 1955.

Milmed, B. K. *Kant and Current Philosophical Issues.* New York, 1961.

Natorp, X. P. *Kant über Krieg und Frieden.* Erlangen, 1924.

Prichard, H. W. *Kant's Theory of Knowledge.* Oxford, 1909.

Paton, H. J. *Kant's Metaphysic of Experience.* 2 vols. New York, 1936.

———. *The Categorical Imperative.* Chicago, 1948.

Paulsen, F. *Immanuel Kant: His Life and Doctrine,* trans. J. E. Creighton and A. Lefèvre. New York, 1902.

Ratke, H. *Systematisches Handlexikon zu Kants Kritik der reinen Vernunft.* Leipzig, 1929.

Reinhard, W. *Über das Verhältnis von Sittlichkeit und Religion bei Kant.* Berne, 1927.

Stuckenberg, J. H. W. *The Life of Immanuel Kant.* London, 1882.

Smith, N. K. *A Commentary on Kant's Critique of Pure Reason.* 2d ed. New York, 1950.

Tonelli, G. *Elementi metodologici e metafisici in Kant dal 1745 al 1768.* Torino, 1959.

Vleeschauwer, H. J. De. *The Development of Kantian Thought.* London, 1962.

Vorlander, K. *Immanuel Kant der Mann und das Werk.* 2 vols. Leipzig, 1924.

Vuillemin, J. *L'héritage kantien et la révolution copernicienne.* Paris, 1954.

Webb, C. J. *Kant's Philosophy of Religion.* Oxford, 1926.

Weldon, T. D. *Kant's Critique of Pure Reason.* Oxford, 1945. 2d ed. 1958.

Wolff, R. P. *Kant's Theory of Mental Activity.* Cambridge, Mass., 1962.

Wundt, M. *Kant als Metaphysiker.* Stuttgart, 1924.

## Other Studies

Wiegershausen, H. *Aenesidem Schulze.* Berlin, 1910.

Zynda, M. von. *Kant, Reinhold, Fichte* (Kantstudien Ergänzungsheft). Berlin, 1910.

# INDEX